QUIET CRISIS IN INDIA

John P. Lewis, presently a member of the President's Council of Economic Advisers, is on leave from Indiana University, where he has been Director of the International Development Research Center and Chairman and Professor of Business Economics and Public Policy.

A graduate of Union College, he received his Ph.D. degree from Harvard. Dr. Lewis has taught at Union and served as a staff member of the Council of Economic Advisers before going to Indiana in 1953. Overseas he has served as an economic consultant to the United Nations in Korea and to AID in Liberia. In 1959-60 he spent twelve months in India as a senior staff member of the Brookings Institution, doing the field work that resulted in this book. His other publications include *Business Conditions Analysis* and *Reconstruction and Development in South Korea*.

QUIET CRISIS IN INDIA

Economic Development and American Policy

John P. Lewis

Anchor Books
Doubleday & Company, Inc.
Garden City, New York
1964

Quiet Crisis in India was originally published by the Brookings Institution in 1962. The Anchor Books edition is published by arrangement with the Brookings Institution.

Anchor Books edition: 1964

FOREWORD TO THE 1962 EDITION

The United States is far more than an interested observer in India's concerted effort to speed her economic expansion. As John Lewis emphasizes in this book, India's development program is the first and, in many ways, the most significant non-Communist economic experiment in Asia. Americans have a vital stake in India's attempt to achieve radical economic transformation by constitutional procedures.

This study was begun in 1958 as an analysis of the role that the United States could play in India's development during the 1960's. The author quickly discovered, however, that it was impossible to investigate the issues of the American role in India without at the same time dealing directly with the prospects for Indian development itself. The result is a book addressed equally to Indian and American readers. For this reason, Brookings is pleased that as this edition becomes available to the American public, the Asia Publishing House of Bombay will publish a paperback edition for readers in India.

The author has dealt selectively with his subject. After explaining India's general development strategy he devotes two chapters to what he considers the most difficult of all the issues of the development effort—the questions of rural policy—first in agriculture and second in the formation and "centering" of local regions. His findings in the chapter on "The Role of the Town in Industrial Location" are controversial, provocative, and worthy of close attention. One chapter is devoted to the outlook for private enterprise, both domestic and foreign, and another to the export problem. Policy makers in both India and the United States will be especially interested in his three chapters on the operation of the American foreign aid program.

Professor Lewis, who served as a member of the senior staff of Brookings' Economic Studies Division while doing the field work for this study and who is a part-time member of the

Institution's Foreign Policy Studies Division, is Chairman of the Department of Business Economics and Public Policy at the School of Business, Indiana University. He recently has been appointed Director of the new International Development Research Center at that university.

Professor Lewis and the Institution gratefully acknowledge financial support from the Ford Foundation, which made this study possible. They also wish to acknowledge and thank a great many Indian and American officials, businessmen, scholars, and other strategically placed individuals and organizations for their interest and help. These include the Department of Applied Economics at Cambridge University and its Director, W. B. Reddaway, who provided work facilities during the summer of 1960; the School of Business, Indiana University, and its Dean, Arthur M. Weimer, who provided research assistance; and the study's Advisory Committee: Henry Hart, University of Wisconsin; Edward Mason, Harvard; Max Millikan, Massachusetts Institute of Technology; and Robert E. Asher, Brookings. The study was started under the guidance of Ralph J. Watkins, former Director of Economic Studies at Brookings, and completed under Joseph A. Pechman, the present Director.

ROBERT D. CALKINS
October 1962   *President*

AUTHOR'S PREFACE

One can never adequately or comprehensively acknowledge the debts he incurs in the course of preparing a study like this one. In my own case this is especially true of the great number of Indians who were so largely responsible for making my visit to their country in 1959 and 1960 unusually informative and enjoyable. I must, for an accumulation of reasons they will best understand, mention the names of two—Lakshmi C. Jain, General Secretary of the Indian Cooperative Union, and Pitambar Pant, Chief of the Perspective Planning Division of the Government of India's Planning Commission. But I hope that the scores of others, in private enterprise, in academic and research institutions, and in other walks of Indian life who might almost as well be listed specifically, will accept my profound, if not particularized, thanks for the informed concern and friendliness with which they received and assisted me.

It is likewise necessary to resort to a blanket vote of thanks to the many Americans and others in India, Washington, and elsewhere, who contributed importantly to what I understand of the Indian development process and of American policies toward it. These were people both in official capacities and in private business, with such organizations as the Ford Foundation, the Rockefeller Foundation, the Massachusetts Institute of Technology Center for International Studies, and the American International Association for Economic and Social Growth, or on study ventures similar to my own. I am grateful to them all.

In addition to the acknowledgments in Dr. Calkins' foreword I must add my personal salutations—for what, for me, has been a most felicitous association—to the Brookings Institution in general and particularly to Ralph J. Watkins, Director of Economic Studies until last July, and to Herbert C. Morton, Director of Publications, and Virginia Haaga, who have handled the publication and editing of the manuscript with great forbearance.

Acknowledgments are due also to B. M. Patel, Dayal Singh, and Joseph Walka who, as graduate students at Indiana University, assisted me with the project, and to Anna Lee Abbas and Elizabeth M. Alani for a cheerful typing of the manuscript.

The book is affectionately dedicated to my wife, June Ryan Lewis, who contributed to it in a number of subtle but important ways because her perceptions of things Indian proved to be unusually acute. She shares my hope that our introduction to India, which this book reflects, will prove indeed to be no more than a beginning.

Bloomington, Indiana   JOHN P. LEWIS
October 1962

CONTENTS

1 WHY INDIA? AND WHY THE SIXTIES?

India in the early nineteen-sixties stands at a critical juncture in its long-range program of economic development—a program that began more than a decade ago. The accomplishments of this program in the next few years will largely determine India's political future and will have a heavy bearing on the future of other Asian and African countries. Its success should be a primary concern of American foreign policy in the years just ahead. These are the basic propositions of this book.

It will not be easy to convince Americans of the urgency of India's claim to special attention. As a nation they must weigh her claim not only against a wide range of domestic preoccupations but also against the competing claims of other foreign countries. American anxieties since World War II have skipped fleetingly from country to country and continent to continent—from Greece and Turkey to Western Europe to Iran to Korea to Vietnam to Formosa, Quemoy, and Matsu to the Near East to Hungary and Poland to India and Pakistan to Cuba to the Congo and Subsaharan Africa to Algiers and Northern Africa to Berlin to Laos and Vietnam to Latin America to Western Europe and back again—usually at the beck of some new (or renewed), immediate, and demanding crisis.

While India has had its share of American attention on occasions, the United States showed a limited interest in its affairs during the early years of the economic development program. In 1958, however, the Indian foreign-exchange crisis precipitated a wave of activity by the World Bank, the United States, and other Western countries. American interest in India burgeoned, resulting in a period of greatly improved relations between the two governments. In the Cooper-Kennedy Resolution, the United States Senate recommended that the Administration "invite other friendly and democratic nations to join in a mission to consult with India on . . . joint action to assure fulfillment of India's Second Five Year Plan and the effective design of its Third Plan." There were also some substantive and procedural improvements in the Indo-American aid program; and there was a new stirring of interest among American private business firms in exploring possible investments in Indian operations.

But by the summer of 1962, when this book was being put in final form, the view seemed to be spreading in the United States that Indo-American relations had taken a distinct turn for the worse. Those who remarked such a change cited, among other factors, the American response to India's seizing of Goa in December 1961 and the Indian reaction to that response; new friction over United States military aid to Pakistan and over India's scheme for obtaining military jet aircraft of Soviet design, allegedly prompted by its concern over Pakistani air power; the more leftward-leaning composition of the Indian Cabinet as reconstituted after the general election of 1962; the serious, if unsuccessful, attempt that was made in the United States Congress in 1962 to prevent any increase in the second annual installment of American assistance for India's Third Five Year Plan; American disappointment at shortfalls and delays in the initial implementation of that Plan; Indian disappointment over the pace and character of foreign aid operations on the American side; and various instances of irritability that authorities of both countries lately had displayed vis-à-vis each other.

However, any complex association between two countries is bound to experience temporary ups and downs that, of themselves, count for little. It is my opinion that the recent lapse in rapport between India and the United States has been considerably exaggerated by the press in both countries and is of relatively little consequence.

What *does* count, however, is the danger of a lasting erosion of American concern for the Indian development effort while the need for the concern still persists. Whether or not it is already well advanced, such an erosion plainly is to be expected if particular efforts are not made to forestall and reverse it. For the emergence of newer anxieties about Africa, Latin America, Southeast Asia, and the European Common

Market considerably narrowed the share of American attention that India was getting as recently as 1959 and 1960. Moreover, Americans are likely to feel that, compared with the disarray in other places, the Indian development effort has been going relatively smoothly and that if hard choices must be made, India's further needs are relatively postponable.

I shall not here pretend to debate the relative importance of India—to indicate over which other particular countries or regions it should take precedence in the allocation of American concern. But of this I am certain: Gauged by the standard of American self-interest, India's true claim upon American attention in the sixties is very high, and higher now than superficially appears. For not only is the long-run outcome of the Indian development experiment as critical for American security as that of any being conducted anywhere; the experiment has now entered a period of extreme urgency. Despite the orderliness and, on the whole, the intelligence with which India's effort is being conducted, its outcome is far more uncertain than Americans generally have been made to realize. And, thanks to a conjunction of economic and political circumstances, time is a more crucial factor than the Indians themselves like to admit.

In short, the test that India of the nineteen-sixties poses for Americans is whether they have the good judgment to recognize a monumental crisis while it still remains quiet—to see, indeed, that the success of what Americans should value most in the Indian experiment will be measured by whether the crisis of the sixties can be kept reasonably quiet and orderly. It will be kept that way only through extraordinary effort, including American effort.

The Importance of India's Undertaking

Many Westerners can agree, almost intuitively, that the West has a vital stake in the success of the present Indian economic development effort, but few can assign adequate reasons for their belief. Frequently, for instance, India's size is cited as the crucial consideration; and this, of course, *is* a factor. A nation of 440 million people—at least a third of the total population of all the economically underdeveloped nations whose development the United States is likely to be aiding any time soon—cannot be unimportant.

But the importance to the West of India's effort depends on more than sheer size. Also it depends on more than India's alleged readiness for rapid economic expansion. Indeed, the picture of her readiness actually is a very mixed one. On the one hand, India's leadership is among the most sophisticated in the economically underdeveloped world and its intellectual elite the largest. Much of its "organized" (that is, larger-scale) industrial and commercial community is of very long standing. The country has a highly experienced, extensive set of financial institutions. The Indian Civil Service (now Indian Administrative Service) has a proud, if paternalistic, tradition of competence and integrity. Even if this tradition has become somewhat frayed since independence, the present level of administrative morality and reliability is far above average for an underdeveloped country. Moreover, the government, down to this point, has a record of political stability; the stock of social overhead capital and industrial "infrastructure" has been long building and is substantial; and the country has had a half dozen years of systematic development planning with a good deal of material progress to show for them.

But there is another side to the picture. India, for all of its sophistication, remains one of the world's most deeply impoverished countries. In many ways it is a prime case of a "dual society," in which an industrializing urban minority is drawing away from a stagnating traditionalist rural community. Land reforms have carried only part way to their intended target in most Indian states and may now have lost their momentum. Much of the social structure, organization, and traditional leadership in the countryside is still highly resistant to rapid economic change. Even in the cities the appetites of policy-makers, both public and private, for greater productive efficiency are being dangerously jaded by the omnipresence of unemployment. Moreover, the vaunted experience of the Indian business and financial communities is not an unmixed blessing. Some of their members still hold to the conservative, low-volume, high-margin, "Scotch banker" traditions of the limited, stagnant market in which most of their experience accrued.

Even the erudition of the planners and administrative elite is not without its drawbacks. Virtually every Western social scientist who arrives in India fresh from one of the Southeast Asian countries exclaims over the wonderful crackle of concepts and insights he finds in New Delhi, packaged always in the superb Indian ability to articulate. But if he stays a while, he is almost equally sure to become critical of the "implementation." The Indians are better talkers than doers, better planners than executors. Their very erudition means that they already have heard everything—and tried very nearly everything, after a fashion. But too often the execution is half-hearted, inept, or bogged down in cross-purposes. As a result, there is a rapid deterioration of good policy ideas; they grow shabby before their time.

As will appear, I sound these negative notes not out of any lack of enthusiasm for Indian prospects. But I think that it is well to recognize that the peculiar "readiness" of India for rapid development is easily exaggerated. Development is always a tough job. It almost always takes extraordinary leadership and skills and some degree of dedication. There always are major obstacles to be surmounted. No developing economy is ever completely "ready" for the "big push"; if it were, the push already would have occurred.

Perhaps we should say simply that India is important to the West because it is regarded as the foremost of the world's poorer neutrals. It is foremost, not only in terms of size and of the scope of the indigenous development efforts already under way, but in terms of the international image that Jawaharlal Nehru has given India. And latterly, particularly since 1957, the United States has come to recognize that it has a major strategic stake in the economic fortunes of those economically underdeveloped countries that have tried to remain neutral in the East-West power struggle. The stake, as now seen, is of two sorts.

First, within the one-dimensional (East-West) framework that has so largely ordered United States foreign-policy decisions since World War II, there is increasing appreciation of the economic wooing of third parties as a less hazardous, more viable form of competition between two rivals who are determined to compete but are reluctant to get blown up in the process. This appreciation of the competitive significance of its aid and other policies toward a country like India has been sharpened for the United States, of course, by the serious and skillful way in which the Soviet Union has taken up the game in recent years.

However, there also has been a growing awareness in the United States that a second major dimension must be added to the American foreign-policy framework. Even if all Communist organizations were wiped from the face of the earth, the very poverty of the underdeveloped countries would present a fundamental long-run threat to the security of rich countries, including especially the richest, now that the poor nations have become self-determining and have acquired massive appetites for material improvement. This threat, it is recognized, will grow at least as long as the welfare gap between the economically advanced and the economically backward countries continues to widen rather than narrow. It is for this issue that the label, "the North-South problem," lately has been contrived—thereby effectively (if inaccurately) distinguishing it from "the East-West problem."

The Reaction to China and Its Dangers

But the importance of India to the West, especially to the United States, inheres also in two distinctive factors. One is India's juxtaposition to China. Much of the surge of American concern about India after 1958 reflects a fear of China—a fear that personally I am not yet prepared to count unjustified. During most of the fifties the Chinese production record, however discounted, appeared to be tremendous, and the Chinese regime's apparent organizational mastery within its own borders was awesome. After generations of profound disorder and of subjection to foreign indignities, mainland China seemed to burgeon with power; it was aggressively disposed; it had started to lean on its neighbors to the south with a motive possibly no more artful than that of sheer bumptious self-assertion; and it had chosen the United States as its particular devil. It was no wonder that Americans found Chinese prospects alarming. Moreover, there is still no justification for any radical revision in this attitude. The evidence of travail and breakdown that lately has been emerging from mainland China is far from conclusive. Thus one can have no particular quarrel with the American impulse to back India as the only possible counterpoise to China. It might be more admirable to be concerned about the Indians just for their own sake, but the comparison is inevitable, and the Indians themselves long have been highly mindful of it. With the Chinese model of development being spread before Asian eyes, it will take a massive, thriving Indian alternative to provide an effective foil.

What are objectionable, however, are the dimensions to which many Americans have insisted on confining the Sino-Indian comparison. These are the dimensions of aggregative economic performance—the rates of growth in real Gross National Product per capita, in capital formation, in agricultural output, in per-capita consumption, and the rest. Always, until very recently at least, repeated use of these comparisons showed India at a marked disadvantage, even in the case of consumption, where the Chinese consumer's smaller share of a more rapidly expanding output was said by the late fifties to have overtaken Indian per-capita consumption.

Such comparisons ignore India's greatest asset, the nature of the development process she has chosen. Until the latest hints of massive economic collapse began to filter out of China, that country seemed almost certain easily to outstrip India in growth rate except possibly in the very long run. If the present regime retains power in China, this may still be the prospect, partly because of differences in temperament and climate, but mainly because of the ruthlessness of Chinese development techniques. Should this be so, however, it need not mean that, viewed as a whole, the Indian alternative would come off second best in the eyes either of the Indians themselves or of other bystanding countries—unless constant emphasis on comparative growth rates meanwhile has closed too many minds to the procedural differences between the two development experiments.

India's Distinctive Development Process

By all odds the most distinctive feature of the Indian effort is its deep commitment to an orderly, peaceful procedure under which personal rights are respected—in short, to a constitutional procedure—of radical economic change.

There may be dispute about the depth and reliability of this commitment of India's. Certainly there are divisive forces at work, some of them on the increase, and the view is being expressed that Western parliamentary democratic forms are not after all suited to Indian needs. I shall return to these issues later. For present purposes, suffice it to say that so far there has been close adherence to constitutional processes; that the electorate, through the instrumentality of parties, legislatures, and elections already wields a considerable veto power over the formation of national policy, even though the great majority of the voters remain illiterate and ill-informed; that "the rule of law" signifies an institution, not just a slogan; that the courts are reasonably independent and evenhanded; and that Indians enjoy a broad freedom to dissent and to organize peaceful opposition. They have substantial and reliable personal security against arbitrary government action. India's present constitutional commitment is plainly a good deal sturdier, for example, than that of France. The institutions of orderly national and state government probably are the most deeply rooted element of India's British heritage, and they are richly fortified by the Gandhian tradition that the means of reform take precedence over the ends.

In this general characteristic, India stands virtually alone in continental Asia and nearly alone in all the economically underdeveloped world. Clearly, this characteristic is the ultimate reason for United States concern over the success of the Indian development experiment. For most Americans, upon reflection, would agree to this: that it is just such a commitment to an orderly, constitutional process of social change, in which individuals retain a high measure of personal security and discretion and settle their differences over social policy without armed conflict, that is the highest value in their own system. It is this rather than any particular objective of social change—whether economic affluence, or income equality, or more or less private ownership of productive facilities, or whatever, that remains their own primary national goal. It may not be the most heroic national purpose, but it is the most civilized.

The trouble in part is that by now this value is so secure in our own system that we Americans take it too much for granted when we confront a country like India. We forget what an extraordinarily difficult and improbable achievement constitutional democracy is for any relatively new nation. Accordingly, we forget that internal constitutionalism and responsibility are apt to make a new government somewhat cumbersome and angular in the conduct of its foreign affairs. We complain that it is easier to get things done with the slick autocracies—we of all peoples, who were one of the stiffest-necked and most prickly to deal with during our first century and a quarter as a nation. Moreover, our appreciation of the basically constitutional character of India's development process is diluted by our concern over central planning and over the emerging alignment between the public and private sectors of production—two separable and subsidiary issues.

Still further, there is some danger that those who are shaping American policies toward underdeveloped countries latterly have come too much under the influence of a new kind of economic determinism—one that, while a far cry from the old-fashioned Marxist kind, nevertheless measures the success of all national development programs by standards that are chiefly quantitative and economic. This kind of analysis tends to imply, for example, that two different economies in process of raising their saving rates from 5 to 15 percent are undergoing essentially the same phase of development experience and are likely to achieve essentially similar results, no matter what differences there may be in the institutional forms in which the mechanics of development are packaged. One is apt even to get the feeling that the composition of the capital formation doesn't matter; it is the total investment rate that is mainly important. Such analysis generates the impression that the rate of growth in real GNP per capita is the overwhelmingly important measure of development "progress." It leads directly to the kind of comparisons between India and China that have already been mentioned.

The old dictum that, if you offer the peasant of a poor country the ballot box (and personal freedom) or bread, he will take the bread probably is right—up to a point. He will if he's hungry enough. That is why my argument is in no sense a plea for blind support of constituted authority, for inattention to economic progress, or for institutional standpatism. The appetite for material improvement is now such in India—and in most of the other poor countries—that the only government with any chance of adhering to constitutional procedures is one that is determined to achieve radical economic reform and expansion and that is capable of so doing. This is obvious.

But the ballot-box dictum becomes a defeatist canard when it is used to assert that the people of a poor country—even when their economic condition is improving steadily and significantly—typically will prefer to make still faster material gains rather than to achieve or retain personal freedom and orderly self-rule. I am persuaded that such is not the case in India in any event. As will be said in the next chapter, I see no reason to dispute the considered judgment of India's leadership that the attainment of a rate of growth in real per-capita incomes of 3 to 4 percent annually is essential if constitutional processes are to survive. This, of course, does not mean that the rural and urban masses have any direct comprehension of this statistic, but the figures indicate the expansion in production that will be needed to provide clearly perceptible, continuing, broadly distributed improvements in diet, clothing, public services, and other categories of private and public consumption. However, if the country *should* manage to achieve this kind of economic performance, it is very unlikely that it would abandon constitutional processes in quest of still more accelerated performance. For one thing, the nation's leadership, present and foreseeable, would be hostile to such a choice, and the public, while perhaps largely unaware of the basic ideological decision it would be making, would tend to reinforce the constitutional growth process simply by participating in it.[1]

Despite the conventions of economics textbooks, consumption is not the end purpose of human existence, and the Indians do not regard it as such. It is unlikely that most of the other uncommitted countries do either, nor should the government of the United States do so in charting policies toward these countries. Not only is it consistent with our own presumed values (for not we but the Communists, after all, are supposed to be the materialists of this world), but it is to our own practical advantage to keep emphasizing to ourselves and others the procedural uniqueness of the Indian experiment. On balance, it would be better for us to think of Indian development as an essentially political phenomenon requiring major economic implementation than to put the matter the other way around.

The Economic Urgency of the Sixties

The skeptic may concede the importance of the outcome of the Indian development scheme but still boggle at the claim that the program has entered a peculiarly decisive decade. American legislators, he may argue (and one must sympathize with this point), are constantly being presented with alleged crises. Such are the stock in trade of advocates of particular policies who are competing for legislative attention. Is not the alleged urgency of the sixties for India a case in point? By common admission, after all, there is more political stability in India today than in many underdeveloped areas, and there is a systematic development effort already under way. It will be regrettable, of course, if the Indian development schemes

[1] I am indebted to Henry C. Hart for the following formulation of this last point: ". . . Growth launched constitutionally builds up effective demands for further growth (and resistances to further austerity to get it) and thus begins vesting an interest in carrying it forward constitutionally."

have to be slowed down, but why would it be disastrous? Why cannot the Indians do in the seventies or eighties whatever they don't get done in the sixties? Since American resources are not unlimited, why isn't it prudent for the United States temporarily to channel the great bulk of its overseas efforts into situations that are more immediately critical than India's?

To such queries there are two answers, one chiefly economic, the other political.

The economic answer is one that will be developed at some length in these pages, especially in Chapter 2. Briefly, it is that the massive expansion program to which India now is deeply committed is one whose momentum cannot be slowed much below its designed pace without grievously disrupting the economy. Such a slowdown could lead to protracted, debilitating drains on India's foreign-exchange reserves, and, worst of all, could waste some of the precious psychological resources for further development that have been accumulated during the past decade. Among the latter, for example, are the desire of cultivators for commercial fertilizer, the willingness of villagers to hold their savings in institutional forms, and some improvement in the public's receptiveness to higher taxes. Each of these attitudes has been painfully difficult to inculcate. Each now is catching on, thereby broadening the opportunity for an accelerated expansion in production. Each could be frustrated and set back by a development slowdown.

Official Indian planning actually proposes not a slowdown, but a substantial speedup in the development effort during the sixties. In particular, it pivots on the assumption that the country's net imports (that is, foreign aid) can surge upward to a peak level during this decade. In part, as we shall see, this planning pattern is a reaction against inadequacies in the Second Five Year Plan and in the performance of that plan. But in the main the ambitious level of both the indigenous and foreign inputs programmed for the Third and Fourth Five Year Plans is simply a by-product of the long-term development design that India has adopted. This is a twenty-five-year design that, I shall argue, is predominantly sound, is probably minimally ambitious for political purposes, and, in its effort to carry India to a condition of self-support in the international market by 1975, has to posit a bulge in net imports in some prior period. That period happens to be the sixties. Such a scheme can no more be chopped into a series of time segments that can be speeded up or slowed down without regard to what has gone before or is supposed to follow than it can be broken up into a collection of discrete industry-by-industry projects that can be started or stopped without significant impact on one another. The whole development process must be carefully integrated both among industries and through time, and the momentum it has now attained cannot be interrupted without serious waste if not complete breakdown.

I confess to some distaste for the popular phrase, "the take-off into self-sustaining growth." It is altogether too mechanical a metaphor, and it suggests a much too soaring type of progress after "take-off" occurs. But in the present context the figure does have one great merit in that a "take-off" is not an instantaneous process. It is an exercise that requires time and from which, after a certain speed has been attained and a portion of the runway used up, there is no turning back or even safe throttling down. This is India's present situation. The only safe course for the sixties is to pour on the fuel to the designed degree.

Such is the tenor of the case that will be made for the economic urgency of this decade in India. If anything, the political case is even more compelling.

The Coming Political Crisis

Despite its effectiveness during the nation's first decade and a half of independence, India's constitutionalism—her commitment to an orderly, peaceful, majority-ruled, minority-protecting, cohesive political system—is far from secure. The conjunction of at least three problems—that of the succession to an "indispensable" prime minister, that of an aging majority party, and that of regional, communal, and factional divisiveness—means that the system will face a critical test before this decade has ended.

Jawaharlal Nehru—sometimes called "The Banyan Tree" by

Indian political columnists—has dominated the landscape since India achieved independence, extending an inspirational, yet active, informed, painstaking leadership to a remarkably large majority of the departments and aspects of the nation's life. No one else has begun to match his charismatic, mystical communion with the Indian masses, nor his skill at cajoling the myriad mosaic of Indian society into retaining the form and, increasingly, into assuming the common identity of a nation. No one else, in short, has Nehru's talent for projecting the image of the New India to herself. And yet, like the banyan, Nehru has cast such a massive shadow that no worthy successors have seemed to grow at his feet.

Nehru's party, moreover, which he has led as long as he has his country, has grown old with him. The Congress commonly is alleged to be tired and to be getting tainted with corruption. It is said not to be generating fresh, dynamic leadership in its middle echelons. And in the great rural bulk of India the Party's grass-roots organization is still very much in the hands of traditionally privileged groups, which are suspicious of economic and social reforms.

The notion, familiar in the West, that India has a one-party political system is incorrect. The Congress won a plurality of only 47 percent of the total votes cast in the 1957 national parliamentary election and 45 percent in the 1962 election. At the state level it has failed in two instances so far to form a government of any kind after a state election. In several other cases Congress has been returned to power by only a plurality or as a member of a coalition. Its substantial parliamentary majorities at the Center thus far—in 1961, for example, 376 out of 507 seats in the Lok Sabha (the lower house) and 171 of 236 seats in the Rajya Sabha—can be credited to the fact that the Indian Constitution fortunately adopted the Anglo-American pattern of single-member-district, instead of proportional, representation.[2] Under the latter system the Party's recent parliamentary control would at best have been highly tenuous.

[2] The Congress' total Lok Sabha delegation in 1961 included ten "nominated," or appointed, members. Twelve seats were vacant at that time.

It is true, nevertheless, that Congress, as the post-independence extension of India's Independence Movement and bearer of Gandhi's mantle, has thus far been able to pre-empt the great middle range of the national political spectrum. Of competing secular parties which are concerned primarily to mount programs for the nation as a whole, there are only three of consequence, and only two that share Congress' commitment to constitutional processes of development and reform. These have been able to win significant support only at the extremes of the array of non-Communist opinion. On the far right, the "Swatantra," or "Freedom," Party was organized in 1959 with an aura of respectability supplied by the venerable C. R. Rajagopalachari, India's only native, post-independence but pre-Republic, Governor-General. Swatantra, reputedly financed largely by a few major industrialists, seems thus far to have been serving mainly as a vehicle for the aspirations of a few disgruntled ex-Congress intellectuals and politicians who have been using its forum to preach an extreme brand of economic conservatism. It captured 18 Lok Sabha seats in the 1962 election. Unless it alters its program, Swatantra probably has little chance of assembling a major popular following. At the other end of the spectrum of constitutionally committed parties, the (democratic, non-Marxist) Praja Socialist Party has some intellectually brilliant leadership and a significant following among industrial workers, especially in the Bombay area. But its organization is weak in most parts of the country, and it has achieved very little support from the rural masses, who still account for four-fifths of the Indian population. The Praja Socialists' Lok Sabha delegation was reduced from 16 to 12 in the 1962 election.

The range of opinion and of groups that the Congress spans between these extremes has two implications. It means that, almost by definition, Congress, as it is now constituted, is less a party than a consortium of sub-parties that have been held in uneasy coalition by the exigencies of retaining power and by the dominion of Nehru's personality. However, the party's present range also means that if the nation is to evolve a continuing constitutional leadership for the decades ahead— or better yet, a constitutional leadership *plus* an effective, responsible, and loyal opposition—it must find them (probably both of them) within the present ranks and subdivisions of the Congress.

Meanwhile, at the extreme left, the Communist Party of India, unencumbered by any durable commitment to constitutional processes, poses a direct threat to the nation's political stability. In view of that party's recently rising electoral strength in Kerala,[3] in West Bengal, and elsewhere, this is not an inconsequential challenge even in the short run. The Party won 29 Lok Sabha seats in the 1962 election, one less than it had had before.

In the eyes of most thoughtful observers of Indian politics, however, the internal Communist danger in India would not be very great were it not being nurtured by a much more deeply indigenous threat to the maintenance of orderly national government. That is the age-old, now possibly resurgent, tendency of the Indian body politic to splinter into regional and communal fragments. An indication of this tendency is the fact that most of the non-Congress votes in recent central and state parliamentary elections have gone, not to the Congress' national party rivals but to such religiously-, regionally-, and tribally-oriented groups as the Jan Sangh, the Moslem League, the militantly Sikh Akali Dal in the Punjab, and the Dravid Mummetra Kazhakam in South India. It is evinced, further, by divisiveness within the Congress, especially within the structure of the language-based states to which Mr. Nehru gave his profoundly reluctant acquiescence in 1955. Moreover, within many of the states, the regional splintering is deeply cross-hatched by caste-group rivalries that not only are divisive within their own areas but do not even have the saving grace, it is said, of building much sense of interregional community within their own strata.

The most careful (and disturbing) recent analysis of these disunifying forces is the work of the American political sci-

---

[3] Although the Communists "lost" the 1960 election in that state, thanks to a coalition among the Congress, Praja Socialist, and Moslem League parties, they polled a significantly larger plurality than they had in gaining power in 1957.

entist and journalist, Selig Harrison.[4] Harrison emphasizes, above all, India's peculiarly tortured language dilemma. Throughout the country he finds a predictable anti-colonial reaction against English, and he notes the violent opposition of the Dravidian-tongued South Indians to the proposal that Hindi become the national language. Judging that there is, for the time being, a politically irreversible trend toward official promotion of the fourteen major regional languages, which already have become the determinants of state boundaries and represent cultural identities, literatures, and values that those who speak them cherish, Harrison concludes that India faces a progressive deterioration of easy interregional communication. He cites as two particularly ominous indications of this trend the official decision (as yet largely unimplemented) to make the local regional tongues, rather than English, the languages of instruction in Indian universities and the parallel demands that even Administrative Class civil service examinations be given in the local languages.

Harrison is brought to the melancholy view that the nationally disintegrative forces—language among them—presently are in the ascendency. He does not forecast an actual breakup of the nation-state into autonomous fragments. But he does expect that the disintegrative drift will be arrested and reversed only by the strong arm of a revolutionary totalitarian government. As to whether the latter will be a rightist military dictatorship or a Communist regime, Harrison thinks probably the former. But he emphasizes the possibility of either, and he senses that, in view of the procedural uniqueness of the Indian development experiment, constitutional breakdown of the first kind would be almost as tragic as the second.

Harrison plainly is right to focus on the unity issue as the theme of India's coming political crisis. The other problems that have been identified—namely, those of succession for the Congress Party itself, as well as for its leadership—fix the form the crisis will take and, roughly, its timing. The issue comes down to this: Can the nation hold together easily under the

[4] *India: The Most Dangerous Decades* (Princeton University Press, 1960).

shocks of Mr. Nehru's retirement and/or a division in the Congress? Will it manage, under more routine leadership, to make an orderly transition to an effectively integrated two-party or few-party system of national government within the existing constitutional frame? Or will the nation so nearly come apart at the seams during the course of a succession crisis that constitutionalism will be swept aside?

One can recognize the validity of Harrison's question without accepting his answer. He may not have allowed sufficiently for the erosion of interregional and intercommunal barriers that is being worked by the broadening of markets, the facilitation of transport and communications, the location of new branch factories and central government projects, the interregional posting of personnel, the attempts at central programming, and other factors that are inherent in the economic development process itself. These aspects of that process are, as Harrison implies, the very ones that generate hostility in divisively-disposed local groups. But there is no a priori reason to assume that the unifying, integrative dynamics they set in motion are weaker than the disunifying reactions they provoke.

Harrison may well have underestimated the degree to which the commitment to constitutional methods, despite its origin as a colonial import, has become rooted in Indian values. Even in the case of the language problem, the optimist can find some reassurance in the way Indian officialdom, including Center and state cabinets as well as their secretariats, has been slow to implement its polylingual legislative mandates. This may be one of those instances in which cooler-headed administrators deliberately stall when unworkable legislation is enacted as a means for venting popular passions and then is partially retracted before it can do much damage.

Other arguments purely political in nature can be cited to contest the pessimistic forecasts of the Indian political future. There is, for instance, the point that, because a major purpose and effect of Nehru's charismatic leadership has been progressively to implant the constitutional habit, the prolongation of his tenure has been steadily improving the chances for an orderly transition thereafter. There is the related point that the banyan-tree figure after all is overdrawn —that there are several potential prime ministers who would be capable of giving the country better-than-routine leadership, as long as they did not have to hold the nation together by sheer personal magnetism.

However, the overwhelmingly important fact for our purposes is that India's political future will turn very largely on what happens to the Indian economy during the next few years. When one is talking about economically underdeveloped countries in general, it is dangerous to regard economic progress as a guarantor of orderly democratic political evolution. But India presently is a special case. She already has such a political evolution well established, and the question is whether she can muster sufficient cohesiveness of national purpose to confirm her adherence to this pattern in the face of the divisive forces certain to be triggered on the occasion of the Republic's first major political succession. This is a question that the economic record during the period leading up to and beyond the political succession very probably will decide. Nothing else is so likely to thwart the Communists, end the agitation of the communal parties, show the merit of an integrated nationwide development effort, and build a sense of national accomplishment under existing constitutional auspices as will a sustained, clearly perceptible, widely shared surge of material advance during the early sixties.

Thus India's political future probably quite literally depends on the success of the Third Five Year Plan. If the near-term economic program that now has been laid down and that we shall be examining can substantially achieve its objectives, it is easy to imagine India emerging from the sixties with the Congress split into two, but no more than two parties, the left having joined the Praja Socialists and the right having absorbed whatever is consequential in the Swatantra movement. The country thereby would be presented with a choice between two national, constitutionally responsible major parties with different economic programs. Either could bid for a national parliamentary majority or, if the Communists gained strength, at least for a sufficient plurality to organize an effective government. And in states where the Communists proved exceptionally powerful, the other two parties could join forces in an effort to keep state governments in the hands of officials who govern by constitutional means. Within party organizations, in such a transition, there might be some net shift in the balance of political power away from the Center toward the states. But with the need for, and the effectiveness of, coordinated national economic policymaking proved by the Third-Plan experience, the Center would retain its lead in economic matters, the law of the federal constitution would be undisturbed, and, in any event, the redistribution of political power in favor of subnational units would be no more extreme (probably less so) than that with which we are familiar in the United States. The transition, in short, could be to a political system that—while political scientists criticize it on some grounds—would be workable and viable.

On the other hand, if the Third Five Year Plan should fail, probably nothing would forestall the outcome Harrison predicts. The formidable forces of divisiveness already in evidence would be in full control after five years of economic disappointment and frustration. To a large extent, moreover, the damage that could be done by the resulting political breakdown would be irreparable. India's still-novel constitutional habit would be broken, and there would be no assurance that she would find her way back to it from whatever pattern of authoritarianism intervened. And certainly the procedural image that India presently holds out to the rest of the developing world would be shattered.

It should be patently clear to the Congress Party, the government of India, and the government of the United States that India's political future for as far ahead as is significant for policy purposes will turn on the economic accomplishments of the next few years.

2 BASIC DEVELOPMENT STRATEGY

Under the quarter-century scheme of economic development adopted in 1951, India's Third Five Year Plan, which covers the period beginning in April 1961, is the third in a series of five such plans, and it can be sensibly appraised only in this light. It reflects a development strategy that, while not inflexible, is already well established as to its basic outlines and continuity from plan to plan.

The great majority of Indians who have any real awareness of public affairs, moreover, are broadly committed to the essentials of the strategy. As was emphasized in the preceding chapter, India faces the prospect of major political change and the possibility of political upheaval before the sixties are ended. But upheaval is likely only if the objectives of the strategy that we shall be reviewing in Chapters 2 and 3 are not achieved.

Besides the Communists, who may safely be assumed to be procedurally at odds with the official development strategy and who would alter many of its substantive features if they came to power, there appear to be, among all of the Indian groups primarily concerned with national policy issues, only two that are fundamentally opposed to the kind of development effort the government is trying to lead. One of these is the small, hardy phalanx of Independence-Movement veterans, rural reformers, ascetics, and intellectuals, who, as the legatees of pure "Gandhian economics," are committed to the ideal of the self-sufficient individual village economy as the appropriate base for the regeneration of the traditional Indian community. The more sophisticated neo-Gandhians, including their most distinguished spokesman, Jayaprahash Narayan,[1] can see very well that their ideal is quite inconsistent with the efficient scales on which most modern indus-

[1] See particularly his so-called "thesis," *A Plea for Reconstruction of Indian Polity* (Akhil Bharat Sarva Seva Saugh, 1959).

trial processes must be conducted—even when one allows for extensive adaptations of modern technology to labor-intensive Indian conditions. But they are willing, accordingly, to let modern industrial processes go hang. The other basic dissenters are the sprinkling of extreme laissez-faireists in a few of the nation's private businesses, business organizations, and universities who deny the legitimacy of any centrally conceived and directed development effort.

The neo-Gandhians and the ultra-laissez-faireists both are highly articulate, and in diversity-tolerant India both get a good hearing. The neo-Gandhians, in fact, have an affectionate, almost deferential audience; they offer Indian intellectuals and men of affairs a vicarious asceticism that appeases one traditional strain in their culture. But the point is that both the neo-Gandhians and the ultra-laissez-faireists are now cast inescapably in the role of respected crackpots. Neither is likely to win any substantial number of practicing converts. Meanwhile, the great mass of informed Indians remains agreeably disposed toward the kind of development effort to which the nation is officially committed.

As I shall be at pains to emphasize, none of this means that the Indian development scheme, either long-term or short, is frozen, or completely and adequately articulated, or incapable of useful amendment. All the same, the present issue for responsible foreign promoters of Indian economic development is not so much what basic design they would recommend if the effort were starting again from scratch. The issue is whether the design already established or shaping is worth backing and, if so, how and how much.

The Goals

India's attempt to develop economically is primarily an effort to raise national output—or, what amounts to the same thing, national real income—in such fashion that continuing growth becomes self-sustaining and eventually India can become self-supporting in the international market. The pro-

gram, of course, is not and could not be exclusively production-oriented. It aspires explicitly to promote social equity
for low-caste and other traditionally underprivileged groups;
it seeks greater equality of economic opportunity and of income distribution among the populace; it is concerned to
reduce the massive, if unmeasured, unemployment and under-
employment that demoralize and enervate the Indian economy; and, as underscored already, it proposes to pursue all
of these substantive aims by constitutional democratic procedures. Nevertheless, the three operational goals to which
Indian development strategy is mainly addressed are those
indicated at the beginning of this paragraph:

First, the strategy undertakes, in any Plan period, to promote a stated minimum increase in real income per capita.
In view of the tendency of some Indian Plan documentation
and also of much Western economic commentary to dwell
almost exclusively on the capital-formation aspect of the development process, it is worth insisting that this per-capita-real-
income-and-output target, not the investment total or any other
magnitude, is the number around which the whole quantitative design of the program turns. Investment is only one
among a variety of related means for achieving the need of
higher product per capita.

Second, however, while it is always the purpose of the
strategy to raise product per capita in the next Plan period,
whether this be the next year or the next five years, it is also
the purpose to set in motion a continuing, self-sustaining expansion of output, and of the net-investment, technical-skills,
managerial, and other input flows necessary thereto. Accordingly, there are circumstances where, via investment and other
policies, a fraction of the maximum possible output gains in
the near term must be sacrificed in order to reinforce the
advance later on.

The third of the dominant operational objectives of Indian development strategy—one, as we shall see, that becomes
pivotal in program design—is that the expanding economy
shall, within a limited period, be enabled to pay its own way
in the international market. Its imports and exports shall be

brought into balance, except for that margain of net imports that may, for a long time, continue to be financed by a net inflow of foreign private investment.

Population Estimates and the Inter-Plan Continuity of Production Goals

Since its formal inauguration in 1951 the Indian development effort has been addressed explicitly to the pattern of goals just indicated. The First Five Year Plan was scarcely a "plan" at all if one chooses to restrict that term to a cohesive, internally consistent scheme for national economic development. But it did, like its two successor plans, propose to set in motion a continuing, self-renewing expansion in production that would also at some future date become self-supporting in a foreign-exchange sense. And it undertook to attain a modest average annual increase in real income per capita of 1.4 percent during the Plan period. Five years later the Indian authorities raised their real-income-per-capita goal sharply, targeting a growth rate of 3.7 percent a year, or a total of about 20 percent for the Second-Plan period. Now for the Third Five Year Plan, they have shaved their target back to an annual rate of 3.1 percent, or a five-year increase of 16.4 percent.

At first glance, in view of the widely discussed step-up in expansion that the Indians are said to be programming for the Third-Plan period, it may seem strange to think of the Third Plan's goal for product per capita as being moderately lower than the Second-Plan goal. However, the step-up is in the projected rate of *total* expansion in production for the Third-Plan period compared with the rate of actual expansion in total output achieved during the Second Plan. In this sense the acceleration being projected for the period 1961-62 through 1965-66 is a very considerable one, for it has been proposed that total real output be raised 31 percent, or at an annual rate of 5.5 percent, compared with an actual increase of only 20 percent, or about 3.7 percent a year, during the Second Plan. But this difference is explained, not by any increase in the intended per-capita income growth rate, but by three other factors.

In the first place, the increase in total real output achieved during the Second Plan (which, of course, was the increase in per-capita output multiplied by the increase in population) amounted to only about 3.7 percent a year, compared with the 4.6 percent average annual increase that had been projected in the Second Five Year Plan document. Second, it has been known for several years that the rate of annual population growth—1.25 percent—assumed in the Second Plan estimates was much too low. India's 1961 decennial census, from which it can be inferred that population actually grew about 2.1 percent annually during the Second-Plan period, now has revealed that this error was even worse than had been thought. Thanks to these first two factors, actual real income per capita grew an average of only 1.6 percent a year during the Second Plan, instead of at the 3.7 percent rate that had been projected.

In the third place, demographic trends require the Indian planners to assume that the average population growth in the Third-Plan years will be higher than in the Second—about 2.4 percent a year instead of 2.1 percent. This will require a greater total productive expansion to make good a given per-capita rate of growth. In combination these three factors mean that the Indian authorities are targeting a 5½ percent annual advance in total output for the 1961-62-through-1965-66 period, compared with the 3.7 percent rate actually chalked up in the preceding five years. But under the pressure of the unexpectedly rapid population growth the *intended* growth rate in *per-capita* real income has been cut back a bit.

It must be understood that the per-capita growth rate projection in the Indian program rests primarily on a political, not an economic, premise: it is the considered judgment of the Indian government and Parliament that no lesser rate of improvement is apt to support the maintenance of orderly political processes. This is the kind of indigenous judgment that foreign observers, especially economists, should be slow to challenge. It is the business of the economist, of course, to inquire whether such a goal, politically "necessary" or not, is economically feasible, and that we shall be doing. But one can say straight away that if an expansion goal as relatively temperate as the one the Indians have adopted were indeed to prove impractical for an economy possessing the momentum that theirs already has acquired, it would be a dismal omen for the prospects of non-authoritarian development techniques generally.

The Role of Government

The focal quantitative objectives of the Indian development experiment, then, really are not very startling or controversial. The specific quantitative program that has been adopted for pursuing these objectives during the 1961-66 period is considerably more complex and interesting (and controversial) than the goals themselves, and accordingly in Chapter 4 we shall take a reasonably close look at the Third Plan per se. However, summary renderings of the Plan's numerical architecture are unlikely to be very illuminating unless one understands the essential theories of development design that underlie them. Consequently in this chapter and the next I want to dwell a bit on these matters of theory, attempting to identify the general strategy that the Indians have adopted for achieving their goals.

One element of the strategy—the proposition that it is the business of government to be the principal planner, energizer, promoter, and director of the accelerated development effort —is so fundamental and so little disputed in India that one probably would not bother even to mention it to an Indian audience. However, Americans generally are ideologically more sensitive to this issue, despite the fact that they have projected their own government into an essentially similar role in every period of acute national crisis in this century. And recently in the United States there has seemed to be a particular anxiety about excessive government domination of the Indian economy. A few writers prominently noted in the American press have contended that the central and dominant economic role being played by the Indian government is, on balance, retarding the rate of expansion by sapping the well-springs of private entrepreneurship, shackling private business with controls, displacing it from investment opportunities, and pre-empting its financial resources; that government direction of the economy guarantees an inefficient, misdirected use of resources; that the present "socialist" regime is slipping toward and may lead directly into communism; and that there really isn't much to choose between the two anyway.[2]

In two later chapters, one dealing with the nature of Indian economic planning and the other with the outlook for the private business sector, including its outlook vis-à-vis public enterprises, I consider two major but limited aspects of the whole role-of-government issue. But except for these, there is not the space here to enter into a full-dress debate with the anti-government view. I do want to emphasize, however, that nothing could so utterly demolish the effectiveness of United States economic policy toward India as would its commitment to an extreme laissez-faire position.

Given the space, it is easy enough for most careful observers of the Indian economy to refute the laissez-faire case on its substantive merits. It can be argued, for example, that, except for the very first of the industrializing economies (Great Britain) and the uniquely circumstanced case of the United States, virtually every national economic development of consequence has, in its early stages, been inspired, led, and engineered by government. It can be noted that particularly in India, where government was the most highly developed of all modern institutions at the time of independence, it was natural for the political authorities to take the lead in development.

One can reasonably contend that, in an economy grinding in upon itself in a condition of low-level stagnation, some agency must take the initiative in breaking loose from the

---

[2] In India these views have been most extensively expressed in the many writings of Professor B. R. Shenoy of Ahmedabad University. The most systematic statement of them to appear in the United States is that which P. T. Bauer prepared for the American Enterprise Association and which that organization published under the title, *United States Aid and Indian Economic Development*, in 1959.

clutch of stagnationist expectations to set a general advance in motion and that, as soon as the informed minority of a traditional society becomes reasonably aware of such possibilities, a responsive government could not avoid making such an effort, even if it wanted to. There is also the familiar collateral argument that government can do what private decision makers, unassisted, cannot or on profit-seeking grounds will not, do. It can provide "infrastructure"; in its investment decision making it can value those external benefits of a project that would fall outside an individual firm's calculation; and, by promoting a concerted development in which industries that are each other's customers grow roughly in parallel, government can cause a whole group of investments to be simultaneously rewarding that would not be so if undertaken one by one.

In the Indian case there is the related point of fact that the official program retains a broad scope for private enterprise. Far from inhibiting private business activity, on balance, the development program is supplying it with an unprecedented array of market prospects and investment opportunities. Indeed, the private sector began to display its true potential for expansion only after the Second Five Year Plan had created an enlarged and convincing growth frame.

One can make the further argument by analogy, though it can be overdrawn, that an accelerated development effort invites a swift, closely-calculated reallocation of scarce resources that is not unlike that called for in a mobilization period in Western countries. It is precisely in such periods that the United States has been unwilling to accept the vagaries, delays, and perversities of market allocation. And further, the price distortions and market imperfections that characterize India, like most underdeveloped economies presently, combined with the radical realignment of relative prices that is bound to accompany the economic transformation now under way, render the rule of the market doubly inappropriate as a primary guide for resource allocation.

Finally, as should be apparent from the preceding chapter, it can be argued that the extreme laissez-faire position outlined above contains two grave political errors. First, the idea that an economically strong central government of the present type will lead the nation by degrees into communism is simply a poor political forecast. On the contrary, the country's best hope for foiling the Communists lies in maintaining an effective center and left-of-center democratic coalition that can hold the country together and offer a positive alternative to the Communist economic program. Second, the notion that Communists and Indian "socialists" of the Congress type are more alike than different depends upon an inversion of values. The similarities, such as they are, in the economic roles of government in the two systems are far less vital than are the deep differences between the two over the appropriate political procedures for economic and social reform.

For the American who is trying to decide what is the appropriate posture of his government toward the cause of Indian economic development, however, the really relevant point is simply that the Indians, in any event, already are deeply committed—one may safely say, irrevocably committed —to a central economic role for their government during their period of initial accelerated expansion. There would be no chance whatsoever of talking them or bargaining them out of this general position, even if one thought it were appropriate to try. It may be quite possible for outsiders, including outside aiding governments, to recommend specific administrative reforms, including a greater decentralization of certain kinds of decision making. They may urge the simplification of regulatory procedures or point to a number of limited industry and market contexts where greater constructive use might be made of market forces as allocative and energizing agents. And perhaps they may influence the assignment of responsibilities between the public and private sectors enough so that some close choices are tilted in favor of the latter. But the basic decision as to the role of government is set. It has been decided in India that it is the duty of government—and it cannot be delegated—to create and maintain that "growth perspective" which, Albert Hirschman has rightly insisted,[3] is the one *sine qua non* for successful economic development.

[3] Albert O. Hirschman, *The Strategy of Economic Development* (Yale University Press, 1958), p. 10.

Outside supporters of the Indian development process who refuse to accept this proposition well-nigh disqualify themselves from the outset.

The Strategy's Dominant Theme: Surmounting Critical Scarcities

As the Indian development designers view it, the task of launching the economy on a course of self-renewing growth is primarily one of freeing it from the grip of certain enervating shortages. As these critical deficiences are eased, the Indians expect that it will become increasingly easy to maintain a sustained productive expansion without extraordinary effort. But meanwhile there is an array of key bottlenecks to be broken, barriers to be breached, and restraints to be loosened.

One can go a long way toward identifying a particular country's development strategy simply by asking what it conceives its critical scarcities to be. Which of its alleged scarcities are not really disturbing? Which are important but overrated? Which others may be underrated? And which are the really pivotal ones?

An Alleged Scarcity: The Will to Work

A good many interested observers of the Indian development experiment are doing most of their worrying about the wrong shortages. As an extreme example of such a misallocation of anxiety, I would cite the concern in many Western and some Indian quarters that Indians, on balance, just are too other-worldly, too disinterested in material gains and the hard work they require, ever to generate and sustain the motivation required for a proper economic expansion. This cannot be dismissed out of hand as absurd. Individuals and groups certainly do differ in the strength of what the psychologists call their achievement-motivation, and so may whole nations. I am inclined myself to suspect (unscientifically) that even in the transformed, modernized India the appetite for material improvement may never become, on average, quite the consuming passion that it is in the United States or parts of Western Europe or Japan, or that it may turn out to be in China.

But this is by no means to say that India is a culture where the scarcity of discontent with the economic status quo is so great as to place an effective restraint on the development process. Westerners who have begun to puzzle over the economic implications of the other-worldly bits of Hindu philosophy they have encountered must remember that extraordinary diversity is the hallmark, not only of India as a whole, but of Hinduism itself. Asceticism is a specialized function in Indian culture, and for every ascetic cult there seems to be some other deviant group whose materialistic inclinations are exceptionally aggressive. Westerners must remember, too, that many of the appearances of weak productive motivation that one presently encounters in India trace to quite different causes—in many instances to sheer malnutrition, in many others, to the country's massive unemployment problem and the make-work philosophy it engenders, and, in still others, to the lack of effective market mechanisms for converting producers' wants into incentives to work harder and produce more. All of these drags on production should give way progressively under the assault of a well designed development program; none is rooted in motivations that are inherently anti-developmental.

It would be hard for anyone to live in India very long and not come to believe that its people are amply endowed with an appetite for material improvement. The urban population, certainly, already is broadly infected with a desire for rising living standards. And every veteran observer of Indian villages whom I know confirms the impression that the typical rural Indian is abundantly equipped with the urge to improve his family's material lot. Too often, as I shall be saying, he is not yet in an administrative and commercial environment that does a good enough job of harnessing these impulses to the cause of productive expansion. But the impulses are there.

There is, obviously, an important place in the strategy of Indian development for an educative and propaganda operation that strives constantly to increase the people's awareness of their national program and of the new possibilities, choices, and issues it poses. It may well be that the extensive resources being devoted to this effort are not yet sufficient. Nevertheless, it is fair to say that inherent popular apathy is not one of the critical restraints on the development process.

The Publicized Scarcity: Domestic Saving

A less extreme, but far more important, misdirection of anxiety, in my judgment, is the almost consuming concern that commentators on Indian economic development so commonly express about the country's shortage of internal saving. The new "conventional wisdom" about underdeveloped countries holds that the inability of poor countries to form capital is the overwhelming restraint on their productive expansion. It holds, further, that this inability to form much capital is explained by a poor country's inability to save much at subsistence or near-subsistence levels of income. Prior to the development push in a country like India, for example, the fraction of the national income being saved and invested is unlikely to exceed 5 percent. And (the familiar argument continues) if the situation approximately parallels the relationships between capital and output that seem to have characterized a good many other economies historically, a 5-percent-a-year saving and investment rate will support only a 1- to 2-percent annual growth in total productive capacity. Thus, if population is growing at least that fast, there can be no net improvement in per-capita incomes, no improvement, therefore, in the internal ability to save and finance noninflationary investment, and no acceleration in total productive expansion beyond the rate that barely matches the growth in population. Such, this diagnosis concludes, is the essential nature of "the low-level equilibrium trap" in which poor economies are caught and from which development programs must break them loose.

This most popular of the current development theories, which is a direct descendent of some highly simplified, capital-oriented "growth models" produced by Western economists during the nineteen-forties, prescribes as clearly as it diagnoses. The way to start raising per-capita income is to break the savings bottleneck and step up investment. (One sometimes feels that almost any kind of investment will do.) And there are two ways to do the latter: tighten belts domestically or bring in foreign capital (public and/or private) as a supplement to domestic saving. Actually most developing economies rely on both internal and external sources of increased savings, the theory continues, but a democratic development experiment like the Indian is peculiarly dependent upon foreign aid since its procedural inhibitions cut it off from the kind of "agony capital" formation that is the forte of totalitarian regimes like the Chinese. Foreign aid permits the climb in domestic investment to run ahead of domestic saving, thereby speeding the advance in real incomes that, with the help of appropriate tax and financial policies, allows the domestic saving rate to pursue and eventually overtake the investment rate.

This last finally brings us to the rather neat formulation that savings-centered development theory offers for the "self-sustaining growth" and "self-supporting growth" goals that I have attributed to the Indian program. According to this reasoning, the two goals are a single objective seen from two angles. When the fraction of the annual national income invested has been raised, say, to 15 percent, it should, if we assume an investment-incremental-capacity ratio of 3 to 1, support a 5-percent-a-year advance in total output and, assuming an annual population growth of 2 percent, about a 3-percent-a-year advance in output per capita. This may be enough to satisfy the program's minimum welfare goal. But the expansion will have become self-sustaining only if the level of incomes that now has been reached is sufficient to generate enough current domestic saving to match current investment. If this happens, and if we adopt the theory's assumption that whatever the economy is willing to save will indeed be invested, we can assume that the expansion process has become self-renewing. By the same token, since a balance between domestic saving and investment means no net inflow of foreign capital (if we wished, we could modify the picture a bit to allow for some continuing net inflow of private capital), we can reason that the country's international payments and receipts must also be in balance. It has also achieved its goal of self-support.

One does not attack lightly the theory I have just sketched. Besides its advantage of having been impressed on nontechnical readers by such exceptionally gifted writers as Barbara Ward and Walt Rostow, the theory has an intrinsic air of profundity that derives from its classic simplicity. It seems to go straight to the heart of the matter and make simple and enduring sense of the whole development puzzle. As a result, a great many people have found it a convincing justification for policies, especially in the foreign aid field, in which I believe there is great merit. One hesitates to challenge the basis for these policy convictions without supplying a substitute that is equally simple.

Moreover, on the merits of the theory itself, it would be easy to carry one's criticism too far. For certainly there *is* a general scarcity of capital in poor economies; capital is vastly more scarce, for example, than unskilled labor, and it deserves to have a relatively high price attached to it. Plainly it is harder for a poor economy than a rich one to forego consuming the same fraction of its national income, and, accordingly, a good deal of attention does need to be given to the design of responsible internal financial policies in any intensified development program.

Disagreement with the savings-centered theory of development is likely to seem particularly formidable to any student of Indian development, for at first sight the Indian program looks for all the world like a textbook illustration of the theory. For one thing, the numbers fit. Investment and domestic saving, according to the planning documents, were both on the order of 5 percent of the national income when the First Plan was started. Then, with investment taking the lead and net imports filling the gap, they moved up to 7.3 and 7.0 percent, respectively, by the end of the First Plan and to about 11- and 8½-percent levels by the end of the Second Plan. The investment rate is slated to reach about 14.5 percent and the saving rate, about 11.5 percent by 1965-66; it is proposed that they reach values of about 17 to 18 percent and 15 to 16 percent respectively by 1970-71; and they should be coming into line with each other (the economy should be approaching a self-sustaining, self-supporting performance) at the 18-to-20-percent level by 1975-76.[4] Moreover, the organization and the slogans of the Indian program, which include special high-level national committees on savings, a continuing "small savings campaign," and, in general, very strong representation of financially oriented (as opposed to "physically oriented") agencies in the planning process, suggest a preoccupation with the savings bottleneck. At a number of points the formal official articulations of the Indian program seem to be almost slavishly rooted in the savings-centered theory. Particularly is this true of the earlier chapters of the Second Five Year Plan document, possibly the most lucid statement of development rationale that the government of India has yet issued.

Be all of this as it may, I am persuaded of two things: First, an Indian development strategy that was in fact based primarily on savings-centered development theory would be grossly misguided and ineffective. Second, however, the Indian strategy, despite appearances, is not really of this sort.

The trouble with the savings-centered theory is not so much that it is descriptively incorrect; it is normatively misleading. It is altogether likely that soon after India achieves a real-per-capita-income growth rate of 3 to 4 percent a year (and, therefore, a real aggregate growth rate of 5 to 6 percent yearly), the domestic saving rate will indeed be approaching a level of 15 percent or better and will be nearing the investment rate. But this does not mean that it is helpful from a policy viewpoint, to regard the rise in saving as the *cause* of the rise in real income or to think that the main function of net imports is simply to supplement total domestic saving. The error lies in interpreting past statistical relationships between saving and output to mean that policies bearing directly on the volume of saving per se are the handles one must grasp to

[4] Government of India: Planning Commission, *The Third Five Year Plan* (1961), p. 28. (Cited hereinafter as Third-Plan document.)

engineer an expansion in production. A far more appropriate
assumption is that the saving rate is a symptom, a reflection,
of the economy's productive performance, which, in turn, is
determined by a whole collection of variables, of which the
private propensity to save is only one of the lesser.

One must be careful, to be sure, not to overdo this argument to the point of implying that domestic saving literally can
be no problem—that a sufficient supply of it always automatically will be forthcoming to meet the requirements set by a
development program. This, of course, is not so. The supply
is not fully automatic; it requires conditioning by appropriate
domestic financial policies; and, if severe enough, a scarcity of
domestic savings can, through the mechanism of an unacceptable or disruptive rate of price inflation, hobble a development
effort. Thus it is possible to conceive of an underdeveloped
country in which a narrowly savings-centered development
strategy would be appropriate. But such a country would have
to satisfy a rather peculiar combination of conditions: on the
one hand, its savings bottleneck would be very narrow and
brittle; on the other hand, the country would be free of other
major growth-inhibiting scarcities.

In the Indian case, in the first place, the domestic saving
bottleneck is *not* an overwhelming problem. Despite the low
level of average incomes, the very unequal distribution of incomes indicates a considerable capacity to save in the upper
income groups. Moreover, there is increasing evidence that
even average Indian villagers do a good deal of saving—in
defiance, as it were, of Western concepts of a "subsistence"
level of income. Evidence also is accumulating that many
cultivators and other small enterprisers are prepared to step up
considerably their rates of saving out of existing incomes as
fast as they become convinced that their opportunities for
profitable direct investments have improved. Most convincing of all is the point that the Indian central and state governments, with their large budgets and extensive government enterprises, are in a position to provide needed supplements to
private saving by raising taxes and/or widening the cost-price
spreads in commodities the government markets. While the
scope for such steps usually faces close political limits at any

given moment, a strong government has a sizable opportunity to increase government savings in the longer term.

The other side of the matter is that India is far from being an economy that, aside from the savings problem, is "free of other major growth-inhibiting scarcities." The savings-centered theory's gross oversimplification of the development process is misleading in the Indian case, first, because of its unwarranted assumption that the community's propensity to save is the only, or principal, determinant of how much it invests and, second, because of its unwarranted assumption that the volume of total investment is the only important, or at least the only readily variable, determinant of productive expansion. In India, as we shall be noting in the following sections, the really problematical issues for development are certain specific needed inputs of commodities, skills, organization, and foreign exchange. The appropriate strategy is one that is geared to these specific scarcities. It must, as I have emphasized, include a responsible domestic financing (or domestic savings) program, but it nevertheless can be drawn on the principle that any development scheme that is physically, technically, and organizationally feasible, and that makes sense on the foreign-exchange side, need encounter no insurmountable domestic financing difficulties. By way of contrast, a narrowly savings-centered strategy would have a sterile, enervating, single-tracked pre-occupation with consumer austerity and would offer little in the way of positive attacks on the other dimensions of the problem.

The actual Indian development design, as I have indicated, is much more of the former than of the latter sort. It is true that the designers, including the many drawn from the Ministry of Finance, the central bank, and other financial backgrounds, do a lot of talking about savings and sometimes exhibit more nervousness about inflationary risks than I, for one, would like. As I shall be suggesting in the next chapter, they have in the past allowed this anxiety greatly to inhibit their approach to the problem of mobilizing the economy's idle resources. But for the most part they have torn through the veil in which conventional savings-centered theory shrouds the development problem and have come to grips with the real issues—to some of which we now turn.

Shortages of Decision Making, Skilled Manpower, and Technique

We do not need to linger long at this point—especially because several of the issues involved will come in for specific comment in later chapters—over the fact that the Indian development effort depends critically upon a variety of know-how and organizational inputs. Albert Hirschman has made the point that "the ability to invest" (by which he means the capacity to identify new investment opportunities, to organize, administer, and risk resources in pursuit of them, and, in general, to perform those functions that in Western thought we lump under the heading of entrepreneurship) is likely in most underdeveloped economies to place a closer limit on capital formation than does the ability to save.[5] This, as I have implied already, has a good deal of validity in the Indian case. Moreover, the Indian economy is striving for a wholesale transformation of its technology, and it is finding that in many instances, because of the differences in factor proportions and costs, or for other reasons, it is not particularly satisfactory to take over the advanced economies' existing productive techniques and processes whole cloth. Thus not only is India encountering a shortage of relevant, especially novel, technology; it is plagued by a scarcity of specialized professional and skilled personnel to press the transformation and man and administer the new processes. Moreover, as we shall be noting, it is troubled by public-administrative and other organizational deficiencies.

Measures to ease all of these scarcities have their place in the next phases of the official Indian development scheme, and we shall be encountering a number of them as we proceed. Yet it is fair to say that it is the sense of current Indian programming that the factors mentioned now constitute only limited restraints on the design of the development effort and

[5] Op. cit., pp. 35ff.

that they are well on the way to being surmounted. The comparative confidence with respect to these variables derives from two kinds of sources. For one thing, India started its intensified development experiment much stronger in most of these respects than are most underdeveloped economies even today. It arrived at independence with a comparatively experienced government, a thoroughly structured bureaucracy, and a public service of high average competence and training in its upper echelons. It also possessed a sizable, although inadequate, number of able, highly trained technical personnel, and (in terms of both personnel and institutions) the core of a university, research, and applied scientific community. And, while there may not have been enough existing "entrepreneurship" to satisfy all of the requirements of a developmental push, there were many thoroughly established, vigorous, well defined entrepreneurial groups together with most of the institutional structure needed for a substantial scale of operation.

The second source of confidence on this score is the record of achievement during the past decade. The clearest example (so prominent as to be almost inconspicuous) is the massive supplement to entrepreneurial decision making that has been supplied by a functioning central economic programming mechanism—for such, in an important sense, is precisely the effect of the latter. This is not to say that the provision of facilities and adoption of policies to broaden the incidence of modern private entrepreneurship does not remain a lively issue (see Chapter 8) or that there is not plenty of room for improving the government's machinery for making and implementing new investment decisions (see Chapter 5). Nevertheless, in India during the past decade government intervention plainly has knocked Hirschman's inability-to-invest bottleneck out of the line-up of principal obstacles to development.

Less dramatic but substantial, mostly steady, progress also has been made toward easing many of the manpower and technique scarcities. Experience has accrued with a variety of arrangements for importing technical assistance and, perhaps more important, for seeding and multiplying its indigenous impact. A seemingly endless array and variety of training institutions and programs have been inaugurated. Many promising research institutions have taken shape. And in the fields both of public and of private business administration a fairly active pursuit of improvements is under way.

The general impression one gets from the Third Five Year Plan—that the solutions to the nation's decision-making, organizational, skilled-manpower, and technique problems are, for the most part, progressing well and that the present Plan can move them all along another notch without their becoming (except in a few rare instances) major restraints on over-all development design—is not, I shall be saying, an entirely correct view. In the realm of technological policy and with respect to certain organizational matters, particularly in the countryside, it borders on dangerous complacency. But insofar as this view permits a direct focus upon the most constrictive of all the scarcities with which Indian development strategy must come to terms—namely, the simple matter of foreign exchange —I cannot but have sympathy for it.

The Pivotal Foreign-Exchange Scarcity and the Doctrine of "Balanced" Development

The fact that the country's shortage of foreign exchange has not been generally recognized as the pivotal scarcity facing Indian development planners shows that social scientists are sometimes inclined to be too sophisticated for their own good. For this certainly is the easiest scarcity to see, and it cannot be put down simply as the superficial manifestation of an underlying inability to save enough or produce enough total output. This is for the obvious reason that there is no perfect, or even approximate, domestic substitute for some of the foreign products India needs. India now has, and will continue to have, many specific needs for imports. Moreover, the problem will not be solved automatically by the development of a surplus of domestic production (over domestic uses of that production) large enough to match the import requirement. For there is no automatic assurance that all of this exportable surplus will be of types and qualities that can be successfully marketed overseas.

It is no adequate answer to this point to argue, along the comparative-cost lines of neo-classical economics, that if the Indian and international markets both were perfectly free and competitive, the country's exportable surplus eventually would adjust to a product and price composition that could be fully sold abroad. For, in the first place, the markets are not perfectly free and competitive. Second, the aggregate rate of growth in national output that would be consistent with such a self-equilibrating trade balance, as well as the factor-price adjustments it might imply, very probably would not yield the minimum rates of welfare improvement that the Indian program is positing as politically necessary. And, third, it is likely that long before enough time had elapsed for an automatic import-export adjustment to have worked itself out, India would have exhausted its foreign-exchange resources and thereby, thanks to the consequent interruption of expansion, have been plunged into political chaos.

Moreover, to pin down an earlier point: the proposition that the availability of foreign exchange per se can constitute a decisive restraint on development in a case like the Indian one is not disturbed by the accounting truism that, on an *ex post* basis, the excess of the country's imports over its exports (that is, its net use of foreign exchange) always equals the excess of its investment over its domestic saving. The accounting identity provides no indication of causation. It is possible, of course, for the tightest real bottlenecks to be lodged in the savings sector, so that the shortfall of domestic saving relative to investment does indeed causally determine the net-import requirement, as savings-centered development theory suggests. But it is just as possible for the causation to run the other way. An independent foreign-exchange bottleneck, by limiting domestic investment and production through its rationing of the complementary imports upon which they depend, and by influencing the volume of domestic saving through its influence on the rate of expansion of real income, can just as well determine the domestic investment-saving balance. As between these two extreme possibilities, the latter, I am saying, is more nearly the actual situation in India.

While, according to the official Indian development design, the country's needs for imports will be heaviest in the next few years, one can clearly see the reason for this design only if he looks ahead to the balance-of-payments problem that the Indian economy will tend to have in the longer run if it achieves the kind of steady expansion in real income per capita that the planners are projecting. The fact is that for a very long time to come India will find it very difficult to sell enough exports to pay for the importing that it will be disposed to do at rising income levels. If the country were to keep relying on foreign suppliers for all of those types of goods and services it now procures abroad, imports would rise precipitously—much faster than total income—as income rises. Such will be the effect of the changing composition of consumer, enterprise, and general-government demand associated with expanding incomes.

But there will be no corresponding automatic growth in exports. On the contrary, the secular demand for several of India's traditional commodity exports, such as jute and tea, appears sluggish; the country can anticipate, to say the least, no exportable surplus of staple foods; the export markets for its minerals and other raw materials constitute, at best, highly volatile, unreliable bases upon which to rest the internal development program; many of India's conventional fabricated products, notably textiles, are among the first items that other newly industrializing countries start making for themselves; and, while India should eventually become a major exporter of such heavy industrial products as steel and of light engineering goods, it will be some time before Indian producers in these lines have their costs, capacities, and marketing arrangements in shape for doing very successful battle with such competitors as the West Germans and the Japanese.

This longer-run balance-of-payments outlook has a variety of implications for policy. It means, for one thing, that the Indians themselves must work hard to promote exports and that India's friends must be prepared to accept and encourage such efforts. I shall enlarge upon these points in Chapter 9. The prospect of a persisting foreign-exchange shortage means too that we must expect the Indian authorities to continue restricting the entry of nonessential imports. Most important of all, however, India's long-term foreign-exchange outlook tends to shape her whole indigenous development design. For it means that the economy must do all it reasonably can to develop domestic substitutes for its otherwise rapidly expanding import requirements. Insofar as the central question of development design involves the composition of the output expansion that is to be promoted, the foreign-exchange bottleneck supplies the crucial answer: As far as is feasible, the production pattern of the expanding economy should be designed to supply the needs of its pattern of consumption and other end uses.

Such basically is the route India has chosen for achieving self-supporting, self-sustaining growth, and personally I know of no other that is equally reasonable. But it should be emphasized that this pursuit of the goal of longer-run self-support primarily via the route of import substitution is just what makes for such a heavy net-import requirement in the shorter run. For among all types of current indigenous production it is the creation of new facilities for new industries that typically generates the greatest need for current imports. Consequently, in one of its most important dimensions, the Indian development scheme boils down to this: It calls for very heavy foreign-exchange deficits temporarily as a means of forestalling an endless, chronically unmanageable foreign-exchange crisis later on.

In Chapter 5, which deals in part with Indian planning techniques, we shall be noting that the key principle of the development design (import substitution) is, of course, not an absolute. Obviously there is no intention that India shall strive to produce those raw materials for which she has wholly inadequate natural resources. Nor must she, in all instances, stop using materials that she cannot produce domestically, or, indeed, turn out every last product of which she is physically capable without regard to differentials between domestic and foreign costs. As a matter of fact, the Planning Commission's projections show the country's "maintenance" imports rising in absolute quantity throughout the sixties.

Nevertheless, the foreign-exchange bottleneck does mean that, in reaching marginal decisions about whether to continue importing or to start producing certain commodities, the planning authorities must attach a much higher price to foreign exchange than the rupee's official rate would suggest when they compare foreign with domestic costs. And as a matter of fact, the Indian production program that has resulted from the application of such criteria is exceedingly varied and comprehensive in its commodity composition. To many Western eyes it is surprisingly so. For example, to cite a minor but illuminating detail, the program does not envisage that India will ever produce a satisfactory domestic substitute for fine Swiss watches, and it contemplates a modest continuing importation of such watches. But it does provide for the early establishment of an Indian factory (with a private foreign partner) that will make serviceable cheap watches to begin meeting the mass demand for such timepieces, especially in the countryside.

My own view is that the Indian effort to move forward simultaneously on a variety of production fronts—and particularly, as I shall be arguing in the next section, in heavy industry and agriculture—is not only justified but essential. However, students of Indian affairs should emphasize that the same prescription is not necessarily applicable to other underdeveloped economies; it fits India's particular set of circumstances. One of the latter is the prospect of the continuing foreign-exchange scarcity that we have just been discussing. This is the *motivating* circumstance that causes development design to push as far in the direction of self-sufficiency as is feasible; and this circumstance, I increasingly suspect, may characterize the great majority of the underdeveloped economies. But in India there are also the following *permissive* circumstances that allow development designers rationally to pursue a long way the self-sufficiency impulse. First, the economy is enormous, and so are the potential sizes of its markets. Even in the near term there is a great variety of products for which demand will be sufficient to permit efficient scales of production by at least a few plants. Second, India is blessed with a fairly good mix of natural resources for servicing the foreseeable material and energy needs of her development program. A striking example is the country's resource base for steel making. Third, India's human and institutional resources include a body of administrative, technical, and scientific sophistication that, although thinly spread, is unmatched in most newly developing economies.

The line of argument I have been pursuing in this chapter already has suggested by implication that it might be a useful exercise for American public-policymakers to try classifying the various backward economies with which they have to deal into categories differentiated by their pivotal scarcities. As an extension of such an analysis, they might find it very helpful to divide the large category whose pivotal scarcity is foreign exchange into subgroups characterized by different combinations of the *permissive* circumstances noted above. In any such classification the Indian case would emerge as an extreme. It is one in which a production-expansion program aimed toward self-sufficiency not only is exceptionally appropriate for foreign-exchange reasons; it is exceptionally feasible.

It is mainly because of the characteristic we have just been discussing that the Indian scheme often is called a plan for "balanced development." When the latter concept is being used carefully (and often it is not), it suggests an attempt to effect concurrent expansion in a wide variety of industries so that the pattern of domestic end-product output would tend to match the pattern of domestic end use and so that the expansion of social overheads and of primary and intermediate products would meet the requirements set by end-product output. In other words, "balanced development" is essentially a production plan based on the import-displacement principle.

Since this general design for development, which seems to me so appropriate for the Indian situation, has been the subject of apparent attack by Albert Hirschman,[6] for whose general analysis of the development process I have already indicated a good deal of respect, I want to say a word about the applicability of Hirschman's critique to the Indian case. Economic progress, Hirschman argues, never has proceeded via a pattern of perfectly synchronized and complementary inter-industry relations. The way of the world is that one vigorous sector thrusts forward ahead of the pack, thereby creating dynamic tensions that induce the decisions that are necessary

[6] *Op. cit.,* especially Chapters 3 and 4.

if other sectors are to catch up. Then some of these other sectors more than catch up, a new set of dynamic tensions is created, and development continues its crab-like progress by a process whose very essence is the generation of, and the reactions to, a series of strategic imbalances. Hirschman, who (as we have noted) believes that the typical underdeveloped economy's scarcest resource is its supply of autonomous, expansion-actuating decisions, would have development planners build their design around this same kind of process. They would concentrate their energies on creating strategic imbalances that would set in motion sequences of induced (not specifically planned) development decisions, thereby maximizing the leverage of the planners' own limited capacity for autonomous decision making.

One would be foolish to claim that this analysis has no relevance to the Indian case. Certainly it is historically relevant. The expanding economy, even under central planning, has made its way from one inter-industry imbalance to another. And, as Hirschman suggests, the imbalances have tended to induce, after a time, corrective or overcorrective responses, not only in the private sector but in government programs by jarring loose the inertias and inconsistencies with which they are often afflicted. Such seems to be precisely the condition, for example, of India's current coal production program.

Moreover, Hirschman's point does have some policy relevance. The imagination and will to venture, to innovate, and to invest is by no means so copiously distributed throughout the public and private segments of the Indian economy as to merit no leverage. I shall be pointing to some tactical aspects of the Indian program, and shall be suggesting the addition of some others, that would activate just the sort of decision-making multipliers Hirschman has in mind.

Nonetheless, as *strategy*, as over-all design, the deliberate-imbalances approach simply does not fit the Indian case. Part of the reason was cited earlier: For all of its limitations and imperfections, developmental decision making in contemporary India is not nearly as scarce a resource as Hirschman posits. The rest of the reason is far more compelling: In any event, India cannot afford the luxury of a program of deliberate imbalances. For such an approach can be enormously costly in ways that those who admire its "dynamic tensions" do not emphasize. It can be costly in terms of capital—capital, for instance, that is locked up in steel mills that are not producing to capacity because coal mining and coal washeries have not been brought along as they should have been. By the same token, the approach can be costly in terms of lost output. Above all, it can be costly in terms of foreign exchange, for which there is an unforeseen need, for example, to import supplements for bottlenecked domestic industrial production or to fill a widening gap between income and domestic food production.

The foreign-exchange restraint that circumscribes and shapes the Indian development design is simply too severe to allow the government of India to turn a foible into a creed and accept unbalanced development as an ideal.[7] Even if government initiative should not be able entirely to fill the decision-making gap that Hirschman foresees, it would be wise of India to settle for a slightly slower but more orderly advance that would minimize the unexpected costs, especially the unexpected foreign-exchange costs, that the development effort generates.[8]

Agriculture and Heavy Industry

Observers of the Indian economy are apt to get the impression that not one but two great economic reform movements

[7] For a similar critique of the Hirschman doctrine, see Gustav F. Papanek, "Framing a Development Policy," *International Conciliation,* Carnegie Endowment for International Peace (March 1960).

[8] In other portions of Hirschman's analysis he notes the foreign-exchange hazards of a "final-touches" first, industrializing backward, kind of development as an "argument for accelerating the establishment of basic industries in developing countries." He so clearly recognizes the considerations emphasized in the text that I can only conclude that his general prescription is made on the assumption that foreign exchange is not a peculiarly inhibiting factor. (See *op. cit.,* pp. 166-73.)

are afoot in the country. One is the program of large-scale industrialization, mainly in such heavy industries as coal, steel, machinery and machine tools, trucks, locomotives, basic chemicals, fertilizers, and electrical generation. The other effort concentrates on the countryside—primarily on agriculture but also on such related matters as community development, local construction and public works projects, rural industries, and cooperatives. These two main strands of the development program overlap, of course; they are administratively as well as conceptually interconnected. But they have different constituencies, different leaderships, different moods, and different preoccupations. And observers often view them as competing efforts. It has been fashionable to charge that India went overboard on heavy industry in its Second Five Year Plan; that consequently the rural, especially the agricultural, side of the effort got slighted; and that in the Third Plan agriculture ought to be returned to the top-priority spot it is alleged to have occupied in the "more successful" First Five Year Plan.

One thing wrong with this familiar line, it seems to me, is that it misinterprets the history of Indian planning. Agriculture was, to be sure, the top-priority activity in the First Plan, but it won the role partly, at least, by default. Far from being a really comprehensive, integrated economic program, the First Plan was essentially an assembly of whatever development projects the existing ministries and agencies of the government of that time had already formulated. And since the established agencies, like the economy they served, were heavily oriented toward agriculture and its supporting activities, it was natural for the projects assembled to have the same orientation. While the Second Plan, which marked the virtual inauguration of comprehensive economic programming in India, certainly did bring a sharp upgrading of the heavy industry effort (on import-substitution grounds), there was no real intention of downgrading agriculture. That it too was to be emphasized is witnessed by the quite ambitious goals that were set for per-capita food production.

The Second-Plan designers did make mistakes (basically two, it seems to me) that caused them to underestimate the effort needed to make good their per-capita food targets. First, as we have seen, they grossly underestimated the rate of population growth. Second, they probably let the two successive good monsoon years that had occurred late in the First-Plan period color their thinking about the difficulty of raising farm production. They thought the job was easier than it is. But their per-capita food goals were ambitious enough, and these are essentially the same goals (when expressed in annual rate-of-increase terms) that have been carried forward into the Third Plan. The re-emphasis on agriculture in the current plan reflects the revised population estimates and a soberer appraisal of the obstacles that the farm production program must overcome. The Third Plan, like the Second, is supposed to have a double-barrelled heavy industry *and* rural emphasis.

As will appear in Chapters 6 and 7, I share the discontent with the recent agricultural and rural performance in India. But I emphatically dispute the contention that the relation between the rural and heavy-industry elements in the development effort is mainly competitive. For one thing, the two *need* not conflict to any serious extent since the scarce inputs they claim are largely dissimilar. In heavy and other larger-scale industries the bottlenecks that govern the rate of expansion are in imported capital goods and technical personnel. In agriculture and the rural economy, on the other hand, the development problem is primarily an organizational one. The latter if anything is tougher, not easier, for this reason. But its solution does not require heavy outlays of foreign exchange (if we leave aside, for now, the special matter of United States surplus food imports, to which we shall give extended attention later on), nor does it claim many of the specialized human resources needed by heavy industry. This, like most such distinctions, of course, is not absolute. The notable exception to it is agriculture's urgent need for foreign exchange to develop domestic commercial fertilizer capacity. But even in this instance the foreign-exchange needs are quite modest when compared with those of the total industrial program. They do not seriously disturb the proposition that the heavy industry effort and the rural effort can be pressed at their maximum feasible rates in their respective spheres without getting in each other's way—as long as neither pre-empts the support and leadership that the other deserves from the highest echelons of government.[9]

The compatibility of the twin heavy industry and agriculture emphases can be put much more positively than this, however. For the two main strands of the total program are not just largely noncompetitive; they are complementary. Both are needed. They must be pressed simultaneously. And neither can get very far ahead of the other without disruptive consequences. The reason for this most obvious manifestation of India's balanced-development design is, of course, the one explored in the preceding section. The point is plain enough in the case of agriculture: Since it can be confidently predicted that if the country accomplishes its purpose of raising its total real output and income an average of 5 to 6 percent a year during the sixties, its demand for food will increase at an average rate of 4 to 5 percent a year, India is going to have to boost its food output nearly 5 percent annually during the current decade to match this growth in demand, eliminate its present food deficits, and become self-supporting in this sector. This it must do—not necessarily year in and year out but on average—if it does not want to slow down its whole expansion effort. This is so, however, not because, as some Indian political discussions seem to imply, there is some ideological or national-security need for a truly sovereign nation to be able to feed itself. It is so because, in the event of a widening gap between domestic food production and consumption, neither of the two alternative consequences would be acceptable. On the one hand, the country could not afford the extra foreign exchange that would be needed to fill a widening food gap with

[9] This final proviso may well deserve more emphasis than I am inclined to give it at this stage in the argument. The predominant error in commentaries on the interrelationships of the rural and heavy-industry elements in the Indian program has been to exaggerate the necessary competition between them, and it is this that I am presently concerned to challenge. As will be implied in Chapters 6 and 7, however, the two strands in the effort *have* competed to some extent for top programming and administrative talent and, in particular for what might be called the Indian Cabinet's limited supply of adrenaline—with the rural strand often coming out second best. This allocation of top-level concern does require some redressing.

imports. On the other hand, its political fabric probably could not stand, and its administrative structure almost surely could not suppress, the violent inflation of food prices that would result from leaving such a gap unfilled.

Western commentators on the Indian experiment generally are quick to accept this line of argument in the case of food. But, oddly enough, many of them refuse to see that precisely the same basic argument makes the heavy industry program equally essential if the country is to attain both its projected growth rate and eventual international self-support. We know very well that, with rising real incomes, the nation's demands for the products and services of heavy industries also are going to rise—in this instance not only absolutely but relatively. Yet India cannot anticipate enough foreign earnings in the long run to fill most of these requirements via imports. And it certainly cannot afford the disruption of trying to leave them unfilled. Its only real choice is to become self-supplying to a great extent.

Unhappily for the American image in India, the agriculture-first critique of the country's heavy-industrial undertakings came, in the late nineteen-fifties, to be regarded as a peculiarly American complaint.[10] The Indian government suspected that many leading Americans, official and otherwise, who adopted a pro-agriculture, anti-heavy-industry posture were motivated by such comparatively extraneous considerations as, first, distaste for the public-enterprise form in which the Indians choose to organize most of their new heavy industries and, second, fear of eventual Indian competition with

[10] This stereotype was in no small measure set by the widely distributed report, *India's Food Crisis and Steps to Meet It,* made by a team of American agricultural economists employed by the Ford Foundation in 1959 (issued by Government of India: Ministries of Food and Agriculture and of Community Development and Cooperation, April 1959). The first few pages of this document (the balance of which goes on to make a good professional diagnosis of India's farm production problems) draw a disturbing and, it seems to me, considerably exaggerated picture of the required rate of food expansion. Then, adopting the role of general economic programmers, the authors assert that the achievement of these targets must be accorded absolute priority, whatever the consequences for the rest of the development effort.

American industrial exports. Whether or not these were fair suspicions (my impression is that the first was, the second was not, as far as the motivations of the United States government policy were concerned), they greatly narrowed the opportunity for Americans to exert a constructive influence on Indian programming. From here on the United States government will be well advised to accept and support a balance between agriculture and heavy industry as an essential characteristic of the Indian design. For that is the way the Indian authorities regard the matter, and their doctrine makes sense.

3 MOBILIZING IDLE MANPOWER— A SECONDARY STRATEGY

The main line of India's development strategy, as we have seen, is a scheme for overcoming the economy's critical resource scarcities in a way that will maximize the long-run expansion of total output of a roughly specified commodity composition. Along with its problems of scarce resources, however, the country also faces the conceptually distinguishable—and, most certainly, the politically distinguishable—problem of redundant resources in the form of idle manpower. I do not propose to linger over the question of just how great this problem is. Presently there is no really adequate measure of India's total involuntary idleness (including both unemployment and underemployment), and I shall be pleasantly surprised if any is developed for a long time.[1] However, this is one subject about which our need for precise knowledge is not particularly urgent. For it is obvious that, whatever its exact size, the volume of idle manpower (most of it still located in the countryside) is enormous. Since it is also obvious that, under such circumstances, any viable government must, for political reasons, have some overt program for promoting employment, the vital question at present with respect to idle Indian labor is less one of empirical measurement than of policy. What is the government's program for reducing unemployment? Or, in more positive terms, what is the program for mobilizing idle manpower to perform development tasks?

[1] How, for instance, is one to classify the urban in-migrant who, instead of doing absolutely nothing, joins Bombay's army of underemployed bootblacks or Delhi's throngs of self-appointed (and tippable) parking directors, or who becomes an extra, redundant salesman in the yard goods stall of the cousin, who according to custom, is going to have to provide him with bed and board anyway? Or how, for that matter, is one to develop meaningful and consistent measures of the part-time idleness and labor redundancy in a typical Indian village?

These are questions that take a bit of answering. For one thing, they concern an area of Indian strategy that, if I am not mistaken, is still forming. The official view in 1961 was not the same as it was in 1956, and it was still evolving. By the same token the consensus within the government on just what the official employment strategy is remains a good deal less firm than is the case with the main thrust of the production effort—economizing on foreign exchange. There is a further reason why the subject of employment policy becomes rather complex: The questions to which the Indian authorities are still in process of evolving considered answers are not the simpler, grosser issues over which debate in this area usually has been joined. In contrast with Indians generally, the Indian planners already have slashed their way through these grosser matters and are now occupied with some subtler but vital questions that lie beyond them.

Employment, Production, and Productivity

What I mean by the "grosser issues" are the questions whether the country's production and employment objectives are *mainly* compatible or not and (what comes down very nearly to the same thing) whether productive improvements that raise output per man are to be feared on the ground that they kill off jobs. A distressingly large number of Indians have taken the alarmist view. Everywhere one turns he encounters publicists, politicians, labor leaders, bureaucrats, and even private business managers of a make-work mentality who sense a fundamental conflict between the nation's employment needs and the kind of expansion in production the government is pressing. Innovations in production technique are feared because they may put people out of work. Repeatedly, even from high-level experts, one hears the statement that in agriculture the effort should be to raise output per acre, not output per worker; and in industry, not labor productivity, but capital productivity.

The bulk of professional economic opinion, Indian and otherwise, is arrayed against these views. Their basic fallacy, the rebuttal contends, is in the assumption that employment goals ever can be divorced from output and income goals. Any society, if it could rid itself of enough technique and capital, could keep every one of its ambulatory members fully employed grubbing for roots and berries. But that is not what is wanted—in India or elsewhere. The desire is for rising employment *with* rising per-capita real incomes. The only way India can achieve this objective is through a program that raises output per member of the total labor force, both employed and unemployed. (Indeed, the only reason for worrying about the productivity of land and of capital is a concern that these scarce factors be spread around in a way that will maximize the productivity of the total labor force.) And the only way to raise general labor productivity is through improvements that increase the output of particular fragments of the labor force. The fact that these specific improvements may force particular workers and firms and even whole trades to change their employment should not be allowed to disguise their generally beneficial character. For, while there may be humane or political reason for cushioning the impact of such dislocations, the dislocations themselves are the essence of progress in any economic system.

Moreover, the circumstance in the West—namely, a deficiency in aggregate demand relative to the economy's total current productive capacity—that sometimes allows improvements in productivity to have an adverse effect on total employment, ought to be one of the last things that India should have to worry about in this era. For the country is faced, after all, with towering needs for development outlays, and it is equipped with an effective, fiscally sophisticated government. An alternative possibility cannot be dismissed quite so readily. That is that particular improvements in methods of production may chew up so much of the economy's limited supplies of foreign exchange, domestic capital, land, or other scarce resources that not enough of these resources are left to provide minimal tools and facilities for re-employing any dislocatees. For the scarcities of these complementary factors are generally thought to be the principal reason why an economy like the Indian is suffering mass unemployment in the

first place. However, it seems unlikely that a system of allocating scarce resources, either by the market or by a planning commission, that is rational for purposes of maximizing
output will miss very far in maximizing employment. (At this
point, as we shall see, the conventional economic argument
becomes a bit shaky, especially for an economy that is trying,
for foreign-exchange reasons, to maximize not just total output but rather total output of a roughly predetermined composition.) At any rate, the static aspects of the issue probably
are overwhelmed by the dynamic. That is to say, if present
mass unemployment is indeed the result largely of comple-
mentary-resource scarcities, in the long run the facilitation
of employment that the official program of "balanced" industrial expansion will accomplish by augmenting the domestic
supplies of such scarce resources as steel, machinery, mechanical energy, and trained managerial talent is almost certain
far to outweigh any restraint on the multiplication of employment opportunities that the composition of the program
entails in the near term.

Accordingly, as to the "grosser" issues of Indian employment policy, most responsible economic opinion takes the
position that the government's best means for promoting employment is, by all odds, simply to press its effort to expand
output; that whatever palliatives for the unemployment problem are adopted should not be allowed to dull or dissipate
the main thrust of the production program; and that, in particular, everything feasible must be done to exorcise decision
makers' fear of specific improvements in output per worker.
Moreover, I should say—and this, of course, is the important
point—that the Indian planning authorities, at least since 1956,
have adopted the same basic stance. They have been supported in their position by the nation's political leadership.
Statements such as these, of course, never can be absolutes.
With the government's political milieu, and its parliament,
party, and bureaucracy all deeply infected with an unemployment neurosis, it goes without saying that there has been a
good deal of compromising with "softer" employment policies.
But for at least the past half-dozen years, it seems to me, the
development designers' basic principle in this area has been,

when in doubt, to accord the priority to the production effort —a posture that, since it is both politically hazardous and economically sound, deserves a good bit of respect.

However, the Indian authorities also have recognized correctly that this basic employment policy is not entirely adequate. For they have seen, at least since the Second Five Year Plan was formulated, that, for reasons involving both its product composition and its time composition, the main production program they were designing was not a truly employment-maximizing one for the Plan period. It did, to be sure, promise at once to institute a net continuing expansion of jobs, and in the long run, thanks to the dynamics already suggested, it promised to do more for Indian employment (with rising incomes) than virtually any alternative program could. But foreign-exchange considerations dictated the development of types of capacity that were more scarce-resource-intensive than would have been compatible with the aim of quick maximization of employment (*or* of total output, if the composition of production were a matter of complete indifference). Moreover, the lead times involved in putting some kinds of productive capacity in place made it impossible literally to maximize output or employment month by month, year by year, or even five-years by five-years if the objective was to maximize performance in the longer run. Thus the main production effort was destined for some time to leave the economy with a residual unemployment problem—with a labor surplus. To admit this unfortunate circumstance was not to impugn the main development design, to which the nation was committed for a good and sufficient reason. But it did suggest the need for some kind of supplemental employment promotion that did not get in the way of the economy's chief objective.

It is with respect to this addendum to development policy that an interesting evolution in official Indian thinking lately has been occurring. There are two rational approaches to solving the problem of residual unemployment. One is to accept the nature and size of the problem as given and to consider what reasonably can be done to mitigate it—or, even better, to capitalize on it. The other intelligent response is to consider again more carefully whether, without altering the structure of the basic development design, there are not adjustments that can be made in its particulars—specifically in the particular technological choices the design entails—that will serve further to minimize the amount of residual unemployment the main production program leaves. The strand of official Indian thought that seems to me to have been acquiring new perception and promise, and to which I shall turn shortly, falls into the first of those categories. In contrast, policy "evolution" of the second cited, but logically prior, kind has been disappointing. It is considered first below.

Technological Choices

The theory of rational technological choice in a situation like India's is well known. The very identification of productive "resources" implies a particular pattern of productive techniques. Coal was not a significant resource until a technology became available for making substantial use of it, and whale oil, for reasons that have little to do with its ultimate availability, is no longer the resource for the United States that it once was. By the same token, resources can be called "scarce" or "abundant" only with implicit reference to the requirements of a particular technological pattern. Moreover, just as it makes sense for national economic developers to do what they can to adjust the economy's resource mix to fit the requirements of the processes by which they propose to produce an expanded output, so, conversely, it is appropriate for them to choose, insofar as they can, processes whose input requirements are relatively attuned to the economy's existing resource mix.

In a case like India's, however, the range within which planners who are dedicated to the ultimate goal of self-renewing, self-supporting economic growth rationally can choose labor-intensive instead of capital-intensive or other scarce-resource-intensive techniques of production is limited on two counts. In the first place, the more labor-intensive techniques for producing particular products tend, on average, to be older, traditional techniques; and the older techniques tend, on average, to be less efficient. This is because they reflect an earlier and lower level of scientific knowledge. In practice this means that the savings of scarce resources which those who have to make technological choices in an underdeveloped economy may appear to effect by choosing the more labor-intensive of two processes for producing the same product are often more than offset by the obsolescence costs that may be inherent in the older, labor-intensive alternative. Countries like India soon learn that, factor proportions notwithstanding, archaic production techniques seldom are least-cost techniques.

In the second place, technological choices are restricted by India's commitment, for foreign-exchange reasons, to a comparatively fixed commodity pattern in expanding output. If the issue were simply to match technologies with available resources so that total output would be maximized without regard to the exportability of, or domestic demand for, the resulting product mix, then many of the widest "technological" choices facing planners actually would be interproduct choices. If the only consideration were technological suitability, then it would be plainly advisable, for example, for the Indians to push low-grade machine textiles for all they were worth and to lay off machine tools entirely. As I have emphasized repeatedly, however, little such freedom of commodity choice remains in a development program built around the import-substitution principle.

But the fact that the scope for maneuvering is limited does not mean that there is no room for technological accommodation in Indian development design. On the contrary, the opportunity for two very important kinds of maneuvering remains. First, in the case of many of the products India is undertaking to produce, the existing technological alternatives still contain a real, if limited, range of choice. Even within the framework of a final-demand-oriented production program there is room for making some technologically significant product choices between close substitutes. And in many instances the modern world has evolved alternative ways of making the very same products—ways that all are drawn from the same advanced stratum of scientific knowledge, but differ substantially in their relative factor requirements. There are some alternative techniques, in other words, whose comparative advantages are almost exclusively a function of the relative cost of the factors engaged in them. In such instances Indian planning, if its factors are sensibly priced, should incline strongly toward the more labor-intensive alternatives.

Second, and perhaps even more important, India has an opportunity to introduce new processes of production that are quite as scientifically progressive as those of the advanced economies, but better suited than many of them to India's particular factor endowments. In principle, it seems to me, this opportunity is enormous. For I can see no compulsion for believing that scientifically advanced techniques of production *necessarily* must be weighted as heavily in the capital-using, labor-saving direction as is modern Western technology. Rather, the probability is that innovation is an economizing, not a random, process that has simply suited its output of new techniques to the needs of the increasingly capital-abundant, labor-scarce economies in which it has taken place. If this is so, then modern science presumably contains the seeds of a whole range of potential innovations that the West and, to a lesser extent, even the Soviet bloc and Japan have not had enough economic incentive to develop. But India has that incentive, and, at least among the non-Communist poor countries, it may be the only one that is both big enough and sufficiently equipped with scientific and technical personnel to develop them to an important degree.

The Indian planning authorities are thoroughly familiar with the kind of theory of rational technological choice that I have sketched, and they would assert for the record that their central development design already incorporates its principles. It may seem redundant, therefore, to suggest that the theory offers clues for further adjustments in the design to reduce the problem of residual unemployment left unresolved in the main production program. In practice, however, India's pursuit of the technological opportunities open to it has, I think, been a good deal less than optimal. For one thing, the country's specific investment decision makers—those making concrete technological choices in the development wings of the ministries, as well as in state governments and in government and private enterprises—often do not begin to know the range of existing alternative processes. They may know the British processes for making their product, but not the Russian, or vice versa, and perhaps not the latest versions of either. There have been instances where they have remained innocent for several years of particular highly relevant new techniques that have been perfected in neighboring underdeveloped countries. This is not a peculiarly Indian problem. It is endemic to the economically underdeveloped world. There is unfortunately no central inventory of technological alternatives, maintained under UN auspices or otherwise, to which the authorities of the developing economies can turn for a reasonably reliable and informative summary of the ready-made technical alternatives open to them. The Indian government, however, could do much more than it has done thus far both toward urging some kind of effective attack on this information gap internationally and toward augmenting the technological-choice data available to its own people.

There is also the difficulty of sheer impatience—the understandable urge of decision makers to get on with the job, to seize upon the most accessible process without waiting for the additional investigation that would have to be made of other known, but less familiar, alternatives. And certainly, in the technological realm, there is the further difficulty that Indian decision makers educated in the West or in the Western technical tradition tend automatically to apply Western norms to their choices. This tendency—abetted no little, I am afraid, by foreign technical assistance personnel—not only skews choices among existing techniques; it retards the emergence of a resourceful, creative indigenous technology. For example, the image of ultimate achievement that Indian engineering schools hold out to their young graduates is all too exclusively, I suspect, the reproduction of massive mechanized systems. There is too little appreciation of the creative inventor who contrives some sort of shrewd capital-saving short cut. The government itself, in its own contracting thus far, has shown comparatively little appetite for original, all-Indian, technical design.

A critique of present practice that is limited largely to general impressions and comes to the conclusion only that "there is room for improvement" seldom is particularly persuasive. Yet such is my strong conviction with respect to Indian technological policy. There is a need for a much more explicit formulation of such policy that would, very possibly, lay down three principles: first, that it shall be a key responsibility of the government to supply investment decision makers with greatly improved data on the technological choices open to them and a vital responsibility of all decision makers to inform themselves of these alternatives; second, that all choices among existing techniques shall favor those more labor-intensive techniques that entail neither sacrifice in output nor excessive total costs, reasonably calculated; and third, that the government henceforth shall make a redoubled, many-faceted effort to foster indigenous innovation, especially that which will economize in the use of scarce factors. Such a policy needs to be articulated and to be accorded continuing high priority at top levels of government. Furthermore, it needs to be rigorously implemented and enforced.

This last, of course, is the crux of the matter. As I have noted, the Indian authorities already are saying most of the right things about technology. But they have been saying them for at least a half-dozen years, and I can find little evidence that meanwhile they have sharpened their procedures for adapting technological choices to resource availabilities as far as their basic development objectives allow.

Activating the Residual Labor Force:
Problem or Opportunity?

Now back to the other kind of rational policy response to the problem of residual unemployment—that accepts the problem as given and tries to devise specific supplemental programs for dealing with it. Whatever happens on the technological front, India obviously is going to have a substantial problem of this sort for at least the next ten or fifteen years. For, as we shall see when we review the Third Five Year Plan in the next chapter, the volume of surplus labor presently being projected for the sixties is very large. It is large enough (although there really is no easy way to quantify the matter) that I am confident that not even the most alert and effective technological policy could come close to eliminating the residual labor force entirely.

It is on this secondary but unmistakably significant front, then, that I think I detect an interesting, uncompleted transition in Indian development strategy. The reader should be warned that what follows is highly interpretative. The shift in attitudes that I shall be suggesting is by no means universal among the Indian planning authorities, and, since it is a shift of which I approve, my observation of it may be colored by wishful thinking. Still the observation is rooted in a good deal of discussion with senior Indian officials. And it is partially corroborated by working papers that have circulated within the Indian government as well as by comparative language in the Second-Plan and Third-Plan documents.

The key designers of the Second Five Year Plan, if I am not mistaken, regarded the problem of residual unemployment as essentially a distracting nuisance that threatened to impede the forward thrust of the "balanced" production-expansion program that they were rightly determined to set in motion. They recognized that for humanitarian, to say nothing of political, reasons at least some of the labor force that their main production drive failed to absorb needed to be supplied with supplementary employment opportunities. But nothing very positive or lasting, other than the provision of employment itself, was looked for from these expedient measures; the chief requirement was simply that they not interfere with the planned production effort. The principal solution that the Second Plan hit upon was that of cottage industries: it was hoped that by means of government subsidies, protected markets, and other promotional devices a substantial fraction of the residual labor force could be encouraged to busy itself making traditional consumer goods by traditional handicraft techniques.

Especially in view of Gandhi's lifelong sponsorship of cottage production, there were, to be sure, some historical and cultural bases for this policy choice. Moreover, I do not mean to slip into a blanket indictment of cottage industries on economic grounds, let alone of all small-scale rural industries, whether of the modern or the traditional sort. In the light of Indian factor endowments it is perfectly possible that, with product adaptations and a selective, indigenously innovated modernization of their techniques, some of the traditional industries will be able to compete unassisted in Indian markets for many years to come. I suspect that this may be the case, for example, with some types of handlooming, although emphatically not with homespinning. Moreover a few of the handicrafts offer a significant, if minor, continuing source of export earnings. And I am convinced that a good part of India's long-term economic—and cultural—fate may depend upon the vigorous development of viable rural industries of a progressive character.

But none of these considerations can disguise the fact that the rationale for choosing cottage industries as the principal answer to the problem of residual unemployment was exceedingly tortured. For their expansion had to be engineered at the expense of more efficient, lower-unit-cost competitors. In many cases the market did not value their products sufficiently to accept them at full cost prices; hence the subsidies. For this reason and because promotion of cottage industries entailed the restraint of competitive factory production, the scheme's net productive contribution, even of consumer goods, was very limited. Obviously, its contribution to the economy's long-term productive capacity was negligible. And worst of all, the cottage industry program created expectations of continuing protection among the artisans it favored and thereby spawned pressure groups dedicated to the perpetuation of pockets of economic inefficiency.

Not only was the Second Plan's cottage industry choice inherently unattractive, but in making it, the development designers conspicuously passed up the chance to throw the bulk of their efforts to promote supplemental employment instead into a massive expansion of labor-intensive public works activity. It was as well known in 1955-56 as it is now that there was an almost limitless need, especially in the Indian countryside, for irrigation ditching, bunding, and well digging, for rural road construction, for the building of grain warehouses, schools, and a variety of other structures, for developing the public facilities of country towns, and for any number of other labor-intensive construction projects that have little need for scarce materials and virtually none for imports. It was recognized that many of these undertakings would have comparatively quick pay-offs in additional agricultural and/or industrial output. It was obvious that a massive works program would run a smaller risk of institutionalizing new progress-resisting pressure groups than did the cottage industries program. And the literature of Western developing economies, with which the Indian planners were thoroughly familiar, already was replete with glowing descriptions of the opportunities, in a situation like India's, for using idle rural manpower for indigenous capital formation.[2]

In the face of all this, why in the world did the 1956 planners choose (in terms of relative emphasis) to pass up the public works opportunity in favor of the cottage-industries palliative? Perhaps partly for reasons of tradition and sentiment. No doubt partly because a public-works-dominated supplemental employment policy would have placed a great direct administrative burden upon government, particularly at its local levels. But mainly (if I may continue to be highly interpretative) because the planning authorities' thinking about development finance at the time still was narrowly circumscribed by savings-centered development theory. To be more explicit: They shied away from the public works solution in the belief that it would saddle the economy with unacceptable inflationary pressures.

Some of the Western economists like Ragnar Nurske who had first touted the idea that poor, labor-rich economies could capitalize on their surplus manpower by converting some of

---

[2] See Ragnar Nurske, *Problems of Capital Formation in Underdeveloped Countries* (Oxford, 1953), and T. Scitovsky, "Two Concepts of External Economics," *Journal of Political Economy*, Vol. 62, (April 1954), pp. 143-51.

it directly into labor-intensive investment had relied on the hopeful proposition that, since the idle manpower already was subsisting anyway, it could be put to work without any significant net increase in consumer demand. This notion that the community, as it were, could get additional development work done free had been the theme of some United Nations technical assistance experiments; it represented the basic strategy of rural capital formation in Communist China; in India it was the underlying idea of such altruistic rural movements as that headed by the saintly Vinoba Bhave; and there was a strain of it running through the government's Community Development Program. But the Indian planners in 1956 knew very well that it was unrealistic to expect costless labor to be available on any massive scale in a society as free as the Indian. Instead, newly recruited construction workers *would* demand compensation; they *would* try to eat more and consume more than when they had been idle or semi-idle; and those remaining to do the work on the farms whence the laborers came would not willingly continue to support the latter. In short an all-out public works effort *would* generate a substantial increment in consumer demand without making an immediately offsetting contribution to consumer supplies. Since it was assumed that a response by the economy's productive capacity to such a spurt in demand was impossible in the short run and, even in the longer run, would be narrowly constrained by a savings bottleneck, it was concluded that a sufficient expansion in public works to make much of a dent on the residual unemployment problem would be bound to have dangerously inflationary consequences.

In contrast, the cottage-industries program had the virtue of ostensibly adding to consumer supplies as much as it added to consumer demand. Since, as we have seen, its net contribution to production actually was very limited, its principal effect was not to add to total real income but simply to redistribute some of it in favor of some of the otherwise unemployed. But that was the most that could be expected of a supplemental employment program in a situation where current productive capacity was fixed and where its expansion was a nearly exclusive function of the main production program that the supplemental program was undertaking to supplement.

So ran the 1956 thinking. It is obvious from what has been said thus far that the transition I am pointing out involves a shift of emphasis away from cottage industries and toward public works as the primary response to the residual unemployment problem. I am convinced that such a shift, although far from complete, is under way. But the fact that Third-Plan thinking is now leaning in this newer direction is not primarily a reflection of a livelier appreciation either of the special disadvantages of promoting cottage industries or of the "bonus" contribution to the nation's productive capacity that a mobilization of idle manpower in a public works program can make. Appreciation of both these points has been fairly lively for some time. What is changing, rather, is that the inflation bugaboo attached to labor-intensive indigenous investment has begun to lose some of its force for the Indian planners. And this, in turn, is because they have begun to challenge some of the implicit assumptions of the economic model from which the bugaboo arose.

The development designers lately have begun to appreciate that, in the case of many Indian consumer goods, current productive capacity is neither so precise a concept nor so fixed, even in the short run, as is the case in those advanced Western economies from which the savings-centered development theory emerged. For in India, unlike the industrialized West, not only is there a substantial surplus of labor when the various scarce factors of production are judged, in terms of past performance, to be fully employed; there is a lurking potential for quick expansibility in many of the indigenous "scarce" factors. In an economy that is catching up technologically there are many opportunities for radical capital-cheap improvements in output per man. As we shall see in agriculture, for example, there is a clear promise of such returns with comparatively simple changes in cultivating practice. There are opportunities for highly rewarding organizational innovations in small-scale production and marketing.

Moreover, as was noted in the preceding chapter, there are signs of substantial expansibility in cultivators' and other small private enterprisers' propensity to save in the form of direct investments, once they become convinced of the attractiveness of investment opportunities. Most important of all, at any given moment today in India there is a far greater potential than in any Western or advanced Communist country simply for getting producers to work more and to work harder—for getting farmers not only to produce more but to market more of what they produce, blacksmiths to expand their operations into small engineering works, bicycle parts makers and assemblers to enlarge their scales of production, manufacturers to lay on an extra shift and venture into new lines. There is a great potential for this kind of thing, that is to say, if the producers can be convinced of the utility of so doing.

To accept the view that, in many Indian consumer goods lines that do not depend heavily on imports or other unmistakably scarce factors, productive capacity is quickly and highly stretchable does not require a retreat from the judgment that Indians by and large are neither afraid of work nor lacking in healthy appetites for material self-improvement. The point rather is that lack of knowledge, fear of change, lack of vigorous, effectively functioning markets and of certain supporting administrative structures—especially in the traditional rural economy—all combine to impede an optimal translation of these healthy appetites into productive activity. Catalysts are needed to speed the stretching of latent capacities, and one of the most conventional and promising of such catalysts, rather obviously, is additional demand.

The diagnosis, to keep our theories straight, is not of a deficiency in demand in the Western (Keynesian) sense. There the problem is a shortage of demand relative to existing, overt capacity. Here, in the special circumstances of the Indian countryside, we have instead a situation where the capacity for producing many goods is so variable and can be expected to be so responsive to increases in demand that it can be thought of as being, within limits, virtually determined by demand. Or, as Arthur Smithies has remarked recently, we have the appearance of an almost total inversion of Say's Law that supply creates its own demand.[3]

To the extent that this diagnosis is accepted, it obviously tends to quiet anxieties about the inflationary dangers of a public works program. But it does more than that, for it suggests that such a program not only yields the increments in capacity contributed by its own projects but has a multiplier effect upon consumer goods output and capacity. The argument can be extended a step further: Since rural producers (both in and out of agriculture) can be expected to respond to a better and more accessible assortment of consumer goods by stepping up their output, the capacity expansion can become cumulative. Indeed, it is probably quite literally true that one of the best ways to stimulate rural production—and saving-investment—is to stimulate rural consumption.

Set against the backdrop of pure savings-centered orthodoxy, the thesis just sketched has the lure of a hedonistic heresy. It is dangerous totally to succumb to its enchantment, as did the two distinguished Bombay economists, C. N. Vakil and P. R. Bhramanand in the highly provocative volume, *Planning for an Expanding Economy,* published at the time of, and in reply to, the Second Five Year Plan document in 1956.[4] Vakil and Bhramanand argued that the whole rationale of the official development program should be scrapped. In its place the nation should adopt as its dominant, if not exclusive, strategy one that is premised on the latent elasticities of domestic savings, entrepreneurship, and materials supplies and that therefore concentrates on activating the economy's idle resources by stimulating consumer demand and thence consumer goods production. They would have been content to let the expansion of the heavier industries follow along in due course simply in response to demands derived from the expanding consumer goods area.

In the Indian case the fatal fault of this approach as a dominant expansion strategy is the same one that disqualifies

---

[3] "Rising Expectations and Economic Development," *The Economic Journal,* Vol. 76 (June 1961), pp. 255ff.

[4] Vora, 1956.

Hirschman's (not unrelated) "deliberate imbalances" prescriptions: it overlooks the foreign-exchange problem. No responsible Indian government seriously devoted to the objective of achieving international self-support in the foreseeable future could adopt the Vakil-Bhramanand prescription as its primary development strategy. There is no getting away, in the Indian case, from the "balanced growth" prescription for this purpose.

But it is only a lesser error, not a minor one, to fail to see the potentialities of emphasizing resource activation as a secondary, but still major, strategy peculiarly suited to the circumstances of rural India. It is from this second error, to which only those slavishly committed to orthodox savings-centered development theory are inextricably committed, that the Indian planning authorities are now emerging. They are recognizing that, alongside their main production program, which is based on the principles of scarce-resource reallocation and augmentation and must be closely planned, there exists in an economy with surplus rural manpower and with the institutional characteristics of the Indian countryside the possibility of fostering a collateral, less closely planned, output expansion of uncertain but substantial size that rests on the principle of idle-resource activation.

Certainly there are no signs yet that the Indian authorities are being swept off their feet in this direction. They are careful to note that, once triggered, an accumulative, self-propelling expansion of rural output and income is likely to bring unexpected strains to bear on foreign exchange and other truly scarce resources. They are quick to insist that in such instances the secondary development strategy must accept checks imposed in the interests of the first. As will be emphasized later, the planning authorities (for good political reason) remain particularly skittish about any risk of inflation in food prices that resource-activation schemes may entail (which in turn, as also will be emphasized, could create an opportunity for exceptionally constructive uses of surplus-food imports from the United States). Nevertheless, one does now sense a new awareness among the key main-line planners in the Indian Planning Commission that there is no need for the adversary relationship that often in fact has obtained between them and those other planners and administrators within the government who have been charged with promoting supplemental employment policies; that idle-resource activation can be a vital, essentially complementary development strategy; that its pursuit requires a more permissive program with a quite different set of attitudes toward austerity and inflationary dangers than has become habitual with the mainline program planners; and that the potential returns to the public works elements and to the other appropriate ingredients of a vigorous program of resource activation may justify a considerably bolder, more systematic effort in this direction than has been mounted thus far.

The Crucial Matter of Rural Organization

If, as argued in the preceding chapter, the Indian development scheme's first pivotal issue, around which the design of the program predominantly turns, is that of foreign exchange, its second pivotal issue, upon which the success of the effort is more likely to hinge than any other, is that of rural organization. It should be plain by now that the analysis in this book is not that of an "agriculture-firster." I have emphatically endorsed the considered view of the Indian planning authorities that, while a vigorous expansion of farm output is essential to the reasonable aims of the development effort, it is no more so than is a vigorous expansion of heavy industries. And, while suggesting that a bold effort to activate idle rural resources can make a distinctive and sizable contribution to the total expansion effort, I have also indicated a belief that in the Indian scheme of things such an effort must remain subordinate to the "main" (foreign-exchange-oriented) development design. In short, my analysis offers no support for the view that the peculiarly rural aspects of the Indian development puzzle are its intrinsically most *important* aspects. However, like many other observers, both Indian and non-Indian, and like many of the Indian planning authorities themselves, I have become convinced that the rural aspects of the puzzle are, by all odds, the most *difficult* ones—and further convinced that the problems in the countryside are primarily organizational.

"Organizational," so used, is a broad term. It embraces the basic question of what political and social tactics are best calculated to achieve an economic transformation of a traditional rural society in its own bailiwick by noncoercive means. There are questions of local public administrative structure, personnel, and function; questions involving educational, training, and communications facilities; questions concerning the organization and monetization of markets; and others concerning the provision of credit, purchasing, marketing, and other business services through such media as cooperatives, industrial estates, and small-scale industry programs. I shall want particularly to extend the concept of "organization" to encompass questions concerning the emerging spatial organization of economic activity in the Indian countryside, which in turn embraces such matters as industrial location, rural-urban migration, local agro-industrial interrelationships, and the comparative concentration or dispersion of the centers in and around which the population of India will be grouping itself during the next several decades.

The excuse for such a sprawling concept of "organizational" problems is that all of these matters, by whatever common term they are labelled, are so closely interconnected that the questions they raise must be threshed out in concert. The result is an extraordinarily complex set of problems, to which Indian development authorities have devoted more thought and more analytical manpower over a longer period than they have to any other subject. And yet the accomplishments in the field of rural organization seem on many counts to be the development effort's most disappointing ones. This state of affairs is so intriguing and, if I am not mistaken, so hazardous, that I want to devote considerably more space to it than to any other aspect of the Indian experiment. Hence, we shall return to this peculiarly difficult part of the development strategy in Chapters 6 and 7.

The Development Strategy: Summary Appraisal

The general rationale of the Indian development program that we have been examining in these two chapters makes good sense. The central purpose of the effort, namely, to achieve a clearly perceptible and, as quickly as possible, self-sustaining and self-supporting expansion of real per-capita incomes certainly is reasonable. The Indian government's assumption of an activist role in this venture not only is justifiable on a variety of counts; it is immensely popular. The logic of the design of the main production program (reflected, for example, in the allocation of planned investments) actually is a good bit sounder than some official Indian verbalizations of that logic would suggest. For whereas these verbalizations might lead one to believe that the central strategy of the effort were simply one of breaking India's domestic savings bottleneck (a phenomenon that appears to be partly illusory), the designers actually have been grappling with the economy's critical scarcities of technique and materials and, above all, with the pivotal scarcity of foreign exchange. Viewed as a response to the prospect of a chronic foreign-exchange shortage, their scheme of a "balanced" expansion in production, including its early emphasis on heavy industries as well as agriculture, appears not only reasonable, in a country with the size and endowments of India, but necessary.

Partly perhaps because of an excessively "savings-centered" approach to the problems of development finance, Indian authorities have been disappointingly timid thus far in their schemes for employing the idle manpower not claimed by the economy's primary expansion strategy. But there are some signs of increasing boldness on this front and, indeed, on the whole matter of activating idle rural resources. In the latter area, the strategy has some exceedingly complex organizational problems yet to resolve. Its policies with respect to technological choices—more particularly, its implementation of these policies—leave something to be desired. And there are other causes for complaint, some of which will be ex-

amined in subsequent chapters. Yet there can be no real
doubt, it seems to me, that the Indian development effort in
its general design is eminently deserving of support.

We now are in a position to examine more specifically the
chronological segment of their strategy that the Indian planners have adopted for the years 1961-62 through 1965-66.

4 THE THIRD FIVE YEAR PLAN

The Third Five Year Plan, as finally published by the Planning Commission and approved by the Indian Parliament in August 1961,[1] proposes that from 1960-61 to 1965-66 Indian real net national income be raised 31 percent, from a level of about Rs. 14,500 crores to one of about Rs. 19,000 crores, both measured in 1960 prices.[2] The proposed average annual increase in net output is 5.5 percent. This compares with an average gain of 3.6 percent during the Second Five Year Plan years.

The Third Plan's total output goal, as suggested in Chapter 2, originally was based on a real-income-per-capita target and on population assumptions for the period 1960-61 through 1965-66 that were derived from the demographic estimates available in 1958-59. As soon as the initial 1961 census estimates appeared at the end of March 1961, it became evident that these population assumptions were not high enough. Both the estimated level of population at the start of the Plan and the projected rate of population growth during the Plan had to be raised. But by this time it was too late to recalculate all of the output and all of the investment and other input magnitudes in the over-all program. Nor were the planners confident that a larger-than-expected population automatically would generate correspondingly larger financial resources. So, at this final stage in the plan-preparation exercise, the adjustment made in response to the 1961 census ran contrary to the goal-setting logic employed up to that time: the per-capita output goal for 1965-66 was lowered to compensate for the upward revisions in the population projections. Instead of the average annual advance of about 3½ percent assumed in the

[1] Government of India: Planning Commission, *The Third Five Year Plan* (1961). (Cited hereinafter as Third-Plan document.)

[2] The Indian term "crore" denotes ten million. Rs. 4.76 equals $1, which means that one rupee is worth about 21 U.S. cents.

Third Plan's "Draft Outline" (published in June 1960),[3] the
final document calls for an annual gain of only 3.1 percent.

The planners plainly were shaken by the unexpectedly high
census figures. One suspects that several statements in the final
document's early chapters—for example, the one in Chapter 2,
that "special efforts should be made to reduce the rate at
which population is increasing"[4]—were last-minute insertions.
Also, the proposed government outlay on promotion of Family Planning during the Third-Plan years has been raised to
Rs. 27 crores from the Draft Outline's figure of Rs. 25 crores
and the mere Rs. 3 crores that were spent during the Second-
Plan period.

Except for its last-minute subordination of per-capita goals
to total-output-and-investment goals, the Third Plan reflects
the broad development strategy outlined in the two preceding
chapters. But the Plan document is an enormous book, and it
would be neither feasible nor particularly useful to supply a
comprehensive digest of it. Instead I shall focus most of the
following commentary on a few key structural issues, concerning the size and composition of the 1960-61-through-1965-66
program, that generated significant controversies during the
course of the Plan's formulation.

The Question of Size

From its beginning in 1958, the primary issue in the debate
over Third-Plan design within the Planning Commission, between the Planning Commission and other government agencies, and between government and interested private groups
was simply the question of how much should be attempted during the 1961-66 period. While the general vector of the Third
Plan already had been set in the Second, a good bit of shading
of the effort, either upward or downward, was possible, and
there were strong proponents of both alternatives. On the one

[3] Government of India: Planning Commission, *Draft Outline
of the Third Five Year Plan* (1960). (Cited hereinafter as Draft
Outline.)

[4] Third-Plan document, p. 20.

hand, the advocates of consolidation and conservatism could say that the Second Plan had turned out to be excessively ambitious, had over-extended the country, particularly in the realm of foreign exchange, and had had to be pruned back. Accordingly now was the time to play it a bit safe and set comparatively modest targets. On the other hand, the proponents of boldness could and did argue that the Second-Plan shortfalls were the very reason why the nation had to be galvanized into making up lost ground during the first half of the sixties; that the Second Plan's long-term scheme was basically sound; and that, in many critical areas, momentum had been established that it would be most unfortunate to lose. Now was the time for redoubled effort to implement the scheme.

The debate over size was couched very largely in terms of finance, or of what the Indians call "resources." For one thing, of course, it was recognized that the scope of the Plan depended critically on the amount of foreign aid that could be posited and obtained. This issue is considered separately below. But the size question also was argued heatedly in terms of domestic resources. Some business groups in Bombay and Calcutta, which would have held the Plan's total investment outlays to less than Rs. 7,000 crores, harped on the theme that the 1961-66 expenditure program should be "tailored to existing resources." Whether this was taken to mean that development outlays should literally be restricted to amounts consistent with the absolute levels of savings, taxes, and net incoming foreign capital in 1960-61, or only to the savings, tax, and foreign investment *rates* in effect in the late Second-Plan years, plainly it was a defeatist prescription. For the whole domestic finance theory of an accelerated development effort is that the tax and saving rates can be expected to increase as the expansion of real income proceeds, thus making it possible for development to generate more and more of the resources for its own perpetuation. Actually, no major group within the government openly subscribed to the ultraconservative view that Plan outlays should be tailored to pre-Plan resources. Nevertheless, even within the narrower range of responsible intra-governmental debate, the essential cleavage was between those primarily responsible for charting finances, who counseled caution, and the physical planners, who urged boldness.

The advocates of boldness, who held the initiative in the debate almost from its beginning in late 1958, were helped no little by the fortuitous circumstance that Rs. 10,000 crores, which happened to represent a quite bold investment figure for Third-Plan purposes, is a nice round number. Given the unfortunate Indian penchant for thinking and talking about planning in investment-focused rather than production-focused terms, the catch-phrase "a 10,000-crore plan" became entrenched in popular discussion early in the Plan-formulation period and thereafter undoubtedly exerted an upward influence on the judgments of the more timorous. The political difficulty of cutting state Plan requests to a figure that would be consistent with a total investment of less than Rs. 10,000 crores re-inforced the big-plan advocates. Moreover, the more influential pieces of foreign advice to which the government was exposed tended to support an ambitious Third Plan. This advice came from both the Soviet and the American government missions that conferred with Indian officials in 1959 and early 1960; from a World Bank mission in the spring of 1960; and, perhaps most influentially of all, from the "Three Wise Men" team of international bankers who, at the request of World Bank President, Mr. Eugene Black, made a survey of Third-Plan proposals that same spring.[5]

Within the Indian government the key advocates of an ambitious Third Plan pressed their case unswervingly; once consent had been won for a "10,000-crore plan," they re-examined their estimates of the needs and possibilities and raised their sights a few hundred crores higher; and once the feasibility of a somewhat larger program had been conceded, the big-plan proponents nudged their asking figure up still another

[5] Only the findings of the last-named group, Mr. Herman Abs of West Germany, Sir Oliver Franks of the United Kingdom, and Mr. Allen Sproul of the United States, were widely distributed: "Letter to the President, International Bank for Reconstruction and Development, Washington, from . . ., Members of the International Economic Mission on Problems of Development in India and Pakistan," (March 1960) (mimeo).

notch. The somewhat bizarre result, since advocates of caution, although giving ground, also clung to their principles, is that the controversy over size has been carried forward, quasi-unresolved, all the way into the final Third-Plan document itself. Thus in Chapter 2 of that document, which obviously is the product of the Planning Commission's Perspective Planning Division, it is stated that during the Third-Plan period as well as during the succeeding ten years, real national income should be raised "as nearly as possible" by an average of 6 percent a year, or about 34 percent over five years. Yet in Chapters 4, 5, and 6, which show the hand of somewhat more cautious analysts elsewhere in the Planning Commission and in the Ministry of Finance, the annual growth target is phrased as being "something in excess of 5 percent a year," or 31 percent from 1960-61 to 1965-66. Similarly, whereas the Third Plan's financial program calls for a public outlay of Rs. 7,500 crores for investment and other development purposes, the price tags of all of the specific projects that the physical planners have incorporated in the program add up to a total of more than Rs. 8,000 crores.

The published Third Plan, of course, does not leave these discrepancies in the form of bald inconsistencies. There is some suggestion that the higher "physical" targets should be viewed as goals for even more strenuous financing efforts over the period of the Plan than it has been possible to think through in advance. However, the reconciling rationale that the document emphasizes is a different one—namely, that the (higher) physical targets assume a perfectly articulated and phased program, whereas, in fact, some hitches and bottlenecks are bound to eventuate. Consequently (the argument continues) it will be unnecessary to provide quite as much financing as the physical program may appear to require, as long as the development budget can be kept reasonably flexible with respect to the reallocation of funds among projects.

As we shall see later, there is a good deal of realism in this position. Yet to highlight such a proposition at the very beginning of a basic planning document is to carry candor almost to the point of defeatism. Despite the rather blurred image that these dual targets impart to the program, however, it is plain that the outcome of the debate over Plan size was a relative victory for the proponents of boldness. For even the lower of the two sets of total-output and investment projections in the Third-Plan document is approximately equivalent (even after adjustment for the rise in prices from 1957-58 to 1960-61) to what appeared to be the upper end of the debated range at the time the issue was first joined.

Moreover, considered independently of its pre-legislative history, the Third Plan is indeed an ambitious program in most respects. It projects a rate of output expansion half again as large as that achieved in the Second-Plan period. It proposes substantial rises in both the investment and the domestic saving rates (from a 1960-61 rate of 11 percent to about 14½ percent in 1965-66 in the case of investment, and from 8½ percent to 11 percent in saving). Its tax requirements are fairly formidable. And, as noted already, it requires substantial foreign assistance.

At the same time, I find nothing in the quantitative outlines of the Third Plan that condemns it out of hand as being unrealistically ambitious if its needs for net foreign exchange can be met. To be sure, a few Western economists can be expected to question the program's implicit aggregative capital-output ratios. But these objections need not be taken very seriously, except possibly as imperfect reflections of difficulties that can be discussed better in more direct and specific terms.

As far as "incremental capital-output ratios," as such, are concerned, many off-the-cuff analyses of the Third-Plan data are apt to be misleading on two counts. First, there will be a tendency to compare the First, Second, and Third Five-Year investment programs with the actual or projected output gains during co-terminous periods. If this is done, it appears, as the top line of the A/D, B/F, and C/H ratios in Table 1 indicate, that the total incremental-capital-output ratio, after rising sharply from the First to the Second Plan, is projected as falling markedly during the Third Plan. It may seem over-optimistic to anticipate such an improvement in over-all capital productivity at this stage of the development process. However, it is obvious that the impact of investment on productive capacity (and therefore on output) occurs some time after

TABLE 1. *Estimates of Investment, Increments in Output, and Investment-Incremental-Output Ratios in the First, Second, and Third Five Year Plans*

(Rupee items in crores)[1]

Item	Net Investment during			Increments in Net Domestic Product during 5-year period ending in						Investment-Incremental-Output Ratios					
	1st Plan (A)	2d Plan (B)	3d Plan (C)	1955-56 (D)	1957-58 (E)	1960-61 (F)	1962-63 (G)	1965-66 (H)	1967-68 (I)	A/D	A/E	B/F	B/G	C/H	C/I
All sectors	3,530	6,750	10,400	1,900	1,800	2,400	3,400	4,700	5,100	1.8	2.0	2.8	2.0	2.2	1.9
Agriculture, community development, major and medium irrigation	n.a.	1,255	2,110	1,110	990	1,076	1,310	1,474	1,590	n.a.	n.a.	1.2	0.9	1.4	1.3
Organized industry and mining[2]	n.a.	2,045	3,370	230	200	181	530	1,479	1,860	n.a.	n.a.	11.3	3.9	2.3	1.8
Village and small industries, power, transport and communications	n.a.	2,160	3,223	160	220	573	890	1,187	1,190	n.a.	n.a.	3.8	2.4	2.7	2.7
Other[3]	n.a.	1,290	1,697	400	390	570	670	520	460	—	—	—	—	—	—

[1] The product data are in constant 1960–61 prices. While it is not specified in the source, presumably the investment data are in current prices. If so, the investment-incremental-output ratios shown for the First and Second Plans are moderately lower than they should be.

[2] Investment data also include net additions to inventories.

[3] Includes, for investment, social services and miscellaneous; for net domestic product, other services. Ratios relating these would be of doubtful significance and therefore have not been calculated.

Source: All data derived from the Third-Plan document; those for First-Plan investment from the chart, "Selected Economic Indicators, 1950–51 to 1960–61" following p. 30; those for Second- and Third-Plan Investment from Chapter 5, Table 3 (p. 59), and the those for the size and composition of net domestic product in 1950–51, 1955–56, 1960–61, and 1965–66 from the chart, "Net Domestic Product by Industrial Origin," following p. 76. Similar estimates for 1952–53, 1957–58, 1962–63, and 1967–68 were interpolated and extrapolated from these data, account being taken of the average annual percentage changes in total and sectoral outputs during the relevant Plan periods.

investment outlays are made. Therefore, the output experience that is related to a particular span of investment experience should be lagged for some period behind the latter. The "average" such lag in an economy is a peculiarly amorphous concept and, at any rate, is not known precisely in India at present. However, the assumption of a two-year lag of capacity effects behind the average timing of investment outlays clearly is preferable to the implicit assumption of no lag at all. In the Indian case when, as can be seen from the columns headed A/E, B/G, and C/I in Table 1, the investment-incremental-output ratios are recalculated on this assumption, the effect is not only to lower most of the ratios (since, in an expanding economy, the recalculation raises most of their denominators); it also changes their behavior through time, since there are substantial differences in both total and sectoral output growth rates in the several Plan periods.

In Table 1, in order to make the figures for 1952-53 and 1957-58 comparable with 1962-63 and 1967-68, I have used estimates for all of these lagged terminal years that are representative of the output trends experienced or projected for the entire five-year Plan periods into which they fall. As indicated in the table's explanatory notes, the recalculated ratios are, at best, very rough, approximate figures. Yet they probably are reliable enough to be significant, and they show a virtually constant total incremental-capital-output ratio over the course of India's first three plans. Actually, very little should be made of such a finding; there is no good reason to expect such regularity in the relationship between two such composite totals. As can be observed in Table 1, the virtual identity of the all-sectors ratios for the Second and Third Plans is the accidental result of offsetting trends in their component ratios. However, the recalculated over-all ratio does at least offer a fitting rebuttal to those who think they can convict the Third Plan of unreasonable optimism simply by juxtaposing its total investment and total output figures.

The second error that is likely to distort discussions of the Indian program's capital-output ratios is a failure to distinguish between output and capacity. It is the latter not the former, after all, that investment affects directly. Indeed, we are interested in capital-output ratios only as imperfect indicators of the capital-*capacity* ratios, of which we have so few direct measurements. But this means that any abnormal lag in output expansion behind capacity expansion (that is, any abnormal rise in idle capacity) can yield a misleadingly high capital-output indicator. Quite obviously, this is what happened in the larger-scale Indian manufacturing and mining enterprises during the late fifties and the early years of this decade.

The Third Plan's proposal that investment per rupee of (lagged) additional output in the so-called "organized" mining and manufacturing industries be cut in half (Table 1, third line, items, B/G and C/I) represents no delusion that the capacity added per rupee of investment can be doubled. On the contrary, the thinking of the Indian authorities on this point is based on some reasonably careful industry studies. (It will be noted that this is the only major sector in which they are projecting a decline in the incremental-capital-output ratio from the Second-Plan to the Third-Plan period.) What they are counting on primarily is that the economy, by breaking imported raw-material and imported spare-parts bottlenecks, by substituting two- and three-shift for one- and two-shift operations, by acquiring additional working capital, and by general improvements in management, can achieve much fuller use of its existing operable industrial capacity, much of which was added during the Second-Plan years. Second, the planners are confident that in the Third Plan's major industrial projects the average lag between investment outlays and the emergence of additional operable capacity can be reduced significantly below its Second-Plan level, partly by better project administration, but also partly by a relative shift of emphasis toward projects with inherently shorter gestation periods. For example, the Third Plan calls for a relative shift toward thermal electric power plants, which take far less time to bring on the line than do hydroelectric projects.

Despite the fact that discussions of the Third Plan became preoccupied early in its formulation period with the matter of the program's total investment figure, the subtotal that is provided for the organized industry sector was not arrived at by a from-the-top-down type of rationing that tempted the planners to spread a limited allotment of investment over a larger number of projects than it is technically feasible for the investment to support. Instead, the investment numerator and (in a somewhat looser sense) also the incremental-output denominator of the sector's Third-Plan incremental-capital-output ratio are simply aggregations of cost and benefit estimates that have been worked up for the particular projects included in the program.

My impression, as I say, is that the project studies upon which the aggregates are based have been reasonably careful and competent. In the next chapter I express considerable skepticism about whether Indian planning and administration have yet achieved enough technical refinement (particularly with respect to phasing problems) and enough administrative skill to make all of these projects proceed on schedule and fit together. Consequently, when these uncertainties are added to the foreign-exchange uncertainty, I am not particularly sanguine about India's ability to step up sufficiently both the execution of new projects and the use of existing capacity to make good the Third Plan's implicit capital-output ratio for the organized sector. But I have no reason to believe that the targeted performance is not, on the whole, technically feasible. In short, while the size of the program in this sector— the only one about which the projected capital-output trend signals any warning—is ambitious in its presumption of improved administration, there is no reason to think it unreasonably so.

Paradoxically, the count on which the Third Plan is perhaps over-ambitious and the one on which it is excessively timid both entail predominantly rural phenomena. The first is the projection for agricultural output. In spite of a readiness to raise investment per unit of additional farm output (Table 1, second line, items B/G and C/I), the Plan's hypothesis that the average annual gain in real farm output can quickly be raised more than a percentage point, from the less than $3\frac{1}{2}$ percent achieved during the fifties to the $4\frac{1}{2}$-percent annual growth called for during the period 1960-61 through 1965-66, is a dubious one—unless, as will be suggested in Chapter 6, we can anticipate a considerably more sweeping transformation of Indian rural policy than the Third Plan overtly suggests. And yet, as we have seen already, the successful accomplishment of India's balanced-growth scheme depends crucially on just such an acceleration of agricultural expansion.

On the other hand, the Plan is excessively timid, as we shall see shortly, in its proposals for activating idle rural manpower. I shall be suggesting that the kind of policy adjustments that would be best calculated to correct the second of these weaknesses would also strengthen the Plan's chances of making good its farm production goals. This in turn will pose the question whether there is enough room within the Third Plan's present financing scheme to stand the strain of any extra manpower mobilization. Meanwhile here, as an initial judgment concerning the size of the over-all plan, we can say that it would be disappointing to see India attempting anything less; at the same time, probably it would be politically and administratively unrealistic for them to try very much more—except in the field of residual employment policy.

The Allocation of Investment

The noisiest of the sub-debates conducted during the formulation of the Third Five Year Plan was that between the advocates of intensified (particularly "hard-core") industrialization and the advocates of an increased emphasis upon agriculture. Early in 1959, partisans of Indian agriculture, supplied with ammunition by the report of the Ford Foundation "Food Crisis" team[6] and represented within the government in the Ministry of Food and Agriculture, began to intensify their appeal for what I have called an "agriculture-first" allocation of investment in the Third Plan. Arguing that the Second Plan had overdone the relative shift of outlays toward industrial expansion, they contended that, in the new Plan, agriculture's share of investment should rise sharply and industry's decline.

[6] Government of India: Ministries of Food and Agriculture and of Community Development and Cooperation, *India's Food Crisis and Steps to Meet It* (April 1959).

The partisans of industry—particularly organized industry (public and private)—counterattacked quickly. In August 1959 the nation's chief private industrial organization, The Federation of Indian Chambers of Commerce and Industry, published a suggested Third-Plan investment program, and by October of that year a hard-core-oriented working paper on the matter of investment allocation was receiving careful and, on the whole, favorable consideration within the Planning Commission. Both of these documents, although providing for substantial absolute increases in investment in agriculture, community development, and irrigation (see Table 2), would have reduced the combined share of these sectors of Third-Plan investment to about 16 percent. This compares with a share of 22 percent that had been projected in the Second Five Year Plan document. As it subsequently turned out, the actual share of investment claimed by agriculture and related activities for 1956-57 through 1960-61 was less than 19 percent.

At the same time that it was shaving down agriculture's percentage of investment, the FICCI proposal would have raised the allocation to industry, including village and other small enterprises as well as organized industry and mining, all the way from the 18.5 percent proposed in the Second-Plan document to a full 40 percent of Third-Plan investment. The hypothetical program circulated within the Planning Commission was considerably more modest in this regard, suggesting that industry claim only 26 percent of total investment—actually a slightly smaller share, according to the Third-Plan document, than industry's percentage of investment under the Second Plan turns out to have been. The FICCI made room for its greater emphasis on industry by hypothesizing a sharp cut in the relative allocation of investment to social services, including housing (whereas the Planning Commission's October 1959 working paper would have raised this figure moderately), and by suggesting a far more radical reduction in the percentage of investment going to transport and communications than the industrially oriented planners within the government were ready to accept.

Viewed against this background, the investment allocation that finally has been projected in the Third-Plan document it-

TABLE 2. Investment Allocation in the Second and Third Five Year Plans

	Second Plan				Third Plan					
	Projected in Second-Plan Document[1]		Actual[2]		FICCI proposal August 1959[3]		Planning Commission Hypothesis[4]		Projected in Third-Plan Document[5]	
Item	Rs. Crores	Percent	Rs. Crores	Percent	Rs. Crores	Percent	Rs. Crores	Percent	Rs. Crores	Percent
Agriculture, Community Development	568	11.8 }21.9	835	12.4 }18.6	1,200	12.0 }16.5	1,600	16.0	1,460	14.0 }20.3
Major & Medium Irrigation	486[6]	10.1	420	6.2	450	4.5			650	6.3
Social Services (incl. housing)	945	19.7	1,290	19.1	1,400	14.0	2,200	22.0	1,526	14.7 }16.3
Miscellaneous	99	2.1	500	7.4	700	7.0 }37.5	900	9.0	171	1.6
Inventories									800	7.7
Subtotal		43.7		45.1		37.5		47.0		44.3
Village & Small Industries	200	4.1 }18.5	265	3.9 }26.8					425	4.1
Organized Industry & Minerals	690	14.4	1,545	22.9	4,000	40.0	2,600	26.0	2,570	24.7 }28.8
Electric Power	427	8.9	485	7.2	1,150	11.5	1,000	10.0	1,062	10.2
Transport and Communications	1,385	28.9	1,410	20.9	1,100	11.0	1,700	17.0	1,736	16.7
Subtotal		56.9		54.9		62.5		53.0		55.7
Total	4,800	100.0	6,750	100.0	10,000	100.0	10,000	100.0	10,400	100.0

Source: Indicated in footnotes.

1 Government of India, Planning Commission, The Second Five Year Plan (1956), p. 52.
2 Government of India, Planning Commission, Third Five Year Plan (1961), p. 59.
3 Federation of Indian Chambers of Commerce and Industry, The Third Five Year Plan: A Tentative Outline (1959).
4 Unpublished discussion paper circulated among Planning Commission staff, October 1959.
5 Third-Plan document, p. 59.
6 "Irrigation, flood control, and other projects."

self is striking in that, with respect to the industry-agriculture split, it calls for having one's cake and eating it too. The agriculture, community development, and irrigation share is put at 20.3 percent, higher than the actual allocation received by this sector during the Second-Plan years and a quarter again as high as the share proposed by pro-industry interests earlier in the period of formulation of the Third Plan. At the same time, industry is projected as claiming about 29 percent of total investment—measurably more than even the hard-core advocates of industrialization within the Planning Commission were proposing in late 1959.

Obviously, for the proposed agriculture and industry shares of investment *both* to rise, there has had to be a compensating squeeze in other segments of the investment breakdown. This has not taken place to a major degree in the power, transport and communications, and inventories sectors, which in the new scheme together claim just one percentage point of investment less than they did in the actual Second-Plan breakdown. Instead, planned investments in housing and other social services have been held down to a significantly smaller share of the total than during the Second-Plan period, and to a much smaller fraction than the Planning Commission originally had in mind for the Third Plan.

The new Plan document offers little positive evidence that its relatively conservative policy with respect to capital expenditures in the social services sector necessarily will entail a deceleration in the progress being made in its component fields of housing, education, health, and social welfare. There are substantial absolute increases from the Second Plan to the Third Plan in the investments programmed for virtually all of the larger subcategories under the social-services heading, and in some of these subcategories, such as technical education and scientific and technological research, the Third Plan calls for a pronounced acceleration in the rate of expansion of investment. In other fields the planned provision for noninvestment development expenditures during the next five years is (quite appropriately) more generous than the provision for capital outlays. And in several of the fields the requirements for additional training programs and for additional skilled manpower already are so high, even in an expansion of the scale indicated by the projected investment scheme, that it may be doubted that much additional investment could be usefully absorbed.

Nonetheless, it is a fact that, in firming up their Third-Plan investment allocation, the Indian planners deliberately have undertaken to economize in the social services sector. More than they had earlier intended, they have weighted their investment design toward sectors (agriculture and industry) that promise relatively direct, quick, and predictable payoffs in additional output. Even within the social services area they have favored programs (technical education and technical research) pointed in this direction. If allocation of scarce capital is considered, all of this looks admirable. However, when one considers surplus-manpower prospects, the restraint exhibited in plotting social-services construction appears in a rather different light.

Employment Policy and Idle Manpower Mobilization

The most obviously disappointing provision in the Third Plan—the volume of additional employment that it proposes be generated in India from 1961-62 through 1965-66—comes as no surprise. Despite the large (if unmeasured) backlog of idle manpower the country had accumulated by the mid-fifties, the Second Five Year Plan document set the notably modest employment goal of only enough new jobs to match the number of new entrants into the labor force during its Plan period. By the time Third-Plan formulation began in the middle of the Second-Plan period, it was generally recognized that not even this objective would be realized; the country was going to emerge from the Second Plan with a substantial increase in its volume of unemployment and underemployment. Thus, as they approached the Third Plan, the consensus among the majority of the Indian planners was that the most ambitious objective they could realistically set was one similar to that of the Second Plan, but that this time they should mean it and implement it more effectively than they had in the later fifties.

The number work of the Plan, developed before the results of the 1961 census became available, was drawn up on this basis. But then the new census data intervened, and it became apparent that the volume of idle manpower at the beginning of the Third Plan would be greater than had been supposed and that during the Plan period the labor force would be growing at a faster rate than expected. Yet the planners found nothing in these new demographic data to justify a sudden upward revision in the size of the over-all output expansion that would be physically and financially feasible. Consequently, in their final revision of the Third-Plan document they were forced in all candor to project a five-year expansion in employment (the equivalent of 14 million additional jobs) that falls 3 million short of the revised estimate of probable additions to the labor force during the same period.

As the Plan document emphasizes, its estimates both of the amount of involuntary idleness at the start of the Plan (about 9 million unemployed and 15 to 18 million underemployed) and of the numbers of jobs likely to be created in various industries during the course of the Plan are subject to wide margins of error. However, since these errors presumably are not systematically biased in one direction, there can be little doubt that the residual employment problem the Plan poses is a grievously serious one—or that the document's failure to spell out a quantitatively adequate, financially and administratively feasible answer to the problem represents, as of August 1961, a massive deficiency in Indian planning. The aberration looks especially incongruous when laid alongside the Plan's comparative austerity with respect to the amount of (highly labor-intensive) construction that is to be undertaken in the social services sector.

And yet the document's approach to the idle manpower issue has some saving graces. For one thing, there is the comforting fact that the planners themselves at least emphatically recognize the inadequacy of their present employment target. The generation of 3 million more jobs than those that the Third Plan now projects, they say, "is considered to be an essential objective in the Third Plan." By itself, this expression of dissatisfaction with a scheme that provides for a development *expansion* in unemployment is nothing to cheer about. What *are* encouraging are the policies, albeit still too tentative and hesitant, that the Plan sketches for implementing this extra, supra-Plan, employment objective. For these seem quite plainly to corroborate the constructive, still-emerging evolution of residual employment policy alleged in the preceding chapter.

In the first place, in proposing means for promoting additional employment, the Plan places its principal emphasis on an expanded rural works program. It proposes that, in addition to what is now explicitly provided in the development scheme, such a program be undertaken on a scale sufficient to provide an average of 100 days a year of work for about 100,000 persons in 1961-62, for 400,000 to 500,000 persons in 1962-63, for approximately a million people in the third year of the Plan, and for some 2½ millions in 1965-66.

Second, the document plainly recognizes mobilization of idle manpower as a source of supplemental productive expansion, not just as an anti-unemployment expedient. Its rural works proposal, it says, "is significant not merely for creating additional employment . . . but even more as an important means for harnessing the large manpower resources available in rural areas for rapid economic development. . . ."[7]

In the third place, the Plan's "Employment and Manpower" chapter shows a lively awareness of certain structural issues in the field of rural development that remained characteristically blurred in the rural policies of the fifties. These issues, treated in the present book particularly in Chapters 6 and 7, include the appropriate interrelationships between agricultural and rural industrial expansion, the need for building up a dispersion of country center-towns as foci for integrated local agro-industrial development, and the catalytic role that a bold and imaginative rural works program can play in the activation of such a rural development effort. We find the authors of the Third Plan saying, for example,

It is necessary to develop centers or nuclei of industrial development in each area and link these with one another

[7] Third-Plan document, p. 163.

through improved transport and other facilities. These centers might be in small towns or in centrally situated villages which are able to attract skills and enterprises and to which power and other facilities could be readily provided. . . . It is essential that the program for agricultural and industrial development should be coordinated with the supply of power. Greater concentration of activity at selected points would bring about improvements in load factor.

. . . For many years the greatest scope for utilizing manpower in rural areas will lie in programs for agricultural development, road development projects, village housing and provision of rural amenities. . . . Programs for developing village and small industries, linking up the economy of villages with the growing urban centers, setting up processing industries on a cooperative basis, and carrying industries into rural areas . . . have to be further intensified. . . . While the rural economy is being built up, there is need for a comprehensive works program in all rural areas, and more especially in those in which there is a heavy pressure of population on land and considerable unemployment and under-employment.[8]

Fourth, the Plan document recognizes realistically that, to attain any substantial size or impact, under an expanded rural works program, "in all cases of works to be undertaken in villages, wages should be paid at the village rates."[9] Obliquely, it consigns to a comparatively marginal role Bhoodan-Gramdan type efforts to mobilize idle manpower on a volunteer, unremunerated basis: "Voluntary organizations should also be able to provide local leadership and undertake educational and cultural work."[10]

Fifth, although the following statement is indecisive and, I think, shows insufficient concern about advancing the monetization of rural transactions, the planners display some appreciation of the possibilities for using surplus imports to "finance" an expanded rural works program: "As the pro-

[8] *Ibid.*, pp. 162-63.
[9] *Ibid.*, p. 162.
[10] *Ibid.*, p. 163.

gram develops, it might be possible to consider ways of paying wages in part in the form of foodgrains."[11]

Sixth, the Plan's "Employment and Manpower" chapter quite clearly indicates—even though it treats the subject in very summary form—that Indian policymakers have now developed some far more concrete and cogent ideas about the organization and implementation of a residual employment (especially a rural works) program than were evident in top policy circles as recently as mid-1960.

Finally, in marked contrast to the Second Plan's residual employment policy, the new Plan suggests no predominant reliance upon cottage industries. In addition to a greatly enlarged rural works effort, it proposes, for one thing, that the presently articulated plan (what I have called the "main-line program" in Chapters 2 and 3) be looked at again to see whether it really does maximize employment opportunities to an extent consistent with its other objectives. It proposes, secondly, that an intensified program of rural industrialization be instituted. But in this latter regard the emphasis is upon modern, technically progressive establishments, not on the traditional crafts. It is significant that, while the Third Plan's presently programmed investments in the village and small industries sector are, in total, expected to exceed the Second-Plan level by 47 percent, investments in the small-scale (modern) industries and industrial estates component of this sector are planned to be 106 percent higher than in the Second Plan. Capital outlays on the balance of the sector, comprising handlooms, khadi,[12] village industries, sericulture, coir, and handicrafts are expected to exceed those under the Second Plan by only 20 percent.

Even when they are all put together, these indications of policy intent do not, to be sure, yet add up to an adequate or decisive idle-manpower-mobilization effort. The plainest indication that they do not is that the Plan as it stands makes very little financial provision for their implementation. Financing presently is scheduled, for example, for only a small fraction of

[11] *Ibid.*, p. 165.
[12] Homespun cloth.

the 2½-million force of part-time rural works employees the planners hopefully want to build up. In part, the Third-Plan document's lack of follow-through in this respect clearly reflects a persistence of the inhibiting fear of inflation that was attributed to Indian planners in the preceding chapter. But the unfinished quality of the document's residual employment program may also, in part, be simply an accident of timing. It represents an unfinished revolution in Indian development strategy that by mid-1961 had gathered enough momentum to permit the statement of some lines of policy that are decidedly novel by Second-Plan standards. However, by the publication date of the Third Plan the proponents of this new approach to idle-manpower mobilization had not yet had time adequately to articulate, and to muster consent for, the financial and organizational corollaries that the approach logically implies.

If this last is a reasonable interpretation, then the Third Plan's residual employment outlook remains for the time being in doubt. Given the present trend in official thinking, there is good reason to hope that the necessary follow-through for making good the new intentions will shortly emerge. On the other hand, this may be another area, of which India already has too many, where good policies are chronically debased by ineffective implementation.

The Division of Investment Between Public and Private Sectors

Despite all of the rhetoric that the issue of public enterprise versus private enterprise has generated in India, debate over the allocation of investment between the public and private sectors was not, in fact, particularly heated during the Third Plan's formulation period, nor has the position finally adopted in the Third-Plan document on this score seemed to excite much controversy. However, because of the document's nearly total lack of year-by-year programming data, some of the longer-term implications of the five-year public-private investment split that it projects may largely have escaped attention.

Measured in terms of over-all public-private investment ratios, the range of what might be called "relevant" debate as to the average division of investment during the period 1961-62 through 1965-66 was not very broad. As a practical matter, the designers of the Third Plan could not come up with a public share of less than 55 percent of the five-year investment total, for this would have meant a relative squeezing of the public sector below its average Second-Plan share. In the Second-Plan document public investment originally had been projected as claiming three-fifths of the nation's total capital outlays in that Plan period, but the unexpected buoyancy of the private sector, coupled with lags and bottlenecks in public projects, soon made it apparent that the intended First-Plan-to-Second-Plan shift toward public investment was going to be moderated considerably. The actual 1956-57-through-1960-61 outcome, it now appears, was about a 54-46 split.[13]

Not only did the Indian political terrain and the broad industrial policy decisions taken in earlier planning periods make it nearly impossible for the designers of the Third Plan to project a public-investment share smaller than that actually attained in the Second Plan;[14] within the broad middle spectrum of Indian political and economic opinion also there was a consensus that the country's massive needs for infrastructure, its commitment to the channeling of most basic heavy-industry expansion into the public sector, and the industrial composition of its long-term development scheme jointly argued for at least some further enlargement of the public-investment bulge during the Third Plan. Significantly, although other lesser private business groups took more extreme pro-private positions, the Federation of Indian Chambers of Commerce and Industry, which typically is more concerned with influencing public-policy decisions than with polemics, advocated a 55-45 allocation between public and private sectors for Third-Plan investment in its August 1959 pamphlet. And this, as I have said, became one limit to the effective range of choice.

[13] Third-Plan document, Chapter 4, Table 3, p. 59.
[14] This is so even when account is taken of the evolution of a less brittle, more pragmatic brand of industrial policy subsequent to the Industrial Policy Resolution of 1956. See Chapter 8 below.

The other ostensible limit was provided by those public-sector enthusiasts within the Planning Commission who suggested a 65-35 split for Third-Plan investment. While this ratio, expressed as a five-year average, does not sound as though it would involve an implausibly radical reallocation of investment to the public sector, it would in fact do just that. For it is now estimated that the public share of total investment slipped to little more than equality with private investment in the final year of the Second Plan. (The Third-Plan document puts both at about Rs. 800 crores.[15]) Consequently, to achieve a 65 percent average for the five-year period of the Third Plan, the annual public share presumably would have to rise to 80 percent or more by 1965-66. And such a radical change in the annual distribution of investment was unacceptable to many segments within what I have called "the great middle spectrum" of opinion on at least two related counts.

In the first place, assuming any reasonable smoothness in allocation trends, the attainment of an 80-20 investment split by 1965-66 would imply a very substantial *further* rise in the five-year public-to-private investment ratio from the Third to the Fourth Plan; and while some of the stronger public-sector proponents within the Planning Commission and the government would have welcomed this prospect, there was by no means the same consensus about the desirability of this rise that there was about the increase from the Second to the Third Plan. For if one considers the probable changing industrial composition of the long-term development scheme, the latter can be interpreted as a temporary, almost inevitable, infra-structure- and basic-industry-connected bulge in the public-investment segment that would be perfectly consistent with a subsequent resurgence of the private-investment segment after the economy had become more highly developed. But the same cannot be said of a substantial further Third-to-Fourth-Plan advance in the public investment share; this would imply an aggressive extension of government enterprise into a variety of lighter industry areas in which the government of India latterly has evinced very little interest in operating.

[15] P. 59.

In the second place, if total Third-Plan investment outlays were to stay roughly within the limits indicated by the Plan, the public share could not rise to 80 percent of total annual investment by 1965-66 without forcing an absolute as well as a relative reduction in the volume of private investment. And in the eyes of many middle-of-the-roaders in India, including officials, such a cutback would be wholly inconsistent with the picture of the developing economy's expanding opportunities for private enterprise that the government has been at pains to paint.

The over-all public-private investment split that the Third-Plan document recommends—60.5 percent public and 39.5 percent private[16]—almost precisely supports the flippant forecast that was commonplace in off-the-record discussions in New Delhi throughout the Plan-formulation period—that the planners, after taking judicious account of the 55-45 and 65-35 limits on their range of choice would, no doubt, wind up splitting the difference. Moreover, the fact that the outcome does accord with expectations based upon nothing much more profound than this splitting-the-difference rationale probably explains the notable tranquility with which the organized private sector seems to have accepted this aspect of the official Third-Plan design.[17] Yet in the light of the considerations just adduced, the proposed 60.5-39.5 ratio has some major implications that are not obvious:

1. The recommended scheme adheres to the logic of the long-term development scheme adopted in the Second Plan, which, under the circumstances, virtually requires a significant

[16] If account is taken of the Rs. 200 crores of "public investment" that the Plan provides be transferred to private small enterprises, the allocation can be interpreted, instead, as a 58.6-41.4 split.

[17] At the time of publication of the Plan in August 1961, Shri Karaunchand Thapar, President of the FICCI, remarked that its allocation of resources between public and private sectors was "broadly similar" to that proposed by the Federation. (*Overseas Hindustan Times* [Aug. 24, 1961], p. 11.) Little or no adverse private-industry comment on this aspect of the Plan document was reported in the airmail editions of the English-language Indian press.

rise in the public-investment share from the late fifties to the early sixties.

2. While it implies a very rapid rise in annual public-investment outlays during the Third-Plan period, from about Rs. 800 crores in 1960-61 to about Rs. 1,700 crores in 1965-66, the Plan does also provide for a moderate rise in private investment—from Rs. 800 crores to Rs. 900 crores in the indicated years. In other words, it calls for about the maximum rise in the public-investment percentage that is consistent with a continuing absolute growth prospect for the private sector.

3. To make good a five-year public-investment share of 60.5 percent, the Plan calls for the annual ratio to climb to 65-35 by 1965-66. Thus the planners, in effect, have adopted the public-sector proponents' recommended ratio as an end-year target rather than a five-year average. In so doing (assuming that the ratio is in any event, unlikely to fall as fast as it is expected to rise), they probably have destined the Fourth Plan to have at least a moderately higher average public-investment share than the Third. But this is the important point: they have adopted a design that does not *commit* future policymakers ever to carry the annual public-private investment ratio beyond 2-1. The present design would be perfectly consistent with a further rise in the ratio during the later sixties, but it would be equally consistent with a contraction in the ratio and a relative expansion in private activity. The unresolved issue, in short, has not been prejudged; the new Plan leaves the post-1966 evolution of the relationship between the public and private sectors to be determined largely by subsequent planning exercises.

The Plan's Foreign-Exchange Dimensions

As the Third Plan was being formulated, differences of opinion about its foreign-exchange aspects tended to cluster around three interdependent issues: (1) During the Third-Plan period, how much net imports (and, accordingly, how much foreign assistance) would the attainment of the Plan's objectives require? (2) What feasible timetable for the achievement of substantial national self-support should the Plan reflect? (3) What would be an appropriate export-expansion target for the Third Plan?

On the first count, Indian planning has been growing increasingly realistic. This means, in this instance, that the planners grudgingly have been raising their estimates of foreign aid requirements for the period 1961-62 through 1965-66. I shall attempt no analysis of the psychology that has caused Indian officials characteristically to underestimate their need for outside financial assistance, but such, almost certainly, has been their habit. In 1959 the Planning Commission staff's original sketches of the Third Plan bade fair to repeat the error of the Second Plan in this regard. They suggested that a five-year development scheme of essentially the same aggregative domestic dimensions as that which now has been adopted might be able to get along with Rs. 1,500 crores of net imports. While, as will be explained below, the data that would be required for making a really careful check of such an estimate neither were available to foreign observers then nor are supplied in the final Plan document now, this figure, almost surely, was far too low. Such was the impression voiced by virtually every foreign advisory group that consulted with the Indians about the preliminary Third-Plan thinking, and the Indians themselves adopted a substantially higher estimate of the net-import need on the basis of the somewhat more detailed projections that underlay their Draft Outline of June 1960.

The Draft Outline put the Third-Plan net-import requirement at Rs. 2,100 crores. Further analysis done during the year that intervened before the firming of the final Plan document led the planners to revise their balance-of-payments estimates as indicated in Table 3. Under import needs (that is, "payments"), a more careful examination of project requirements indicated that Third-Plan projects would need, not Rs. 1,900 crores, but at least Rs. 2,030 crores worth of imported machinery and equipment (the bracketed number in column B). The figure of Rs. 200 crores that the Draft Outline has estimated for machinery replacement, spare parts, and

TABLE 3. *India's Balance of Payments, 1961–62 Through 1965–66, as Projected in the Draft Outline (June 1960) and in the Final Version (August 1961) of the Third Five Year Plan*

(Rupee items in crores)

Item	(A) Draft Outline	(B) Final Plan Document	(C) B–A
Receipts			
Exports (merchandise)	3,450	3,700	+250
Invisibles, net (excluding official donations)	120	nil	–120
Net capital transactions (excluding receipts of official loans and private foreign investment)[1]	–500	–550	–50
External assistance[3]	2,600	2,600 (2,730)[2]	0 (+130)[2]
Draft on foreign exchange reserves	nil	nil	0
Total receipts	5,670	5,750 (5,880)	+80 (+210)
Payments			
Imports of machinery and equipment for Plan projects	1,900	1,900 (2,030)	0 (+130)
Components, intermediate products, etc. for raising production of capital goods	200	200	0
Maintenance imports[3]	3,570	3,650	+80
Total payments	5,670	5,750 (5,880)	+80 (+210)

[1] Mainly repayment of old debt.

[2] That the extra Rs. 130 crores of required foreign exchange for which the Plan provides no formal financing should be assigned to the external assistance category is the judgment of the present writer, not of the authors of the Third Five Year Plan who, if they were forced to allocate this amount clearly, apparently would treat it as a need for additional exports.

[3] Excluding U.S. surplus food.

Source: Third-Plan document, Chapter 6.

other non-project-connected capital goods was let stand.[18] But the estimate for maintenance imports was revised upward

[18] At best this category is tenuously differentiated from the other import categories. See Chapter 11 below for comment to the effect that the very concepts of "capital goods" imports and especially "project-connected capital goods" pose serious obstacles to rational programming and further, that the non-project-connected portion of net imports is likely to run considerably higher during the Third Plan than Table 3 seems to indicate.

by Rs. 80 crores, thereby raising the Plan period's total import requirement by Rs. 210 crores.

In considering next the availability of foreign exchange for meeting this increased requirement, the planners found themselves forced first to make two adverse adjustments in the Draft Outline's figures. For one thing, it was now concluded that the joint effects of rising foreign debt servicing charges and diminished Indian holdings and earnings overseas would reduce the net receipts from invisibles to an average of zero under the Third Plan. Second, recalculations indicated that scheduled repayments of outstanding obligations would be Rs. 50 crores higher than previously estimated. These two items, together with the increased need for imports, meant that the planners now foresaw a foreign-exchange requirement under the Third Plan Rs. 380 crores higher than had been projected in June 1960.

After some deliberation the government's foreign trade specialists decided that, in response to this increased need, the Third Plan's merchandise export target could feasibly, and should, be raised another Rs. 250 crores. But they felt that it could not realistically be put higher than this. There was no gainsaying the Draft Outline's position that the nation's foreign-exchange reserves, drawn down radically during the Second Plan, now represented the minimum liquid balances the country required for servicing its international transactions; no further net contribution to Third-Plan financing was available from this quarter. Finally as for the one remaining item under receipts—that labelled "external assistance"—the planners apparently felt that, as a matter of international political forecasting, it was quite impossible to raise their estimate of the foreign aid that would be available during the period 1961-62 through 1965-66 above the Rs. 2,600 crore figure included in the Draft Outline.

Thus they were at an impasse. Their considered estimate of foreign-exchange requirements for the Third Plan exceeded their hopeful best estimate of foreign-exchange resources by Rs. 130 crores. The document's resolution of this difficulty is as disarmingly simple as it is unsatisfactory: For purposes of showing a balanced receipts-payments projection for the Third

Plan (Chapter 6, Table 8) it simply makes believe that the project-connected import requirement is Rs. 1,900 crores, as in the Draft Outline, rather than the Rs. 2,030 crores that, it now has been more carefully recalculated, would provide the minimum needed support for the Plan's production goals. Hence the unbracketed figures in column B, Table 3, that add up to a receipts-payments balance of Rs. 5,750 crores and indicate an apparent net-imports projection (imports less merchandise exports and net receipts from invisibles) of Rs. 2,050 crores. Actually, however, the Plan's projection of required total imports is Rs. 5,880 crores and of net imports, Rs. 2,180 crores; but it contains no satisfactory present answer as to whence Rs. 130 crores of the foreign exchange for financing the latter is to come.

The Plan's answer, such as it is, about the missing Rs. 130 crores is that it poses a need for still further expansion of exports above the Rs. 3,700-crore level. However, it is apparent, without our yet attempting an independent appraisal of the export target, that in the minds of the Indian planners themselves the Rs. 3,700 crore figure already is quite ambitious and that the chances of exceeding it are fairly slim. It is disappointing, therefore, that the draftsmen of the Plan document did not choose candidly to treat the extra Rs. 130 crores as a need for additional external assistance, as I have taken the liberty of doing in the upper portion of Table 3. The document's hypothesis that the Draft Outline's total external assistance estimate[19] of Rs. 2,600 crores is, in some sense, sacrosanct, is undefended and unpersuasive.

Indeed, as the final draft of the Plan is at pains to emphasize, India's foreign-aid prospects became, not only much brighter, but far more tangible in the year following the publication of the Draft Outline. As will be discussed in Chapter 10, in May-June 1961 a consortium of friendly countries organized by the World Bank and led by the United States promised India Rs. 1,089 crores of assistance to be made available before the end of 1962-63. Combined with Third-Plan credits

[19] Net of foodgrains supplied by the United States under its Public Law 480.

of Rs. 305 crores already supplied by the Soviet Union, Czechoslovakia, Poland, and Switzerland and with an unexpended balance of Rs. 365 crores carried forward from Second-Plan authorizations, this meant that three months after the start of the Third Plan India already had aid commitments (over and above Rs. 600 crores of surplus farm commodities that the United States additionally had agreed to supply) of more than Rs. 1,800 crores for the Plan. And most of these were credits specifically earmarked for the first two years of the Plan by lenders and donors disposed to provide additional credits for the latter three years of the Plan period. Certainly there was nothing in these figures, or in the mood of the negotiations from which they emerged, to suggest that the Third Plan necessarily had to conform to some arbitrary limit on total aid that was unrelated to the scheme's carefully scrutinized and programmed requirements for net imports.

The planners have cast the program's external assistance requirements in an unnecessarily unfavorable light in one other interesting respect. In their balance-of-payments projections they have made no attempt to distinguish the inflow of foreign private profit-seeking capital from the other "external assistance" supplied by governments and international organizations. Since a net receipt of such private capital is prompted by ordinary commercial motives and, we trust, will persist long after India has attained a condition of "self-support," the need for aid as such is unfairly exaggerated if foreign private investment is not estimated separately. And, as we look ahead, the exaggeration becomes a progressive one, since net private foreign commercial investment in India, which seems to have averaged less than Rs. 20 crores a year during the Second-Plan period, is expected, in the Planning Commission's present long-term projections, to rise rather steeply during the coming fifteen years.[20]

[20] This is the inference to be drawn from the projection (Third-Plan document, pp. 28-29) for the year 1975-76 of (a) a national income of Rs. 33,000 to 34,000 crores, (b) achievement of national self-support, but (c) a domestic saving rate (saving/income) about 1 percentage point lower than the investment rate. The implication is that non-aid-financed net imports should rise to about

My net impression is that the Third Plan's foreign-aid projection, even when we retrieve the suppressed Rs. 130 crores and use the bracketed figures in Table 3's column B, probably still is a little unrealistically conservative. Yet this is a difficult point to establish, for to do so convincingly would require a fully phased projection of exports and imports by relatively detailed commodity groups; and not only does the Plan document contain no convenient compilation of such data, but there is reason to doubt that Indian planners yet have assembled an adequate array of detailed, annually phased estimates even for their own use. (See the next chapter.) Nevertheless, the Plan contains one bit of aggregative evidence that reinforces the suspicion that the foreign-aid estimate is understated. Table 4, to which we shall be turning our attention next, summarizes the long-term development model outlined in the second chapter of the Third-Plan document. It will be noted that it projects for the final years of the Plan an investment rate of 14 to 15 percent of national income and a saving rate of 11.5 percent. Thus implicitly it projects net imports of 2.5 to 3.5 percent of national income, or anywhere from Rs. 475 crores to Rs. 665 crores for 1965-66. As the second item on line F of the table indicates, this range of alternative end-year net-import possibilities suggests (if we assume a steady year-to-year percentage growth in annual net imports) that total Third-Plan net imports might range anywhere from about Rs. 2,130 crores to Rs. 2,650 crores. But the Plan's official net-imports estimate (even when we add back the troublesome Rs. 130 crores) is only Rs. 2,180; it lies virtually at the bottom of the range of possibilities that the long-term model poses; and it will suffice only if, on the one hand, the saving rate by 1965-66 has risen fully as much as the model proposes, while, on the other hand, the investment rate has attained only the lower end of the range projected.

One is left persuaded that a somewhat bolder estimate of net-import—and foreign-aid—requirements would have been

_____
1 percent of the national income, or more than Rs. 300 crores annually. Put in absolute terms, this seems an implausibly high figure. But the expectation of a radical growth in net private foreign investment is unmistakable.

TABLE 4. *Income, Investment, Saving, and Net Imports in India's Long-Term Development Scheme*
(Rupee items in crores at 1960–61 prices)

	Second Plan	Third Plan		Fourth Plan		Fifth Plan	
	1960–61	total	1965–66	total	1970–71	total	1975–76
line							
A National income	14,500		19,000		25,000		33–34,000
B Investment/ national income	.11		$\left\{\begin{matrix}.14\\ \text{to}\\ .15\end{matrix}\right\}$		$\left\{\begin{matrix}.17\\ \text{to}\\ .18\end{matrix}\right\}$		$\left\{\begin{matrix}.19\\ \text{to}\\ .20\end{matrix}\right\}$
C Investment (B × A)	1,600	10,500	$\left\{\begin{matrix}2,660\\ \text{to}\\ 2,845\end{matrix}\right\}$	17,000	$\left\{\begin{matrix}4,250\\ \text{to}\\ 4,500\end{matrix}\right\}$	25,000	$\left\{\begin{matrix}6,260\\ \text{to}\\ 6,800\end{matrix}\right\}$
D Domestic saving/ national income	.085		.115		$\left\{\begin{matrix}.15\\ \text{to}\\ .16\end{matrix}\right\}$		$\left\{\begin{matrix}.18\\ \text{to}\\ .19\end{matrix}\right\}$
E Net imports/ national income (C − D)	.025		$\left\{\begin{matrix}.025\\ \text{to}\\ .035\end{matrix}\right\}$		$\left\{\begin{matrix}.01\\ \text{to}\\ .03\end{matrix}\right\}$		$\left\{\begin{matrix}0\\ \text{to}\\ .02\end{matrix}\right\}$
F Net imports (E × A)	362	$\left\{\begin{matrix}2,130\\ \text{to}\\ 2,650\end{matrix}\right\}$[1]	$\left\{\begin{matrix}475\\ \text{to}\\ 665\end{matrix}\right\}$		$\left\{\begin{matrix}250\\ \text{to}\\ 750\end{matrix}\right\}$		$\left\{\begin{matrix}0\\ \text{to}\\ 680\end{matrix}\right\}$
G Net imports/ investment (F/C)	.227		$\left\{\begin{matrix}.167\\ \text{to}\\ .25\end{matrix}\right\}$		$\left\{\begin{matrix}.055\\ \text{to}\\ .177\end{matrix}\right\}$		$\left\{\begin{matrix}0\\ \text{to}\\ .109\end{matrix}\right\}$

[1] Assuming constant annual percentage growth from Rs. 362 crores in 1960–61 to Rs. 475 crores in 1965–66, at the lower limit, and to Rs. 665 crores, at the upper limit.
Source: Third-Plan document, Chapter 2.

more realistic. At the same time, the present figures make much more sense than those with which planners began in 1959, and—moving on now to the second of the issues raised at the beginning of this section—we can also say emphatically that in their final drafting of the Third Plan the planning authorities have evolved a notably more realistic timetable for India's longer-run attainment of economic self-support. The change from the Draft Outline in this regard represents much the most important shift in aggregative development design made during the fourteen months intervening between the publication of the two documents. For the Draft Outline, although sketchy on the matter of phasing, clearly assumed that the country's need for aid-financed net imports would peak during the Third Plan, would already be on the decline by 1965-66, and would phase out entirely by the end of the Fourth Five Year Plan. As Table 4 shows, this pattern has now been stretched out a full additional planning period. In an effort to keep the change from appearing too radical and to show net imports declining in some sense during the course of the Third Plan, the authors of Chapter 2 in the Plan document emphasize that net imports will be steadily declining from now on as a percent of investment.[21] But the far more relevant points are that, from the end year of the Second Plan to the end year of the Third, net imports now are shown as, in all probability, *rising* as a percent of national income, that their absolute level is projected as rising very substantially during the same period, that the model contains no clear indication of a declining trend in net imports during the Fourth Plan,[22] and that it suggests a volume of total Fourth-Plan net imports roughly comparable to that in the Third. The multiplied effects of the uncertainties that the model expresses in its income, investment, and saving estimates for the Fifth Plan cause the calculated net-import figure to range all the way up to Rs. 680 crores even for 1975-76. However, this is misleading; the purpose that the numbers are meant to express is that "by the end of the Fifth Plan the economy will be strong enough to develop at a satisfactory pace without being dependent on external assistance outside of the normal inflow of foreign capital."[23]

The fact that the final version of the Third Plan projects a Fourth-Plan aid requirement more than half again as high as the one the Draft Outline suggested would, of course, be no cause for rejoicing among the suppliers of aid to India, includ-

[21] As Table 4 indicates, there is a possibility that they will rise from 1960-61 to 1965-66, even when they are measured on this basis.

[22] However, thanks to the prospect of rising private foreign investment, it is fair to say that the model's average estimate is for some Third-to-Fourth Plan decline in the requirement for foreign governmental assistance.

[23] Third-Plan document, p. 29.

ing the United States, if the earlier scheme for attaining self-support in 1970-71 had been practicable. But rather plainly it was not. For the earlier timetable to have been made good, the Third Plan would have had to have started with a rush, well supplied with foreign aid provided at least a year earlier than the consortium's agreement, and the whole developmental decision making and implementing process would have had to be almost ideally efficient, integrated, and synchronized. As will be emphasized in subsequent chapters, planning and administrative reality in contemporary India lacks a good deal of exhibiting such perfection. Consequently, the practical outcome, had the planners stuck to their goal of self-support by 1970-71, could only have been a bob-tailed, frustratingly inadequate expansion in production. It is for this reason that, despite the adverse implications for American taxpayers, American policymakers who are concerned to support a successful Indian development experience should cheer the Indians' decision to extend their period of heavy dependence upon external assistance another five years.

The final issue mentioned at the beginning of the section—the appropriateness of the Third Plan's export target—is not one upon which I shall dwell at this point. In Chapter 9, which is devoted to export problems, I shall be noting the need for a more strenuous brand of export promotion than India has exercised during the Second-Plan years. However, the Third-Plan document makes the same point with greatest insistence, and its Rs. 3,700-crore target for Third-Plan exports already assumes such an intensification of effort. While one can hope that exports in fact will do even better than this, the process of export promotion will continue to be a difficult one for the time being, and I know of no basis for judging that the Rs. 3,700-crore figure is an insufficiently ambitious forecast of the gains that (with strenuous new efforts) are likely to be achieved. After all, if we assume a straight-line expansion in annual exports, the figure implies an increase of nearly 40 percent in five years, from exports of about Rs. 605 crores in 1960-61 to about Rs. 830 crores in 1965-66. That is a very substantial gain by any standard.

Domestic Finance

We have noted that in the Third Five Year Plan India's financial authorities were persuaded to accept considerably bolder targets than they had initially preferred. As it was, before the end of the preparation process they eventually drew the line and refused to project more than Rs. 7,500 crores of financing (Rs. 6,300 crores for investment and Rs. 1,200 crores for current outlays) for a public-sector program whose projects price out at more than Rs. 8,000 crores. The Plan document, consequently, has the air of a program whose domestic financing scheme already has been stretched just about to the limit.

At the same time, I have criticized the Plan for the inadequacy of its specifically programmed schemes for mobilizing idle manpower and have implied that the official fear of inflation, which has been at least partly responsible for this deficiency, has been largely unwarranted. Obviously, this leaves us with a very important question. Does the financing pattern presently projected look quite feasible of accomplishment, and beyond that even, does it include a safety cushion that could help to dampen whatever inflationary impulses might be generated by an expanded effort to activate idle manpower? Or, on the other hand, does the present pattern promise, at best, to do only a bare-minimal job of containing the inflationary tendencies of the present "main-line" program?

In formulating the issue this way, I am assuming that, whatever its motivations for rationalizing the difference between the Rs. 7,500 crores and the Rs. 8,000 crores, the Plan is correct in its hypothesis that there will be sufficient delays in project execution to cause expenditure requirements to fall at least 6 percent off the pace implicit in the present project targets. (As will appear in the next chapter, it will be gratifying if detailed planning and administration in India avoid any greater performance shortfall than this.) Given this assumption, it follows that any room for enlargement that may exist in the present financial plan could be devoted to the residual employment effort.

Two other general comments are in order before we try to look into the specifics of this matter. First, any answer to the question whether more Third-Plan outlays could be safely financed presumes some judgment as to how much and which kinds of inflation an economy striving for accelerated development can "safely" accommodate. My own judgment is that it is irresponsible for a government with the purposes and conditions of the Indian to attempt to insure a very high or complete degree of safety against inflation. As noted already, to strive to avoid inflation in foodgrain prices is politically sensible. And certainly it is important to forestall the kind of cumulative, self-accelerating inflationary spiral that can be generated by a general excess of demand. But in a situation of rapid development, which is bound to contain many particular supply-demand imbalances and is likely to entail a number of rising import costs, a sufficient restraint upon aggregate demand literally to hold the average price line would signify an insufficiently aggressive expansion effort.

To make this value judgment more concrete, let me say that the kind of inflation experienced during the Second Plan, it seems to me, falls within the limits of what planners should regard as acceptable. While one certainly can hope that the Third Plan can succeed without as large average price rises as those of the preceding five years (30 percent in the general wholesale price index and 24 percent in the working class cost-of-living index), the main point is that the period showed few symptoms of excess aggregate demand tending to push up prices across the board and cumulatively. Rather, much of the actual increase, especially in the last two years of the period, reflected rising prices for particular domestic and foreign industrial raw materials, and another major portion reflected the absence of sufficient foodgrain inventories to cushion the impact of poor monsoons. It is most doubtful that the anti-expansionist effects of any effort to restrain aggregate demand more than it was restrained during the Second Plan could have been adequately justified on anti-inflationary grounds.

The other general comment has to do with the characteristic disposition of the Indian government toward the problem of financial responsibility. In the case of many countries aided by the United States it would be a treacherous abuse of his own country's interests for an American commentator to emphasize the considerations of the last couple of paragraphs. Indigenous fiscal irresponsibility is so endemic in many aided countries that it is appropriate for the Americans addressing them to stress without respite the urgency of anti-inflationary planning. But, I am strongly persuaded, this is not the case with India. The financial instincts of the Indian government, centering in the Ministry of Finance and the Reserve Bank of India, have been, for the government of an underdeveloped economy, peculiarly conservative. This is why it is not patently unrealistic, despite the general tenor of the Plan document's treatment of finance, to approach somewhat hopefully the question whether a larger volume of expenditures could be safely financed. But now let us get down to cases.

Table 5 summarizes the sources from which it is proposed to finance the government outlays projected in the Third Plan and compares them with those under the Second Plan. To begin with, I think we can say that the items on lines 1, 2, 3, 5, and 8, while moderately optimistic in some cases, probably as a group are quite reasonable projections if the proposed expansion of real income is achieved at approximately the intended pace. And if the latter does not prove to be the case, then not all of the projected increases in taxes and savings will be needed on schedule anyway. Much the same can be said of the estimated gains from increased rates and/or kinds of taxation (line 7). However, this is a sufficiently important subject to require special comment. The expectation that the surplus over the government's nondevelopment expenditures of receipts from tax laws and rates existing at the start of the Plan will rise as indicated on line 1 seems to be appropriately related to the income projections and to reasonable intentions concerning improvements in tax administration. It does imply a relatively greater degree of restraint in current general government outlays, especially for defense, than during the Second Plan; but the Indians presently believe that this is feasible.

Some of the estimated changes in earnings in specific industries during the Third Plan underlying the figures on line 3 (for example, five-fold increases in public steel and fertilizer plant earnings) are startling at first sight. However, much new Second-Plan construction in such industries will be moving up to full-capacity operations for the first time during the Third Plan and should be multiplying many times over their total margins over costs. The target for receipts of government-sponsored small savings schemes implies only a 17 percent increase from the Second Plan to the Third Plan in savings per rupee of income, and this certainly does not seem excessively ambitious, especially in view of the promised intensification of the activity of rural cooperative financial institutions. Finally, the estimate for the budgetary derivative from external assistance is pretty cut-and-dried if the Plan's estimate of total assistance—Rs. 3,200 crores, including Rs. 600 crores of P.L. 480 foodgrains—is correct.[24] In the previous section I have suggested that the aid probably will require some increase. If it does, most of this is apt to take a form that would add to budgetary revenues.

The crux of the Plan's financing scheme is its proposal for additional taxes (line 7 of Table 5). India's record on this count is reasonably encouraging. The revenues garnered from newly introduced taxes and newly increased tax rates during the Second Plan amounted to well over twice the target projected in the Second-Plan document and helped to raise the tax share of national income from 7.5 percent in 1955-56 to about 8.9 percent in 1960-61. The present proposal is that the tax take be hiked to 11.4 percent of national income by 1965-66. This will take a good bit of political and administrative courage, but it should be feasible. While the Plan document is far less explicit than an analyst could wish about what the composition of the tax increases is intended to be, it suggests a

[24] Rs. 1,000 crores estimated as "nonbudgetary" assistance will be used for repaying external debt, for loans the foreign lender makes directly to the private sector, for building buffer food stocks that do not directly generate rupee proceeds, and, in the case of a small fraction of those P.L. 480 foodgrains that do generate rupee proceeds, for meeting United States government rupee expenses.

TABLE 5. *Domestic Financing of Government Development Outlays in the Second and Third Five Year Plans*

(Rupee items in crores)

Line	Item	Second Plan (estimated actuals)	Third Plan		
			Center	States	Total
(1)	Balance from current revenues (excluding additional taxation)	–50	410	140	550
(2)	Contribution of railways	150	100		100
(3)	Surpluses of other public enterprises	*	300	150	450
(4)	Loans from the public (net)	780	475	325	800
(5)	Small savings (net)	400	213	387	600
(6)	Provident funds (net), steel equalization fund, and balance of miscellaneous capital receipts over non-Plan disbursements	230	716	–176	540
(7)	Additional taxation, including results of new policies to increase surplus of public enterprises	1,052	1,100	610	1,710
(8)	Budgetary receipts corresponding to external assistance	1,090	2,200		2,200
(9)	Deficit financing	948	524	26	550
(10)	Total	4,600	6,038	1,463	7,500

* Included in items 1 and 6.
Source: Third-Plan document, Chapter 6.

very considerable role for new indirect taxes, especially excises on commodities that, while they do not figure in a bare subsistence standard of living, are bought very widely by those of the masses who are experiencing some improvement in real income. This is an eminently sensible emphasis. It can lead to a tax system that is far more administrable in an underdeveloped economy than would be one that relies primarily on direct taxes; that can have a broad impact and yet be at least crudely progressive; and that can reach into the countryside with increasing effectiveness as fast as the rural population increases its purchases in the monetized market.

The most uncertain issue in the tax field, very probably, is whether the state governments can be inspired or cajoled into bringing off their assigned share of the tax expansion. On the one hand, the growth in state revenues as a result of a rising tax base has been most encouraging recently. But on the other hand, during the first year of the Third Plan, the states fell behind the pace at which the planners wanted them to add new taxes. Particularly because of the major role of the states in the field of rural taxation, this is a problem that the nation's political leadership is going to have to keep after.

Last, we come to the government borrowing items in the table (lines 4 and 9) and to some residual items including certain unspecified capital transactions (line 6). For Americans it is essential first to get a bit of semantics straight: In Indian usage, the sale of long-term government securities to the public represented on line 4 is *not* deficit financing but a device for channelling private savings into public use. "Deficit financing" is limited to gap-filling, non-term loans obtained directly from the Reserve Bank of India. This language suggests that only "deficit-financed" government outlays are made out of newly created money that adds to the money supply and increases government demand without forestalling an offsetting amount of private demand. The terminology would make good sense if all purchases of long-term governments were in fact financed out of current private income and did forestall private spending. But during the Second Plan much less than half of the Rs. 780 crores of long-term government borrowing met these tests. Much of it was accounted for by purchases of government securities by the State Bank of India with P.L. 480 rupees that had been deposited with it;[25] another sizable portion involved direct purchases of government securities by the Reserve Bank of India; and a third part consisted of other purchases of securities by commercial banks. The first two of these categories entailed no mobilization of (*ex ante*) private savings, and the ordinary purchase of governments by the commercial banking system needs entail none if the system's reserve position allows it to lend by creating fresh demand deposits.

Accordingly, the Third-Plan target on line 4 of the table is deceptively ambitious if it is intended that all of the Rs. 800 crores of long-term borrowing shall represent an anti-inflationary offset to public development outlays. Actually, however,

[25] See Chapter 12 for an extended discussion of P.L. 480 rupee financing.

the planners do not seem to contemplate this, for they still expect that some of the Rs. 800 crores of securities will go to commercial banks. And they are counting among the Rs. 800 crores purchases by the various provident funds despite the fact that the financing scheme takes credit additionally for the accumulation of assets within those same funds (line 6). For these reasons and also because presumably not all the "miscellaneous capital receipts" mentioned on line 6 represent withdrawals from current private income, it seems plain that neither the line 4 nor the line 6 item is a solid anti-expansionist figure. Yet, in this respect, some improvement over the Second-Plan record is intended and should be attainable.

In the case of deficit financing proper, the Third Plan is not in as much stronger a position than the Second as Table 5 makes it appear. For during the earlier Plan the expansionist impact of Rs. 548 crores of the deficit was fully offset by an equivalent drawing down of India's foreign-exchange reserves, leaving only Rs. 350 crores of the nominal deficit uncovered. The comparable figure proposed for the Third Plan is Rs. 550 crores. However, as we have just been noting, there is additional expansionist financing disguised elsewhere in the public-sector financing schemes in both Plans, and more in the Second than in the Third. Thus the total new-money financing presently proposed for Third-Plan public outlays—an amount that I should put, very roughly, in the neighborhood of Rs. 700-800 crores—is not even in absolute terms greatly in excess of that in the Second Plan and, taking account of the comparative scales of the two programs, the general inflationary threat that the new scheme poses is distinctly less than that of its predecessor.

Let me put this last point differently—in terms of what we might call the acceptable growth in the money supply. During the Second Five Year Plan the Indian money supply, which the Reserve Bank defines as currency and deposit money with the public, grew 33 percent to a 1960-61 level of Rs. 2,900 crores, thereby accomodating a 20 percent growth in national income, some monetization of rural transactions that previously had been conducted on an in-kind basis, and a good bit of particular-commodity price inflation.[26] Yet (I have already argued) total new-money financing was not sufficient to produce any evident general excess demand. Reasoning by analogy, the Third Plan, which proposes a 30 percent advance in the national income and anticipates a considerably more rapid monetization of in-kind transactions, should be able to handle at least a 50-percent expansion in the money supply (that is, Rs. 1,450 crores in five years) with no worse effects than during the Second Plan. And yet, as I say, the proposed amount of new money to be created for public outlays does not appear to exceed Rs. 800 crores. Even when allowance is made for some parallel creation of bank deposits through extension of bank credit to the private sector, this figure falls comfortably within the Rs. 1,450-crore "limit." Indeed, it represents a substantially smaller fraction of the latter than the fraction of total monetary expansion that government new-money financing alone accounted for during the Second Plan.

An answer to the question whether the proposed domestic financing scheme could reasonably be stretched to encompass a more adequate residual employment program is now apparent. The tax, enterprise-profit, and savings elements in the scheme are ambitious, but, assuming fairly energetic administration, they are collectively realistic. Indeed, significantly more new-money financing—I should say, up to Rs. 200 crores more—would be consistent with what seems to me the appropriate concept of fiscal safety and responsibility for India's situation. Thus it appears that the present financing scheme safely could be stretched enough to accommodate a major residual employment effort. For the price tag that the planners have put on the total supra-Plan, 2½ million-man rural works program is Rs. 150 crores.

Two other considerations reinforce the conclusion that the Third Plan financially contains some room for enlargement. First, if the Plan's foreign-assistance projections do turn out to require amendment on foreign-exchange grounds, this will also automatically strengthen the government's domestic budgetary

[26] The line of argument in this paragraph assumes comparative stability in the velocity of monetary circulation. As far as I know, this is not an unreasonable assumption.

position. Second, there is the line of argument that has been developed at some length in Chapter 3: The outputs of many indigenous goods might prove so responsive to extra increases in rural consumer demand that, if specific defenses could be provided against food-price inflation, the price effects of additional public outlays on labor-intensive construction would be very moderate. Moreover, if joined with an imaginative rural tax program, an expansion of such outlays could supply a significant feedback in the form of additional revenues.

Problems of Physical Feasibility

Although this critique of the Third Five Year Plan is nearly done, there is an important sense in which it could be said only to have laid the preliminaries for a proper evaluation of the Plan's potentialities as an operating program. For, within the broad framework established by the Plan's general architecture, which we have been examining, the actual workability of the program will depend very largely upon such pointed, practical considerations as these: Which particular-industry expansion schemes threaten to cause the most serious bottlenecks in the over-all expansion? Are the rates of growth in production that are being projected in critical industries physically attainable? Has realistic account been taken of such general, nonfinancial bottleneck factors as skilled manpower? In terms of the technical matrix of inputs and outputs they imply, are the various industrial strands of the proposed expansion program internally consistent? And have their detailed time patterns been worked out in a way that fits together through time? Unhappily, these very urgent questions are ones that the present commentary can address with little authority. Partly this is because the commentator lacks sufficient detailed knowledge of Indian industries and their technologies to make worthwhile independent appraisals of the feasibility of the particular-industry programs. Another part of the deficiency can be laid to the Plan documents' paucity of adequately phased data. Still, there are a few useful impressions concerning the Plan's physical feasibility that can be recorded.

In the first place, as will be explained in the next chapter, the inter-industry relationships implicit in the Third Plan's various output targets are based upon what is, for any under-developed economy, a surprisingly elaborate bill of information about the technical coefficients—the ratios of materials and other inputs to output—that pertain among different industrial processes. This is very imperfect information; it is variously dated, from various sources, and in many instances may not reflect the most appropriate technologies for India's circumstances. Nevertheless, as I shall be emphasizing in the next chapter, during the pre-Third-Plan period a great deal of enterprise in the assembly of such information was shown within the Planning Commission. As a result, we can be reasonably confident that there is a fair degree of technical (input-output) internal consistency among the various output targets the Third Plan projects for 1965-66.

Second, while I am not qualified, as I say, to make independent evaluations of the engineering and administrative feasibility of achieving many of the particular-industry expansions the Plan proposes, it was possible, in the course of observing the Plan-formulation process, to identify those particular potential bottleneck products around which planners' anxieties seemed most commonly to center. These were especially coal, electric power, steel, and fertilizers. One gets the sense from the final Plan document that, in some of these areas at least, industry planning has moved in a realistic direction. In the case of coal, where the lag of performance behind intention looked particularly ominous as of 1959-60, there has been no cutback in the 1965-66 target (which both the Draft Outline and the Plan document put at 97 million tons). But in the last year of the Second Plan new production, especially in the public sector, came in with an encouraging rush, raising 1960-61 output more than 1½ million tons above the expected 53 million tons. And for the Third Plan an apparently reasonable allocation of expansion between the public and private sectors (20 million tons for the former, 16.8 million for the latter) now has been settled and with it, I hope, some of the enervating differences that had developed between a particularly intransigent ministry and a particularly stubborn private industry.

After further examination of the Third Plan's electric power requirements, the 1965-66 target for generating capacity was raised in the Plan document from the Draft Outline's figure of 11.8 million KW to 12.7 million KW, thereby calling for considerably more than double the 1960-61 capacity of 5.7 million KW. In one sense, the very substantial lag in Second-Plan power projects, which raised operable capacity only 2.3 million KW by 1960-61 instead of the targeted 3.5 million KW, makes the proposed Third-Plan expansion look unrealistically ambitious. On the other hand, most of the delayed Second-Plan projects will be coming on the line early in the Third Plan, thereby narrowing the new capacity that projects started and finished during the Third Plan will need to contribute.[27] Moreover, a majority of the capacity to be completed during the five years 1961-62 through 1965-66—and a heavier majority of the new projects—is of the more quickly built thermal rather than hydro variety. One further bit of evidence that the Plan document's power program is fairly realistic is the fact that the projected capacity of the Draft Outline's very high-cost nuclear power plant—300,000 KW—has been cut in half. All in all, it seems reasonable to conclude that, while the new power program is apt to fall short of its 1965-66 target and thereby force somewhat stricter rationing of electrical energy than the Plan data imply, it should be possible, with a little luck and strenuous effort, to keep the shortfall fairly small.

The most persuasive evidence that the Third Plan's particular-commodity targets now have been modified by a more realistic analysis of their physical feasibility is offered by the adjustments that have been made in the output projection for such industries as steel, aluminum, and fertilizers. In the first two cases the estimates, not of new capacity to be started in the years 1961-62 through 1965-66, but of the outputs to be realized in 1965-66, have been shaded down slightly in recognition of possible completion and breaking-in delays. In the

[27] However, a small portion (very possibly too small a portion) of the Third-Plan outlays are programmed for power projects that will be finished during the Fourth Plan.

fertilizer case, the Draft Outline's production targets for nitrogenous and phosphatic fertilizers of 1,000,000 and 500,000 tons respectively[28] would have required a whirlwind completion, staffing, and shakedown of projects for some of which not even the preliminary engineering had been started by the beginning of the Third Plan. In the Plan document both targets were cut 20 percent. Yet in these and other instances in which they have adopted more realistic projections of the output gains in particular commodities, the planners do not propose a parallel cutback in projected domestic consumption and, thereby, a retardation in the pace of over-all development. Instead, they simply are facing up to the prospect that India will have to import, for example, 200,000 tons (nitrogen-equivalent) of nitrogenous fertilizer in 1965-66, which the Draft Outline was not prepared to admit. Thus it is apparent that greater realism in foreign-exchange projections, particularly with respect to the economy's timetable for attaining self-support, has facilitated greater realism in physical planning.

A third among the physical-feasibility issues mentioned at the start of this section is the cross-testing of the program with respect to the availability of skilled manpower. Some of the Plan document's specific-industry projections evince careful attention to this variable; for instance, if I am not mistaken, a bottleneck in design and basic engineering talent is one of the more critical limiting factors that have caused the estimated completion rate for fertilizer plants to be stretched out. Moreover, by devoting a whole chapter to the needs for, and means for multiplying, scientific, technical, and other skilled manpower, the Plan document demonstrates a general awareness of the problem. This, in turn, reflects a series of rather careful quantitative studies inventorying requirements for particular categories of skilled personnel that were worked up within the Planning Commission during the Plan-preparation period. On the basis of such incomplete evidence and fortified by the kinds of broad reassurances adduced in Chapter 2, one can

[28] Measured, in each case, by the weight of the active ingredient. Production in 1960-61 was, respectively, about 210,000 tons and 70,000 tons.

tentatively conclude that Indian development probably should
not be as seriously embarrassed by a scarcity of skilled manpower as are most other developing economies. But this is a
very inconclusive finding. As we shall be noting at various
points, the present situation, especially with respect to allocation of the existing supply of skilled persons, leaves a good bit
to be desired; and India still is badly in need of much more detailed, *comprehensive* planning of its total phased requirements for, and supplies of, skilled personnel, as well as of a
comprehensive training program for improving the supply.
The Third-Plan document contains no real evidence that a detailed skilled-manpower budget has been constructed, parallel-
ing and cross-checking the program's commodity and financial
budgets. If my understanding is correct that such a budget does
not exist, this is a dangerous deficiency.

Finally, we come back to a dimension of the physical feasibility problem that is closely akin to the first one we considered. That first consideration was the inter-industry consistency
among the various five-year targets of the Plan. There is, as I
have said, a basis for some confidence that the Plan hangs together reasonably well, if timing is not taken into account,
when it is examined on this point. But one has much less confidence that it hangs together equally well chronologically, on
a year-by-year or half-year-by-half-year basis. There is some
indication of annual phasing in most of the particular industry
and sector programs outlined in the latter portions of the Plan
document. But nowhere in the chapters dealing with the over-
all expansion effort is there any attempt to bring these pieces
together in anything resembling a series of annual requirements and resources budgets. We already have seen enough
examples in this chapter—such as the case of the public-private
investment split—to know what a different pattern five-year
totals and targets sometimes can take on when they are considered on a year-by-year basis. Indeed, the apparent lack of
adequate phasing in the Third Five Year Plan seems so
gravely inimicable to its administrability as an action program
that we shall do well to pursue the matter at greater length in
the next chapter. And unless we find there that the Third-Plan
document's fuzziness in this regard can be attributed simply to

editorial errors, not to planning oversight, we shall be forced in the last analysis to suspend judgment on the Plan's net workability as an expansion scheme until the Indian planners have done a good bit more work on phasing.

Conclusion

The final drafts of democratic political documents—especially of legislative programs—have an inherent tendency to become blurred. This is one of the costs exacted by the processes for organizing consent in an open society, and India's Third Five Year Plan has paid it in good measure. The Third Plan is a considerably blurred document. Its language is frequently fuzzy and equivocal; it tries to put the best foot forward in all directions; it strives to offer something for everybody. Actually this blurring, despite the offense that it may give to rigorous analysts and stylists, is an achievement, for it has done little to corrupt the Plan content to which it supplies protective coloration. Thus far, at least, it seems to have secured, both within India and outside, a surprisingly non-hostile reception for what is, in fact, a very strong program.

The program in its main lines, is a wholly consistent extension of the long-term development scheme adopted with the Second Plan. It follows the import-minimizing strategy, continues to push basic industrialization, and maintains continuity in the evolution of public-private sector relationships without unnecessarily committing the future Indian economy to a pattern of intensified nationalization that it may not want. The program is tough-minded in its assignment of priorities and bold as to over-all endeavor—except in the matter of activation of idle manpower. On this latter score too the Plan has the superficial appearance of an extrapolation of the Second Plan, but in this instance there is evidence of an unfinished transition toward a more fruitful line of policy. And fortunately there appears also to be the financial potential for facilitating such a transition.

Especially in the related cases of residual unemployment and of agricultural expansion, the Third Plan leaves major problems unsolved despite the heavier investments it proposes in the latter. But it contains the hints of solutions; and particularly in its reassessment of the probable duration of foreign-aid requirements and its reappraisal of certain critical industry targets, it reveals maturing, more carefully considered analyses. On the whole it is a hopeful document representing an improving planning process.

But therein lies the nub of the next chapter. For no document should be equated with the decision-making process from which it, its predecessors, and its successors emerge. Even less should it be equated with the administrative processes available for its implementation. Having taken a look at the Third Five Year Plan itself, partisans of the Indian development effort need even more to examine the planning, and Plan-implementing procedures upon which India is depending for making operative the general strategy that the Plan documents embody.

5 PROCEDURES FOR PLANNING AND
PLAN IMPLEMENTATION

In formulating a brief critique of the Indian economic planning process, I find myself disposed toward a quite different set of emphases than would have seemed appropriate two or three years ago, especially for an American audience. At that time central economic planning by government, regardless of type or circumstance, was viewed with alarm by American policymakers. And India, offering what was generally accepted as a nonpareil instance of systematic economic planning in the non-Communist portion of the economically underdeveloped world, was regarded with particular suspicion for that very reason.

In such a climate of opinion it would have been appropriate to spend a good bit of time defending the Indian commitment to planning. One would wish to develop at much greater length some of the points made in earlier chapters—for instance, (1) that the Indian government has a politically inescapable responsibility for leading the development effort; (2) that it has had to provide a growth perspective, fill decision-making gaps, and supply infrastructure; (3) that consequently it must try to do what it does in a way that seeks an optimal allocation of the economy's scarce resources; (4) that Indian markets have a variety of infirmities that make them unacceptable as the economy's dominant allocative machinery during its period of accelerated development; and (5) that the government has a resultant obligation to run an allocative system that implements the development goals in a coherent, internally consistent manner while, at the same time, stimulating, not impairing, idle-resource activation and private productive energies.

However, there is much less need now for such a defense of the very concept of comprehensive economic planning in countries like India. For meanwhile the climate of American opinion, at least official American opinion, has changed radically. As late as early 1960 many senior (and junior) Washington officials still regarded comprehensive national economic development planning as a dubious alien practice, but the shift in attitudes was becoming discernible even prior to that year's presidential election. Today the same kind of planning is officially viewed as an essential concomitant of any national development effort that merits American assistance, and the United States government is urging such planning upon Latin American, African, and Asian governments that do not yet practice it.

This change in posture is mostly sensible and admirable. However, like any sudden switch of views it has run the risk of exaggeration and oversimplification. American foreign economic agencies, after almost a decade in which they regarded all comprehensive planning with suspicion, are not heavily manned with personnel who understand the intricacies of the analytical techniques or administrative procedures of central economic planning. As a result they run the new danger of thinking that "planning" is some sort of discrete, ready-made, problem-solving gadget that a country has only to acquire and plug in, in order to shake loose from the political confusions that have been attending the nation's economic policies and obtain a proper energizing of its aspirations for development.

So far as the American attitude toward Indian planning is specifically concerned, the present danger is that the latter may be idealized too much. India's reputation as a non-Communist country that already has an elaborate array of well-established planning machinery, and that already has practiced comprehensive economic planning very seriously and with a good deal of effect for several years, makes it, in American eyes, a kind of oasis of the sort of expertise that the United States suddenly is concerned to generalize to the rest of the economically backward countries with which it has some kind of rapport.

Yet it could be a serious mistake for American policymakers to assume that the Indians have all of the answers on planning. For the fact is that Indian planning and administration have a number of correctible weaknesses that carefully designed and negotiated aid programs can help to complement or overcome. But the latter is possible only if United States aid negotiators themselves are well enough schooled in planning techniques and development administration to be able to spot some of the foibles of the process in which they are at least peripherally involved.

The following comments, therefore, bypass the question of justifying planning to concentrate instead on certain matters of procedure and technique. Furthermore, they tend to focus on aspects of the process that invite improvement. I hope, however, that both Indian and American readers will appreciate that the whole critique is based on the tacit premises that India does and must have a system of comprehensive economic planning, and that the system is well enough conceived and established now to invite an examination that concentrates on desirable refinements.

Three Contrasts That Can Be Overdrawn

To begin with, it will be useful to straighten out three questions of terminology. Each involves a pair of concepts that can helpfully be distinguished in one's analysis of the Indian—or of any other—central economic planning process. But in each case analysts often talk as though the contrast between the two concepts were greater than it really is.

First, there is the difference between *plans* and *planning*. Nearly everyone would agree that Indian planning is most significantly viewed as a continuing decision-making process, not just as an intermittent production of certain blueprints or documents. Yet the "plans" per se are, after all, nothing but the decisions that the process yields. The issue that those who emphasize this distinction actually are trying to get at is that of the rhythm of the process. In order to allow for the long lead times on many items, to keep planning problems manageably simple, and to economize a country's limited skills and energies for planning itself, it has become customary to program national development efforts in three-, five-, seven-, or other multi-year chunks. However, this sensible procedure can backfire if, by attaching an artificial importance to the economy's five-year (or three- or seven-year) accomplishment, it causes planners to ignore intra-period changes or the need for smooth transitions from the late Second-Plan years to the first Third-Plan years, and so on.

Indian planning never has been totally at the mercy of this kind of astigmatism. In principle the once-every-five-years exercises have never been regarded as more than major stock-takings and reformulations of a longer-term program that is subject meanwhile to constant review and frequent (usually year-by-year) revision and reauthentication. Nevertheless, as we shall see, Indian planning has displayed some unnecessary jerkiness in its inter-Plan and intra-Plan phasing of expansion projects.

Second, in trying to make sense of a planning process, it often is helpful to distinguish between issues of *technique* and those of *administration*. In what follows I shall frequently have occasion to point, on the one hand, to technical considerations that arise out of the planners' underlying economic models or out of the types of analysis they use for particularizing the strategies emerging from such models, or that concern the statistical limitations under which they work. On the other hand, we shall encounter problems that seem to be essentially matters of bureaucratic, political, and/or constitutional structure and relationship. Yet what is striking in the Indian case, I think, is the extent to which we shall find these two procedural strands of the planning process intertwined. Virtually all of the difficulties are ones to which *both* technical and administrative factors contribute. When we talk about problems of planning "technique," we are talking usually about the way issues tend to shape themselves for economist-type planners, whereas the administrative and organizational specialists view the same issues in terms of their own training and experience. Both types of specialists are needed in an effective planning organization, but their concerns are very much of a piece.

Finally, there is the alleged contrast between *planning* and *implementation*. It is convenient to draw a distinction, as I have a number of times in these pages, between development planning and development administration, and it may even have a certain impressionistic validity to say, as I have, that the "Indians are better planners than doers." But, it must be emphasized, no conclusive evaluation of a government's planning can be made in isolation from the quality of its administration. Moreover, this is not just because the pragmatic test of any plan is the action to which it gives rise. The fact is that "planning" and "implementation" are parts of the very same continuum. They are loosely assigned labels for different ranges of the same decision-making process. Seen in one of its dimensions, that process can be graded from general to specific. Typically, we call decision making at one end of this spectrum "planning" and at the other end, "implementation," but in many ways it is the intermediate range of the spectrum that is the most interesting. It makes not the slightest difference whether these intermediate decisions are called "detailed planning" or "(broad) plan implementation," but it means everything to the planning-*cum*-implementation process that they be made in timely and cogent fashion.

This last point is as apposite as any for indicating what this chapter undertakes to add to the present critique of the Indian economic development effort. To appraise the serviceability of the Indian planning process it is not sufficient to conclude, as I have, that the general development strategy emerging from it, while inviting amendment, is on balance eminently worthy of support. For if the strategy is to be made good, it must be connected to specific operational decisions by more detailed kinds of planning. And in the Indian case it is precisely in the realm of such implementational planning that there is the greatest room for improvement.

The Issue of Comprehensiveness and Internal Consistency

In a sense the government of India made its choice once and for all between "piecemeal," or project-by-project, economic planning and "comprehensive" planning back at the beginning of the fifties, when it committed itself to the pursuit of a series of over-all development plans and set up a permanent Planning Commission to provide the central staffing for the effort. However, government's commitment to comprehensive planning meant little as long as such planning consisted simply of assembling a collection of state and ministerial projects that had few requirements for internal consistency other than that the sum of the outlays on particular projects should add up to the total stipulated cost of the program. The First Five Year Plan followed traditional government budgeting practice in this sense; it was a collection of discrete projects with very little interdependence. The major ministries of the government instinctively favored such a planning approach; they were jealous of the new Planning Commission's potential encroachment on their decision-making prerogatives; and, thanks partly to the fact that the Commission's only members of political stature other than its chairman (the Prime Minister) were the ministers of these same line ministries, the latter were able to hold the Commission to a fairly modest role during the early fifties—even though it had accumulated a substantial full-time staff.

The great procedural achievement of Indian planning during the period when the Second Five Year Plan was being formulated was, I think, establishment of the principle of the central importance of internal consistency in development design. Under the aggressive intellectual leadership of a few key planning technicians (notably Professor P. C. Mahalanobis) and with the active personal support of the Prime Minister, it came to be accepted that traditional budgeting practice was an extremely bad procedural model for those major portions of the planning problem that required the balancing of goals and particular expansion programs, of outputs and inputs, of the output of one industry with those of others, and of many variables through time. Here internal consistency was of the essence, and here, it was therefore recognized in principle, the traditional budgetary practice of leaving the initiation of program design entirely to the operating agencies would not work. Instead, if planning were to be coherent, yet not infernally tedious, the initial design would have to be formulated by a central group that viewed the economy as a whole—and then, of course, tested, modified, and recast its scheme in consultation with the operating agencies before submitting the whole program for political approval.

In principle, India has not wavered from this essential planning postulate since 1955. But for reasons that we shall next examine, it achieved only highly imperfect application during the Second-Plan period, and there is still reason to doubt the effectiveness with which it is being and will be implemented during the Third Plan.

Second-Plan and Third-Plan Programming Techniques

In formulating the Second Five Year Plan and during most of the period of that Plan India's central development designers fell far short of fully carrying out the mandate for internally consistent programming. The Second-Plan exercise did start with the development of a so-called "plan-frame" that, for a preliminary document of that period, was a cogent piece of central design work. Nevertheless, the plan-frame itself was sketchy. For example, it and the early chapters of the Second-Plan document that were fashioned after it still, like the First-Plan window dressings before them, placed major reliance upon operationally meaningless and purely notional projections of the economy's over-all capital-output ratio. In many instances the connections between the general Plan framework set forth at the beginning of the Second-Plan document and the more specific industry and sector chapters that filled up the bulk of the book were tenuous; a number of the latter still had the look of piecemeal agency programs.

Worst of all, the phasing of the expansion programs during the latter half of the fifties was highly unsatisfactory. Planners tried to do their decision making too much in a single five-year lump. Perhaps the worst aberration was in the area of private investment, where the entire five-year allocation of foreign exchange for this sector was made available at once. When, to everyone's dismay, private investors proceeded to use up the bulk of this ration in the first two years of the Plan period, the result was the well-known foreign-exchange crisis of 1957-58 and a consequent foreign-exchange stringency that continued to impede, not only further expansion, but current production in many industries during the balance of the Plan period.

Phasing was highly imperfect also in the public sector, where very little provision was made for those projects that would need to be started in the late Second-Plan years and completed early in the Third Plan if a steady thrust of expansion from Plan to Plan was to be maintained. Moreover, as the Second Plan unfolded, many temporary inter-industry inconsistencies developed. Cement capacity was installed considerably before there was a need for it. Steel lagged badly and coal and coal washeries, even worse. There were other similar difficulties. Some of these, of course, were the result of engineering problems and other physical difficulties that could not have been foreseen. But much of the trouble was chargeable to bad detailed planning.

The spotty procedural record of the Second Plan reflected a weakness of programming technique. We have already noted that the excessive deference shown by the Indian planners to orthodox Western saving-centered development theory has tended to curb the boldness of their efforts to activate idle resources. I have argued, however, that India's main production strategy has in fact, despite its saving-centered pretenses, fortunately been foreign-exchange-centered. But now we come to another charge that must be chalked up against the Second Plan's savings-centered orthodoxy. For, while the latter did not particularly impair the production strategy, it did impair the planners' technical implementation of that strategy in two ways.

In the first place, orthodox theory lured the planners into what was, for the time being at least, a technical blind alley. It suggested that the proper analytical sequence for particularizing the production program was first to determine the volume of total (unspecified) investment to be undertaken in the Plan period and only thereafter to go on to the question of investment allocation. And when the working programmer did move on to this "subsidiary" (but, as a practical matter, all-important) question of program composition, orthodox development economics of the time had only an exceptionally arid, abstract literature on "investment-choice criteria" to offer him. Since 1955 that literature has been considerably enriched. We now have had sophisticated endorsements of "social marginal product" as the best ground for investment choice, alternative advocacy of attention to the varying "re-investment quotients" of different projects, fresh emphasis on the applicability of re-fined benefit-cost calculations, and, from the burgeoning field of mathematical economics, some promising speculations about the possibilities of applying linear programming and other relatively sophisticated quantitative techniques to the in-vestment-choice problem.

Nevertheless, I would make the considered (although herein unsupported) assertion that, even today, none of the standard theory on the criteria for investment choice offers a service-able *primary* technique, given the present and near-term avail-abilities of economic data in India, for determining the com-modity and industry composition of the Indian expansion program. The best of the orthodox theorizing offers the In-dian planner some helpful hints, but still no directive guidance. In 1955-56 the hints were even less helpful, and the designers of the Second Plan, after fumbling a bit, simply stopped short of attempting to make explicit linkages between their aggrega-tive plan and the specific investment (or project) choices along the route that conventional development theory seemed to indicate.

In the second place, the homage that the designers of the Second Plan paid to inappropriate theories was partly to blame, I think, for their failure fully to exploit the availability of an alternative, less elegant, but far more workable, tech-nique for linking up specific projects with general expansion goals. This was implicit in the foreign-exchange-pivoting pro-duction strategy that, theory aside, they were in fact evolving. It was the technique of "planning backward" from final de-mand targets, which becomes usable *if* it can be assumed that, by a target year, the economy's production mix should match its consumption or end-use mix quite closely.

The "planning-backward" procedure consists first in estab-lishing a set of broad final-demand goals indicating the mag-nitudes of general government services, of public-sector and private-sector current capital formation, and of personal con-sumption (in the light of the predicted volume of disposable personal income) that can be expected to fit within the economy's expanded real income that is being projected for the target year. Second, these broad demand goals can be broken down into sufficient commodity or commodity-group detail (for example, through the use of studies of income-elasticities of consumers' demand for foodgrains, cotton cloth, and various categories of consumer hardware, and other studies of the typical construction-versus-equipment breakdown of different categories of investment) to establish a serviceable array of final-product output targets for the Plan period. Third, calculations can be made of the outputs of primary and intermediate products that should be available for supplying the requirements of final-goods production. Fourth, once the whole array of output targets is compared with existing capacities, planners can identify those expansion projects (and their several inputs, including particular-investment requirements) that are needed to bring particular industrial capacities up to the targets. And then finally planning backward, the planners can work out the specific phasings required to keep the whole process in concert and on schedule.

Now the foregoing, of course, is a dangerously oversimplified statement of procedure, even for our purposes; no satisfactory programming analysis can be quite as streamlined or one-directional as the one just described. At each of the analytical steps indicated the tentative results must be cross-checked for their physical and financial feasibility, and when this is done, modifications at other, logically prior steps in the analysis frequently will be indicated. Thus, even if it is exclusively of the type I have suggested, programming analysis is more likely to follow a round of successive approximations than a straight line from firm goals to firm particular-industry requirements. Furthermore, practical planning inevitably requires a combination of analytical approaches. At the time of any given planning exercise, for example, there always are some unfinished expansion projects to which heavy commitments of resources have already been made, and almost invariably, whatever the new final-demand projections of the planners are, the opportunity costs of not finishing these projects as quickly as possible will exceed the costs of so doing. Moreover, there are always a certain number of multi-purpose

infrastructure and basic industry installations that so plainly
will be needed by just about any conceivable pattern of expanded production that they can sensibly be pushed before
many of the details of a comprehensive production program
have been worked out. Thus there must in practice be certain
kinds of specific *ad hoc* planning and some "planning forward" from existing capacities and existing uncompleted projects as well as the planning backward from final-demand
targets.

Granting all of this, it nevertheless seems to me that, when it
came to choosing the general technique for Indian programming, the planning-backward approach was the one really
practical one that the Indian planners had available for achieving an effective marriage between aggregative and detailed
planning. As we have seen, the technique's basic objective (to
minimize imports) was highly appropriate in the Indian case.
It would not be sensible or desirable, of course, to seek absolute self-sufficiency. But the Indian economy's need and potentialities for import substitution were great enough that it
was possible to expand the outlined programming analysis to
allow on the one hand, for the omission from the production
program of imports for which there are no substitutes[1] and,
on the other hand, for the addition to it of projectible exports
without seriously undermining the production guidance that
the final-demand projections could afford. Moreover, the series
of quantitative estimates required by this approach—of final-
demand goals, of the latter's commodity composition coarsely
broken down, of the requirements for primary and intermedi-

---

[1] As suggested in Chapter 2, decisions whether to produce or to
continue importing particular items where the answer is not obvious can sensibly be made on a comparative cost basis, but with
the rupee costs of imports calculated at a "shadow" foreign-exchange rate considerably higher than the official (also market)
rate. Such a calculation can assume any shadow rate to begin
with, pursue all of its import implications for the target year, add
them up, and see if the total exceeds maximum projectible exports
plus any net imports that are considered acceptable for the target
year. If it does, a higher shadow exchange rate must be adopted
and the specific decisions to produce or import must be refigured.
By successive approximations the desired hypothetical relationship between imports and exports can be struck.

ate products by major commodity groups, and of the investment and other major inputs required for different industrial
categories—were within potential reach of Indian technical
skills and Indian statistics. While none of these needed estimates could be formulated with sufficient refinement to suit
the taste of an economist who chose the role of a skeptic, it
was possible for the Indians to generate serviceable data at
each of these programming steps.

But now we come to the rub as far as Second-Plan design
was concerned. It was *possible,* I say, to do a reasonably good
job of planning backward from final-demand targets. But it
was not easy; many of the data required were not ready-made.
In particular, two kinds of data gaps needed filling: First, quite
obviously, the approach did call for explicit formulation of
final-demand targets, and this could not readily be done in the
absence of a historical series of final-demand estimates to serve
as a base for the projections. Curiously enough, official Indian
national income statistics included no such series. There was
a related need, moreover, for income-elasticity and other studies to be used in developing a commodity breakdown of final
demand, and these too India in the mid-fifties largely lacked.
Second, and basically more formidable, there was an urgent
need for a great mass of technical-coefficient data showing
what kinds of inputs were required for producing what outputs
—how much steel and cement per average unit of industrial
construction, how much machinery and electricity per ton of
cement, and so on. Such data were essential for translating
requirements for finished goods into requirements for unfinished goods and for converting all output requirements into
investment and other input requirements.

The basic technical shortcoming of Indian planners at the
time the Second Plan was formulated was their failure to bestir
themselves very actively to fill these data gaps that inhibited
the spelling out of a final-demand-oriented production program. It may be argued, of course, that the planners at this
juncture simply did not have enough time to get much accomplished in this respect. However, I suspect that the fact
that the planning-backward approach had little respectability

in the eyes of orthodox development theorists accounts to a considerable degree for the data gaps.

The Second Plan's lack of explicit final-demand estimates and of a comprehensive array of technical coefficient data did not, as we have seen, prevent the mounting of a production program that was more faithful than not to the import-substitution strategy. Demand projections were used in setting a number of particular-commodity output targets, and, on the whole, the planners showed a pretty good intuitive sense of what the shape of target-year final demand should be. But by failing to project and publicize a set of final demand goals the planners robbed themselves of the most cogent justification that could be offered for the mixed bag of primary-, intermediate-, and final-goods targets they postulated; by failing to assemble an adequate array of data on inter-industry requirements, they stumbled into some of the bottleneck problems already noted; and by failing fully to exploit the planning-backward approach, they passed up the best available defense against the phasing errors by which they were subsequently haunted.

By the time the Third Five Year Plan was formulated Indian planning had undergone an inconspicuous but important transition in these respects. Throughout the formulation period and in the final Third-Plan document itself (as was noted in the previous chapter) the Planning Commission persisted in its curious, passively stubborn refusal to present any formal statement of even moderately detailed final-demand goals. Yet I can attest that this time most of the "mixed bag" of commodity output targets were related to final-demand models, not just intuitively, but by explicit calculations contained in some of the Planning Commission's unpublished working papers. Moreover, during the interim there had been a significant accumulation of income-elasticity and other studies that could facilitate the projection of particular final-product categories. Most important of all, the government had acquired a formidable collection of technical coefficient data, thanks mainly to the initiative taken by Pitambar Pant, Chief of the Planning Commission's Perspective Planning Division. These data, as I have noted in another connection already, were, and had to be, assembled catch-as-catch-can. They are of an uneven quality, and there was no assurance that the various technologies they reflected were the appropriate ones for India to pursue. Nevertheless, Pant's tireless effort to assemble these nuts and bolts data and his incitement of the government's operating wings to check and refine them created the opportunity, more than did any other one thing, for Third-Plan programming to be an internally consistent exercise.

These are encouraging developments, and, on the whole, Indian planning seems to be on the way to making good their promise. However, there is still cause for concern about technical problems, particularly over the crucial matter of phasing.[2] This is a particularly slippery subject to judge from afar or through the reading of official documents. However, the last time I saw Indian planning first-hand, in the early summer of 1960, the Third-Plan projections of specific industry growth still, in many cases, were not based on realistic estimates of what the actual (as opposed to targeted) Second-Plan accomplishment would be; the Third-Plan goals had not been broken down into any series of closely calculated *annual* national income, industrial output, and foreign-exchange balances; the majority of the major industrial projects proposed generally for the early years of the Third Plan, had not had their design, contracting, manpower, investment, and import-requirement phasing worked out; and there was serious question still whether the Plan made sufficient provision in its later years for enough Fourth-Plan starts to maintain a steady thrust of expansion into the succeeding period.

While the final Third-Plan document includes some emphatic language, as well as some evidence, indicating a determination to eradicate this sort of programming fuzziness, I think it is fair to include that the radical improvement in Indian programming techniques that had been under way for the previous five years had not yet been fully consolidated at the time of the Third Plan's adoption. There was still room for a

[2] See W. B. Reddaway, "Importance of Time Lags for Economic Planning," *Economic Weekly* (Bombay), Annual Number (January 1960), and "Phasing a Development Plan," Special Number (June 1960).

more explicit recognition of the merits of the planning-backward approach, and there was still need, as a means of implementing that approach, for an explicit formulation of final-demand targets.[3]

[3] In the course of drafting this section I have felt a growing desire to address a conciliatory (if not self-protective) aside to those fellow economists who may have been irritated by my failure, in explaining and advocating the planning-backward approach, to re-emphasize certain programming complications that already have been recognized in earlier chapters. These include the facts (1) that relative commodity and factor prices are sure to change during the course of the development effort, (2) that even within the restraints imposed by a foreign-exchange-economizing strategy, there is room for choosing between readily substitutable products with different input requirements, and (3) that there is also room, in the case of some particular products, for choosing among alternative technologies. It may be asked, how does the planning-backward approach take care of these issues? The answer is that, while it has no special magic for resolving them, as a general programming technique, it can readily incorporate into its analytical pattern any particular solutions to these problems that may be devised. For example, as fast as the opportunities for technological choice and for limited product choice are recognized, the planning-backward approach can adopt the same procedure that already has been suggested in the case of produce-or-import decisions: In spelling out the output-target and input-requirement implications of the final demand goals, it can make its process choices and its product choices on a comparative-cost basis. Throughout its analysis it can make more general use of "shadow prices"—for example, in the case of domestic labor and capital as well as of foreign exchange—if this is deemed appropriate. If acceptable forecasts of (actual) relative price changes become available, these can be incorporated into its projections, and if serviceable estimates of the price elasticities of the demand for particular products also become available, there can be consequent adjustments in the real composition of the projections. In short, the planning-backward approach can encompass all of these refinements or—at worst—none of them. But meanwhile, whatever its degree of sophistication in these respects, it is the one approach that provides the working planner with a way of getting on with his principal, immediate job—which is to come up quickly, and to keep coming up, with comprehensive, presumptively consistent, sets of program numbers that are sufficiently detailed to supply firing-line decision makers with serviceable operating instructions.

Let me add this further aside: To aim the expanding production effort at final-demand targets is in no sense to tilt the economy

Administrative Impediments to the Marshalling of Facts

Indian economic statistics are better than those of many economically underdeveloped countries, and there are instances—notably that of the technical coefficient data already cited—where planners have shown great initiative in assembling the empirical information they need. However, there still are surprising gaps in the national income estimates when one considers that national income accounting and national-income-oriented economic planning both are more than ten years old in India. The country at this writing still has no official historical series on final demand. Even the available estimates of investment are exceptionally weak and sketchy. And planners have been led into the very risky practice of working out their whole quantitative program in a net-national-income rather than a gross-national-product frame (thereby submerging the problem of replacement investment) by Indian national income accounting's perverse failure yet to supply any regular series of historical estimates of the gross national product. There are a good many comparable examples, outside the national income field, of serious deficiencies in the current economic series. There is no reason, for example, for the between-censuses

toward a greater emphasis on the public sector or toward more controls over private enterprise and decision than would obtain under a differently designed production program. In the near term there are going to be some kind of foreign-exchange rationing and some priorities among the encouragements government gives to private investors in any event. But in the longer run, since the final-demand targets, if properly determined, are predominantly *forecasts* of what consumers and other end-users will choose to buy with higher incomes (not the judgments of the planners as to what they *should* buy, like it or not), a final-demand-oriented production pattern (if the forecasts are any good at all) is the very kind that can minimize the need for direct detailed controls over consumer as well as private business decisions. Given the export problem and given India's determination to become internationally self-supporting after a limited period of heavy imports, the long-run prospect for controls would be heightened if the economy muddled into a production pattern that was inconsistent with its emerging final demands.

manpower data to be as generally weak as they are—even after allowance is made for the conceptual difficulties encountered in measuring labor idleness. All in all, it is fair to say that the development of statistics in India has fallen well short of the potential in view of the fact that, in terms of advanced theoretical statistical competence, India may well be the most richly endowed country in the world.

Moreover, these gaps and soft spots in the published economic series are paralleled by a failure on the part of Indian planners generally to marshal as much solid *ad hoc* empirical detail as they readily could use. Many of the top officials, while competent and diligent themselves, seem to be insufficiently aggressive in driving their own staffs, or the staffs in the operating ministries, to prepare needed pieces of information and analysis in time to gear into the general planning exercise. Instead of forcing determined and imaginative assaults on the informational barriers, many key officials spend long hours reasoning and speculating their way around them.

Furthermore, the arrangements for injecting technological expertise into the planning process are less than ideal. Some, but not much, of this difficulty may be the one, usual in an underdeveloped economy, of simply not having enough technically-trained people. Most of India's problem in this regard has been instead first, a failure to distinguish clearly those issues in development design that should be left essentially to decision by professionally trained specialists instead of being submitted for independent decision (and not just authentication) to the bureaucratic-political process; and second, a failure to seat cadres of the best available specialists within the government, or to attach them to it, in such fashion that when appropriate matters of development design are referred to them, they can make themselves heard through the muffling of administrative layers and channels.

The Indian government's muting of technological expertise is attributable partly, at least, to its British-inherited domination by a highly selected corps of "generalist" administrators who are supposed to be intelligent enough and broadly experienced enough to be able to handle anything; who, at the same time, recognize their own limitations in modern technical fields and, withal, have been reared in an administrative system that abhors mistakes. The result is a jungle of unnecessary committees: Intelligent and cautious generalist-administrators, charged with deciding technical issues for which they do not have the necessary specialized knowledge, defer to the collective wisdom of a committee of their peers, most of them equally intelligent, cautious, and ignorant of the matters at hand. The committee typically appoints a subcommittee of the same sort, which typically convenes an advisory committee likely to include a number of distinguished industrialists and academicians. While the latter may be generally conversant with the subject at hand, they seldom have the incisive knowledge of it possessed by half a dozen (often younger, but experienced) specialists in the country, whom no one gets around to consulting.

The Planning Commission's Political Dependency

In any democratic government worth the name, planning in the last analysis must be a political process, and the Indians never have fallen into any delusions to the contrary. Yet this basic circumstance condemns the Planning Commission as a central staff agency charged with performing a quasi-expert, but also quasi-political, function to an inherently precarious, ambivalent set of relationships with the central government's ministries and other major line organizations, as well as India's fifteen state governments. The precariousness of the Commission's position is intensified by the fact, noted already, that, lacking politically strong full-time leadership of its own, the Commission's political bargaining power depends almost wholly on the liveliness of the support it draws from the Prime Minister.

The latter half of 1959 and the first months of 1960 offer a particularly nice illustration of this dependency. This was a time when work on the formulation of the Third Plan was supposed to be at its peak—and indeed it was, *within* the Planning Commission. However, simultaneously a great deal of sectoral and regional decision making also was supposed to be shaping up in the ministries and particularly in the state governments, and many of the planners at these levels found themselves highly frustrated. For the programmers at the operational levels did now, by and large, respect the principle that the Planning Commission had succeeded, with Mr. Nehru's very active support, in establishing back in 1955-61 —that of the Commission's primary responsibility for initiating the over-all development design. Consequently, planners at the state and ministerial levels expected a fairly voluble and steady flow of informal guidance from Commission officials in this formative period of the Third-Plan exercise.

Instead most of the leading members of the Commission's staff seemed to retreat into a strange taciturnity during these months. Most of them hesitated to commit themselves to the kinds of concrete projections that would have been most informative to the sectoral and regional authorities. The proximate reason for this reticence, rather obviously, was that at the time there was much less decisiveness within the government and parliament than there had been five years earlier over such broad issues of development strategy as the agriculture-heavy industry balance, the distribution of investment between the private and public sectors, and the question of joint cooperative farming. But these were questions on which these Commission officials had strong opinions that they usually did not hesitate to express. Their reticence was not just a case of "normal" bureaucratic neutrality; it reflected the fact that the Commission's political stock was unusually low for the time being. And it was low chiefly because Mr. Nehru's mind, up to that point in the Third-Plan exercise, had seemed to be largely on other matters.

The fact that the vitality and the authority of India's central planning operation is so closely dependent on active and interested support from the Prime Minister is not necessarily regrettable. Under a system of democratic political responsibility this in some degree is inevitable, and I am by no means sure that the way to solve the problem would be to give the Commission more independent political strength of its own. It is plain, however, that no evaluation of the efficacy of the planning effort can be complete without attention to the competing distractions under which the Prime Minister, at any given moment, is laboring.

Decentralized Planning and Center-State Relations

Comprehensive economic planning in India must be centralized for the sake of cohesiveness. Indeed, where the struggles and difficulties (many of them not yet fully resolved) that we thus far have encountered in these notes on the evolution of Indian planning methodology have related to the centralization-decentralization issue, my own sympathies—in the interests of cohesiveness—consistently have been on the side of the centralists. Yet comprehensive economic planning in India also must be considerably decentralized to broaden the opportunities for creative development decision making, to exploit the special insights and experience of those closest to local and particular-industry problems, and to protect the central planners from being overburdened and the channels of communication and command from being overloaded. In short, if planning cohesiveness requires centralization, planning vitality requires decentralization. The procedural formula for optimal planning, however, is not just to walk a middle course between the two extremes. Rather, it is selectively to centralize functions where it is important to do so for reasons of cohesiveness *and* selectively to decentralize wherever it is desirable and feasible to do so on vitality grounds.

If the cause of selective centralization is not yet secure in Indian planning, the cause of selective decentralization is even more beleaguered. The country's high propensity for regional and communal divisiveness makes the political leadership at the Center reluctant to delegate planning discretion to the states. Compared with the American, at least, the Indian Constitution leaves the states with heavy legal subservience to the Center. More important, the country's administrative system and tradition tend to discourage initiative and the location of large decision-making responsibilities at lower administrative levels. The career public service has, in the old British style, been engrained with a strong sense of hierarchy, in which command flows clearly from larger jurisdictions to smaller and reputations are built upon one's ability to comply with superior authority and minimize overt local mistakes.

The Indian Administrative Service, the nation's elite bureaucratic corps which mans most planning posts at the state level, extends as essentially the same service, with common entrance requirements, training, performance standards, and possibilities of transfer and promotion, throughout the central and state governments. This means that the professionally ingrained habit of administrative deference upward extends without interruption from the state secretariats to New Delhi. Moreover, the strikingly large status gap between IAS and other officials has meant that most central or state administrators find it quite hard to imagine that the quality of the non-IAS officials in smaller jurisdictions ever could be sufficient to warrant delegating substantial decision-making authority to them.

Add to this the impulse of the central planners themselves, preoccupied with the problems of scarce-resource allocation and still scrambling for enough authority to do a proper job on the cohesiveness front, to resist any dispersion of the planning function; add their *comparative* oversight still of the parallel problem of idle-resource activation, wherein the need for local and regional initiative is seen in its most urgent guise; add their inadequate attention yet to planning's spatial, geographic dimension (a point that I shall try to make in Chapter 7); add finally a traditional distrust among Indian administrators of markets (even of sensibly regulated markets) as decentralized, but serviceable organizing devices—and you have the makings of a planning and administrative structure that tends very substantially to deaden the upward ferment of development impulses, ideas, and decisions originating at the local level.

Under these circumstances the integration of state governments into the central planning process has been very unsatisfactory. On the one hand, in order to reinforce their own often-limited planning experience and skills and to help them key their programs to the national effort, the state officials need a strong, steady flow of lucid information about national development goals, policies, and priorities, targets expected of the states, preferred criteria for choosing among alternative projects, recommended planning techniques, and the like. As we have noted in the 1959-60 case, the flow of such guidance from the Planning Commission to most state governments has often been quite scant. Yet, on the other hand, the states feel that they have little authority and inadequate facilities for undertaking development programs on their own. And if Center-state relations are imperfect in many ways, as I shall be indicating in the next two chapters, the distribution of authority and responsibility down the line from the state level is even less satisfactory.

"The Texture of Operations"

The phrase is that of an American veteran of the Indian Community Development movement who was telling me the reason for his latter-day disillusionment. The whole texture of operations, he said, was discouragingly shoddy. One of the most thoughtful and strategically placed senior Planning Commission officials spent most of our last interview talking from the heart in the same vein—and not just about the Community Development effort. Indeed, one hears about this "problem of implementation" wherever he turns. It haunts perceptive Indians and dulls the hopes of India's friends.

The problem complained about is not primarily that of corruption; this fact, in the case of such a poor country, is in itself remarkable and represents another of those enormous advantages of the Indian situation that it is easy to pass over too lightly. India, I should suppose, has higher effective standards of public morality than almost any other country with comparable poverty. In the press and conversation around the country one certainly hears a great deal about official corruption, but this would seem to signify the public's intolerance of it more than anything else. At least in the eyes of observers who have spent time elsewhere in Asia and Latin

America, there appears to be very little corruption in high places. When any is discovered, it is rooted out by what seem to be independent, dispassionate investigatory and judicial processes. Petty graft down the administrative line is another matter. While there is a good bit of this, undoubtedly, it is very hard for a Westerner to judge its scope or even to make sure he understands the traditional Indian proprieties in this regard. My own impression is that petty governmental corruption is a problem chiefly in its corrosive effects upon the public's attitude toward government and especially on the former's willingness to pay taxes.

At any rate, far more than moral uplift, Indian administration needs morale-uplift and efficiency experts. The problem of petty graft is as nothing alongside the massive sloth and sluggishness of public administration at lower operational levels. This condition is not universal. A number of the new public enterprises may thus far have escaped it as whole units, and throughout the governmental structure—in the central ministries and in the states, the districts, and the development blocks—one encounters individuals with a sense of urgency about them who are struggling to execute a tough, incisive program. But they are struggling against the norm, one that any Western observer encounters in the course of transacting his personal business with the post office and with other minor officialdom and sees again and again in the loitering in government corridors, the untidiness of government offices, the thoughtlessly round-about, time-consuming administrative routines, and the massive redundancy of paperwork.

This is not the place, nor am I the person, to attempt an extended explanation of the loose texture of so much Indian public administration. However, part of the reason—namely, the existence of an elite cadre that, while exceptionally intelligent and competent itself, is too much preoccupied with old routines to impart much sense of mission or adventure to the rank and file—may already have been suggested. As an economist, I am persuaded that an even more important reason (to return to a familiar theme) is the perverse fear of improved labor productivity—of putting people out of work—with which the redundancy of labor has weakened the whole fabric of Indian development thought. It is almost impossible to inject a psychology of efficiency, of the importance of good work, of time-saving, into an organization so long as the inputs of human time itself are not regarded as valuable and scarce. As we have seen, it is essential for the Indian government to be supporting sensible make-work programs at this juncture. But it is disastrous to the cause of effective public administration to bring them into its own household.

Conclusions

The Indian system of planning and plan-implementation is an admirable, indeed a remarkably good, one for any country with a per-capita income of less than one hundred dollars a year. It is an experienced, sophisticated system of high average integrity. But it is also highly susceptible of improvement. In the realm of programming techniques, the Indian planners (encumbered no little by inappropriate economic theories learned mostly from the West) have been groping their way toward a serviceable set of procedures for spelling out a comprehensive, internally consistent production program that is well enough articulated both cross-sectionally and chronologically to be truly implementable. But there are still a number of statistical gaps to be filled, analytical techniques and administrative practices to be sharpened up, and political reinforcements to be provided before the battle for cohesive planning will have been clearly won.

Of the battle for vital planning and administration, much more yet remains to be fought. Indian planning as a whole has tended to be too cautious, too afraid of making mistakes, too little animated with an uncompromising determination to activate idle resources. It still looks too much like what it is—the progeny of an administrative system dedicated to the prevention of wrongdoing rather than to the marshalling and energizing of "right-doing."

From the viewpoint of American policymaking toward India, there need be nothing fundamentally discouraging about these conclusions, to which many Indian planners candidly agree, off the record. The diagnosis should be essentially encouraging because it not only finds the system improvable—and improving—but probably effective enough as it stands to manage much of the development tasks it has set itself. However, it would be foolish policy for the United States to expect the present Indian system to economize perfectly either resources or time. And it would be irresponsible policy on the part of the United States government—or any other concerned outsider—not to do whatever it appropriately can to assist and encourage specific improvements in Indian planning and plan-implementing procedures.

6 THE AGRICULTURAL PUZZLE

India's struggle to achieve a radical economic transformation by peaceful means is apt to be won or lost in the countryside —not because rural problems have some sort of intrinsic priority in a development program over such other issues as heavy industrialization and foreign aid but because of the rural problems' combined quotient of importance *and* difficulty. Of all the essential achievements, success in the countryside may be the hardest to bring off.

By comparison, the foreign-aid prospects, if the pace set by the so-called "Aid-to-India Club" in 1961 can be maintained and if some of the procedural difficulties to be noted in Chapters 11 and 12 can be ironed out, are fairly encouraging. Moreover, for all their complexities and headaches, the problems of starting or expanding large organized industries also are reasonably tractable. For in these cases, despite the need for more adaptive and creative innovation, there *are* opportunities for borrowing a great many technological processes and some whole complexes of processes almost ready-made from the more advanced economies. And these processes tend to bring with them, as built-in adjuncts, the patterns of productive organization and the industrial discipline required for effective operation. Most advantageous of all, perhaps, is the fact that the industrial-core side of the development effort is relatively little inhibited by home-grown precedent. To a considerable degree, it can start from scratch as new construction on new ground relatively remote from the institutional encumbrances of traditional Indian society.

Rural development, by contrast, is a remodeling project. It calls for making over—indeed, by economic standards, for radically making over—the traditional society itself; for introducing many wholly new functions and activities, changing fundamentally many of the old ones, and revamping many of the socio-political substructures in which these activities

are housed while, all of the time, the tenants continue to occupy the premises. To accomplish such a feat without arbi-
trarily coercing the old tenants is, almost by definition, organizationally more difficult than the "new-construction" side
of the development effort.

America's Stake in Rural India

The Indian rural problem is especially insusceptible to the
importation of ready-made Western "solutions." The Indians
must, in the last analysis, thresh it out for themselves. But
this does not mean that it lies beyond the appropriate range
of American concern.

Difficult and remote or not, the problem of rural development is so central to the whole cause of economic advance
and political constitutionalism in India that no foreign party,
governmental or private, seriously associated with that cause
can afford to be disinterested in rural issues. It would be
wrong and futile, in my opinion, for the United States government, in its aid negotiations with the government of India, to
seek to persuade the latter to redirect any substantial portion
of its presently programmed foreign exchange or domestic
finance away from the core industrial area into agriculture.
But there is no reason why American aid negotiators who
have informed views of the Indian rural situation should not
urge them upon their Indian associates. There is no reason
in principle even why American negotiators, having due regard for the net impact on relations between the two countries
and upon India's over-all development prospect, should not
make specific aid offers contingent upon the institution of
particular adjustments in indigenous rural policy.[1]

Moreover, the United States already has some direct and
specific involvements in Indian rural affairs. First, there is the
so-called P.L. 480 program for supplying India with surplus
foods from the United States. As has been suggested already,

[1] It does not discredit the legitimacy (although it does underscore the delicacy) of such bargaining to charge it with "tying
strings." See Chapter 10.

this particular form of foreign aid, which only the United States government among the outside contributors to the Indian development effort has been equipped and ready to supply, can play a peculiarly strategic role in facilitating a rural development effort. Conversely, there are few forms of assistance whose lasting impact on development can be so thoroughly dissipated by misuse.

Second, Americans already have played a surprisingly active role in the design and implementation of many Indian rural programs. Albert Meyer, the tireless and imaginative New York-based city planner who became a prime mover of the pilot rural development project in Etawah District of Uttar Pradesh in the late forties; Douglas Ensminger, as the Ford Foundation's resident in India beginning in 1951; Chester Bowles during his term as Ambassador from 1951 to 1953; Carl Taylor, the sociologist—these and a number of other Americans were instrumental in helping to shape India's single largest rural innovation of the fifties, the Community Development movement.

Both the United States Technical Cooperation Mission, particularly during Frank Parker's leadership of its agricultural programs, and private American foundations operating in India have supplied more technicians, researchers, and specialist advisers in agriculture than in any other field during the past decade. Under International Cooperation Administration (now Agency for International Development) contracts American land-grant universities have been working with state agricultural departments, colleges, and experiment stations throughout India to improve the quality of agricultural education, research, extension, and administration.

Eugene Staley and several of his Stanford Research Institute associates have had a major hand in the development of the Indian government's programs for promoting small-scale (non-traditional) industries, which, according to my terminology, should be considered mainly "rural" in their import. Others, such as Thomas Keehn representing the American International Association for Economic and Social Development and the Cooperative League of the USA, have worked in the fields of cooperation, agricultural credit, and handicrafts. American church mission groups have long been engaged in practical rural development work. And Americans have served on various semi-official evaluative missions, to whose appraisals of agricultural and other rural programs the Indian government has accorded careful attention.[2]

Thus the American people, through a sizable group of their individual countrymen, already have a participant's stake in the Indian rural development effort. They share the credit for the effort's hopeful results during the past decade. By the same token, Americans have advised, kibitzed, and assisted enough by now to have incurred some moral responsibility not to desert a grossly unfinished job.

Implicit Perspectives and Rural Priorities

The few American tourists in India who get the opportunity to visit a representative Indian village usually are appalled. Gauged by Western standards, the absolute level of economic welfare seems so abysmally low that it is hard to imagine that anything really encouraging can be going on. This same sort of parallax afflicts many professional Western economists in their initial contacts with rural India. However, to be overwhelmed with depression about the present condition of Indian villages really is not very helpful. For not only is the present level of welfare as high as most of their inhabitants are used to; there has been some improvement during the past decade. After a generation or more in which total farm output probably nearly stagnated, and per-capita output apparently declined,[3] total production during the fifties appears (when one screens out the vagaries in the weather) to have risen at an average of 2½ to 3 percent a year. This has been fast enough to provide at least a slight growth in output per capita despite the accelerated rise in the population. The coun-

[2] For example, the Ford Foundation's 1959 "Food Crisis" team, mentioned in Chapter 2.

[3] See Daniel Thorner, "Long-Term Trends in Output in India" in Joseph Spengler (ed.), *Economic Growth: Brazil, India, Japan* (Duke University Press, 1955), especially pp. 120-28.

try people are eating better. There has not been a major famine since 1951, and experienced observers touring the Indian countryside in the late fifties reported far fewer areas that showed evidence of general malnutrition than had been the case a few years earlier.[4]

Moreover, the ferment of rural institutional reform touched vast numbers of Indians for the first time during the fifties. The land reform movement, despite disappointments, has had a significant impact on land tenure in most of the states. Many tens of millions of village Indians have become acquainted with the existence and vocabulary of the Community Development effort—with "development blocks," "*gram sewaks*," agricultural extension workers, and the rest. Many have had their initial encounter with cooperatives. Thousands of villages have acquired their first all-weather roads connecting them with the outside world. Thousands more have their first schools, community radios, and other amenities.

The pattern of reform is incomplete, it does not yet go far enough, and some of its elements, I shall be suggesting, are questionable in their very concept. Moreover, the rate of output expansion achieved is not yet nearly up to the requirements for the next decade. But judged by its own past and its direction of change, the current Indian rural situation is basically hopeful, not hopeless. Some momentum in the right direction has been established, and many capable and earnest Indians have enlisted in the cause of rural development.

Perspective has a great deal to do with the judgments one reaches about what the priorities in rural development policy should be. Those who view Indian peasants primarily through the lenses of pity—who see them as poor, benighted, ill-fed, ill-clad, sickly, socially oppressed folk who require extensive personal development before they really can be expected to accomplish much on their own—are inclined to emphasize the overwhelming needs for schools, literacy, health services and facilities, and social-uplift endeavors. These all, to be sure, are essential components of an adequate rural program.

[4] See Daniel and Alice Thorner, *Land and Labour in India* (Asia Publishing House, 1962).

But to argue that a massive expansion of such services and facilities is a necessary *prerequisite* for an accelerated output expansion is a counsel of despair. For rural India is such a vast area with such vast needs that it must find within itself the great bulk of the real resources for meeting those needs. What can be injected from outside are essentially catalysts, little more.

Only when one views rural India as an area teeming with people who have an age-old habit of helping themselves, who have been making considerable progress during the past decade, and who (just as they are, even without further education and better health) have much greater productive capacities than are presently being tapped, can there be much fundamental optimism about the near-term prospects for rural development. Given this perspective, however, it is plain that rural development's top priorities must be reserved for programs that promise directly and fairly quickly to expand physical production—agricultural and otherwise. From the beginning, some improvements in education, health, and general well-being must go hand in hand with the expansion of commodity output. But in the longer run the adequacy of these public service programs (and their effectiveness in stimulating new gains in productivity in the still longer run) will depend upon the size and strength of the local economic base that has been built under them.

"Rural" and "Agricultural"

The words "rural" and "agricultural" are not being used as synonyms. The former refers to all aspects of that area, and of the activities and institutions within it, in which people live in villages, small towns, or other relatively dispersed population centers. (There are very few places in India, other than parts of Kerala, where the rural population is spread out in individually dispersed dwellings in the manner of American farmhouses.) As will appear in Chapter 7, in order to make sure that certain vital aspects of rural-urban and agricultural-industrial relations do not fall between two stools, I find it useful to let the "rural" frame of reference encompass also those quite sizable towns and large industrial enterprises that are situated in predominantly rural environs.

"Agriculture" is an industry, not a culture or a societal area; it is rural India's principal, but by no means its only, industry. It is one of my basic contentions that a serviceable rural development program in India must deal with the several aspects of the rural economy in an integrated fashion. An isolated agricultural development effort unrelated to, and unsupported by, other kinds of rural policies would be doomed to failure almost surely.

Nevertheless, any concrete discussion of the Indian rural scene must start with some particular problem and, as it were, work out from there. So in this chapter we shall start with the matter of farm output and farm marketings and try to make some sense of the program of policy presently being addressed to it. However, since one cannot pursue such an agricultural discussion very far without a growing sense of incompleteness, we shall go on in the next chapter to consider some of the remaining issues that must be included in any reasonably complete rural program or diagnosis of the rural problem.

The Scope for Productive Expansion:
Known Answers and Missing Ingredients

There is a common thread running through a good many expert Indian and Western appraisals of the Indian farm problem that I find persuasive. The following is a bare-bones summary of this diagnosis, which seems to me to be the net burden of the technical findings of the Ford Foundation's 1959 mission of American agricultural experts and is advanced vigorously by a number of the more competent American landgrant college specialists who have been working with Indian agriculture for extended periods at the state and regional levels:

First, the very weakness—both the average over-all weakness and, in particular, the spottiness—of India's present agricultural performance indicates opportunities for radical improvement. Average yield per acre for many major Indian crops is far lower than comparable figures in most other countries.[5] For most areas and most crops the mode of cultivation could readily be a good bit more intensive and effective than it now is. Moreover, there are exceptionally wide ranges of performance, not only between regions and sub-regions but even among the particular cultivators growing the same crops in the same localities. Thus there is an abundant chance, not only for raising the upper end of the performance distribution, but for increasing output simply by inducing the less effective cultivators to adopt practices that already are observable in their own areas.

Second, as suggested already, lack of outside capital is not the principal impediment to rapid expansion in production. To be sure, some supply shortages, notably of chemical fertilizers and, to a lesser extent, of such materials as steel, are critical. But the foreign-exchange and the scarce-capital costs of eliminating these bottlenecks are comparatively modest, and their elimination has now been accorded a very high priority in the Third Five Year Plan. Thus in future even such commodity shortages, wherever they continue to impede agriculture, will represent essentially administrative failures. Most of the other capital formation that agriculture needs is highly labor-intensive; this too, in the last analysis, is largely an organizational matter. And the rural credit problem, viewed in real terms, is entirely so.

Third, Indian agriculture likewise is not seriously constrained for the moment by scientific bottlenecks. Since con-

[5] The 1960 *FAO Production Year Book* supplies the following comparative average annual yields, all in 100 kg. per hectare, the rice figures for the years 1957-59, and the wheat and maize yields for 1959-60.

Rice		Wheat		Maize	
India	12.9	India	7.9	India	8.7
Burma	15.6	Iraq	4.4	Iraq	6.2
Malaya	21.1	Lebanon	8.0	Thailand	15.9
Korea	28.8	Israel	11.8	Japan	21.7
Taiwan	29.8	Japan	23.6	U.S.A.	32.4
Japan	45.9	Canada	12.1		
U.S.A.	35.9	U.S.A.	14.3		

tinuing gains in farm productivity are going to be urgently needed for a very long time to come, to take the present position is in no sense to deny the need for an enterprising and sustained agricultural research effort. Nevertheless, the fact seems to be that in crop after crop a number of simple measures that could greatly improve yields are very well known, not only by foreign technical advisers and by many Indian government and academic experts but often by a widespread minority of the cultivators themselves. These measures include the use of commercial fertilizers and green manuring; better local water management to facilitate irrigation in many areas and to avoid waterlogging in others; reallocations of the available lands and water among alternative crops; differently spaced and/or more regular planting; better weeding; the adoption of simple soil conservation practices; the introduction of certain improved hand tools, such as Japanese-style paddy cultivators; and, in the case of livestock, artificial insemination and scrub bull castration.[6]

Fourth, while India's ability to achieve the expansion in farm output it needs for the sixties may therefore be said to depend on getting millions of cultivators to do a lot of comparatively little things differently, success also typically will depend on getting several of these things done in concert. This is a point especially underscored by the 1959 Ford Foundation team. In many cases, for example, the need is for better water use *and* better seed *and* more fertilizers *and* improved cultivating practices—and therefore, also for better credit facilities and improved availability of supplies. The need is for all of these things at once, and the return if all of them are pursued concurrently will far exceed the sum of the increments in output that would result from undertaking them one by one. This doctrine has now been emphatically accepted by the Ministry of Food and Agriculture, and, in the Third Five Year Plan, it is the theme particularly of the "intensive agri-

[6] The manner in which authorities both at the center and in many of the states are promoting and progressively winning consent for this last as a constructive compromise with Hinduism's taboo against cattle slaughtering is a gratifying example of Indian pragmatism.

cultural district program" that, at the suggestion of the Ford Foundation team, the Ministry has adopted for speeding an expansion in farm production in fifteen especially promising districts, one in each state. It is hoped that a concerted attack in these areas will achieve results that, besides adding substantially to total output in their own right, will exert demonstration effects on agricultural practice in neighboring districts.

Fifth, (to repeat an impression asserted in Chapter 2) there is no endemic lack of self interest among the Indian peasantry. On the contrary, most careful observers seem to find Indian farmers shrewd and pragmatic in their approach to the soil. But native intelligence and an appetite for self-betterment are not enough to facilitate an automatic adoption of the "known" practices that can yield rapid increases in output. The very multiplicity of variables in the average cultivator's situation confuses the learning process. It means that partial, one-by-one changes in practices frequently are disappointing. Conversely, it is hard to pick out from the variety of things that a successful neighbor does differently the particular keys to his success. The peasant's natural conservatism is compounded by the fact that in this realm he is risking his family's subsistence when he innovates; he wants to be shown, and to be sure, before he changes. The official techniques for showing him—for spreading an awareness of the improved practices—leave a good bit to be desired. Furthermore, rural officials commonly are not in a position simultaneously to provide all of the critical supplies and facilities that are needed to implement the adoption of a concerted set of improved practices by cultivators.

Last but most important of all perhaps, most Indian cultivators live much of their time in an environment that lacks adequate grain storage facilities, good local marketing arrangements, and adequate farm-to-market roads. It is an environment that rewards abundant production with low prices, allows the cultivator to be victimized by exploitative middle men and local money lenders, and offers him little incentive to acquire cash beyond what he needs for his taxes, rents, and debt obligations. It is an environment, in short, that does

not efficiently convert the cultivator's latent energies and motivations into decisions to produce as much and market as
much as he can.

The Low Urgency of Further Reorganizations of Production

The two great debates in the realm of Indian agricultural
policy recently—the one over land reform, the other about so-
called "joint cooperative farming"—are both, according to the
present analysis, rather beside the point. Some careful students of Indian farm economics insist that any notable ad-
vances in output must await first a far greater equalization
of holdings than was achieved during the nation's first decade
of nominal land reforms and then, second (partly in consequence of this first necessary change), the gathering of individual producing units into some kind of collectives. It is argued
that the latter, whatever the arrangements as to the property
rights, income claims, and self-determining rights of the participants,[7] is needed to increase radically the average unit scale
of Indian farm production.

The diagnosis just sketched, however, contains an implicit
rebuttal of this viewpoint. It suggests that, if the means for
informing cultivators and harnessing their latent productive incentives can be found, there is abundant scope for expanding
output within the existing productive structure. Furthermore,
there is very little evidence that either further land reform or
producing cooperatives, vigorously pushed, could add much
productive stimulus at least for the time being.

First, with respect to land reform, there are not enough
large landholders left in India for any politically feasible redistribution of land to narrow the range of holdings or broaden
the ownership base very much; nor is there any convincing
evidence that the larger cultivators cannot be effectively actuated by the same incentives that can appeal to the smaller
ones.

[7] While the Indian proponents of collective farming disagree
about these matters of internal organization, in general they incline
toward looser, more voluntaristic forms.

Second, as for joint cooperative farming, the only strong technological case for the assembly, and the common cultivation of, individual holdings (although not for the assembly of fragmented plots within a holding) is one that assumes mechanization so extensive as to be largely irrelevant to India for a long time yet. Meanwhile, those additional services and facilities that are technologically appropriate but that cannot be procured economically by individual cultivators can be had through so-called service cooperatives, or even by rental from private entrepreneurs.

It may be objected that, whatever its other merits, an effort to build a farm program on the organizational status quo offers no adequate corrective for the poverty of farmers with very small holdings and of landless farm laborers. This is a prime example of a problem, however, wherein policy planners cannot afford to treat agriculture as a world unto itself. For clearly the principal solution to the welfare problem of the lowest-income Indian farm families lies in the development of better part-time and full-time nonagricultural rural employment opportunities—in the first instance, for example, in rural public works and, beyond that, in rural industries.

I do not reach a negative conclusion about the present urgency of joint cooperative farming and further land reform with any partisan zest. It should be emphasized to American readers that in India most forms of absentee land ownership already have been greatly reduced and that, despite the failure of the land reform effort to fulfill its original high hopes, the unevenness of land distribution is far from being the problem that it is in many underdeveloped countries. Nevertheless, the case for further land redistribution on grounds of equity is strongly appealing. And cooperative farming strikes me as a perfectly good way to grow crops if the growers prefer it; certainly much of the case made by the adversaries of joint cooperative farming has bordered on hysteria.

However, any advocate of quick, peaceful output expansion in India must be thankful for the lack of urgency of further land-equalizing and collective-farming measures. For as a practical matter it has become quite obvious, since the leadership of the Congress Party and of the government first undertook to espouse joint cooperative farming in late 1958, that the Indian political process is most unlikely to yield radical reforms in farm productive organization any time soon. It would be a pity, therefore, if vigorous expansion had to await such reforms. As it is, the government safely can leave these highly sensitive issues to local experimentation and self-determination. Such is its present disposition.

The Tactics of Farm Reform: Manipulate or Condition?

If the central task of Indian farm policy is to get the present array of cultivators, organized in essentially their present array of production units, to work harder, adopt new techniques, and market more of what they produce, there are two ways to do it. The more direct approach is to prod, inform, teach, exhort, and otherwise manipulate, the individual cultivator into changing his ways. The other, indirect approach is to condition him—to restructure his environment in a way better calculated to harness his built-in motivations to the cause of expanded output. In some measure, of course, any sensible farm program will follow both of these approaches, and it will contain specific elements that might be classified either way. For example, provision of seed and fertilizer supplies may be a necessary feature of a demonstration or extension program that is essentially "manipulative" in concept. Yet if established on a sufficient and continuing basis, such supplies also obviously alter the market environment in which the producer operates. Nonetheless, the present distinction is useful, I think, for judging the predominant style and emphasis of an agricultural development effort, and in that sense the Indian effort to date can be said to have had a manipulative bias.

As my comments on the cooperative and community development movements will make clear, there is plenty of room still for improvement in the manipulative techniques being used in the agricultural field. Many Indian and American farm specialists are particularly aware of the need for better extension work, where a great deal can be accomplished gradually and laboriously by supplying the field with more technical agricultural personnel; by improving the quality, and particularly the practical relevance, of their training; by narrowing the gap between the farmer and agricultural research institutions; by sharpening the cogency of the doctrines of state departments of agriculture with respect to such matters as water and fertilizer use, seeds, and soil erosion; and by intensifying the use of the demonstration technique and of visual aids in the propagation of these doctrines. Improvements in all of these directions invite much more aggressive implementation during the sixties.

All the same, the predominant concern of Indian farm policy thus far has been to reach out and down to the individual cultivator, through the administrative hierarchy of the Ministry of Food and Agriculture, the state agricultural departments, the district agricultural officers, and the block-level agricultural extension officers, and do things directly to and for him that alter his behavior. This is nicely illustrated by the selected district program that, as mentioned already, the Third Plan has incorporated—heightened always by a sense of urgency, of need to make up for lost time. The program is essentially a scheme to pour into a few favored districts (about one-twentieth of the total number) more of everything—more improved seed, more fertilizer, more tools, more credit, and far more technical agricultural expertise—that the existing farm program has been trying to spread across the rural economy as a whole. The scheme is to be a highly managed operation in the crash-program tradition, receiving detailed direction and priority attention all the way up the ministerial hierarchy. In its original formulation by Ministry officers and Ford Foundation consultants in 1960, at least, the program provided that to obtain its benefits, every participating farmer would have to adopt and conform to a specific production plan for the forthcoming season. Although this was billed as being "his own" plan, the logistics of the operation make it obvious that the average individual cultivator was going to have to be bound, with precious little time for reflection, to a production plan selected for him from among a few ready-made models in the extension worker's pocket.

Probably there is nothing inherently bad in such a program. Although it is hard to imagine that it will nurture farmers' enterprise and resourcefulness very much, the result may be a quick extra gain in output. Certainly, as I have said, there is a need for the reinforced extension efforts the selected district program is attempting. However, while there may, therefore, be no absolute over-emphasis on manipulation in the present farm program, there has been most emphatically under-emphasis on conditioning, environment-improving reforms. Hence the focus upon these latter in the next section.

Missing Links in the Harnessing of Incentives

One of the respects in which visiting Western economists are likeliest to differ sharply from the economic policymakers they encounter in the government of India is in their appreciation of the organizing capacities of self-adjusting markets. Westerners tend to admire the ethical and administrative economy that the market mechanism has as an instrument of social policy. The typical Western professional economist these days is quick to admit that the freely fluctuating market is a creation of man, not the Deity, and that government must supply it with a legal and financial framework, must police, participate in, and tinker with it structurally, and must supplement it with positive programs if it is to serve the general welfare. But he does prize it, so conditioned, as a device that can harness to the pursuit of the general welfare the self-seeking motivations of private individuals and groups. Recognizing the mass of interrelated decisions that must be taken to keep a complex economy operating and growing, he respects the self-adjusting market as a magnificent labor-saving mechanism.

By comparison, many senior Indian officials seem totally unexcited about the organizational feats that appropriately structured and disciplined self-adjusting markets can perform. In part, I think, this is a matter of general philosophy; many Indian leaders still are inclined to feel that self-seeking interpersonal and inter-enterprise rivalry is a rather beastly, culturally retrograde business. Probably more influential is the fact that many Indian officials, having accumulated a set of specific grudges against the performance of the narrow, imperfect markets that the Indian economy has known in the past, tend to project these complaints uncritically to market forces in general.

In any event, a principal weakness of Indian farm policy has been the inadequacy of its efforts, thus far, to develop the kind of market environment in and around agriculture that is best calculated to stimulate productive expansion. The shortfalls have been more ones of degree than total oversights, and the Third-Plan document strikes some newly hopeful notes. Yet there is reason still to fear that particular market-building and market-rationalizing efforts may not be pressed with sufficient zest; that some of the positive interventions that the government must make into the rural economy are not being designed with an eye to whether they strengthen or stultify market mechanisms; and that there is inadequate appreciation of the extent to which broadened and quickened markets can multiply the impact of these interventions by generating mutually reinforcing trading linkages and production sequences.

There is, to begin with, the matter of foodgrain prices. Despite all of the past and present concern about promotion of foodgrain output and marketing, there has been little effective use of the pricing mechanism for this purpose. This is not because of any official reluctance to tamper with market determination of foodgrain prices. On the contrary, the country has been beset by a considerable paraphernalia of food price policies and price controls, including a particularly confusing and disruptive set of inter-regional trading restrictions and official price differentials. Yet there has been little sustained attention to the possibility of using incentive prices for the stimulation of production.

Fortunately, from the viewpoint of urban consumers, what is most needed in the realm of price behavior to promote the marketing of foodgrains apparently is not an average rise in foodgrain prices but greater price stability and predictability, both from one year to the next and from season to season. In its discussions of price policy and of agricultural programs the Third-Plan document correctly emphasizes this point. It also clearly recognizes that, in order to improve price stability, the government, rather than trying to impose direct controls, needs to take a strong position in the market itself and promote price stability through its operations as alternately a major buyer and seller.

The Third-Plan document emphasizes the basic facilities the government needs to engage more vigorously in this activity— namely, a much larger public foodgrains inventory and adequate warehousing for food stocks. It notes the solution to the inventory problem that the United States' P.L. 480 commitment for the Third Plan is now due to provide, at least for wheat (far less so in the case of rice), and it programs the necessary central warehousing. And it bespeaks an official determination to use these facilities greatly to step up price-stabilizing efforts. But the document stops a half step short of the kind of policy commitment that would fully reap the production- and marketing-incentive effects that can flow from such an operation, for it does not explicitly commit the government to establishing a system of specific forward minimum price guarantees for the major foodgrains (to be implemented, as required, by government buying). This possibility, often suggested in recent years, was explicitly included in the initial formulation of the selected district scheme by Ford Foundation consultants in late 1959. However, the Third Plan leaves the idea shrouded in vague, indecisive language.

It is important for Americans especially to understand that in India, where the basic agricultural supply problem for the foreseeable future is one of food shortages, not surpluses, a program of concrete year-to-year forward price guarantees will generate little or none of the accumulated long-term problems that similar price supports have in the surplus-biased conditions of the United States. The program would tend to increase total market foodgrains output, thereby implementing the most critical objective of farm policy. Moreover, if, in a year of exceptionally good weather, it resulted in a large excess of government purchases over government sales, this would simply help to equip the nation with the enlarged food reserves it urgently needs. But for years to come there will be virtually no possibility of an excess on the average of domestic output over domestic requirements. Thus the government's reluctance to commit itself to a program of specific, pre-announced price supports must be interpreted as evidence either of fiscal timidity or of insensitivity to the possibilities for actuating incentives via the market. Very possibly it reflects both.

Part and parcel with the problem of disruptive fluctuations in agricultural prices is that of the marketing structure for farm products. As studies of Indian agriculture repeatedly have attested,[8] and as the Third-Plan document once again indicates, the mass of smaller Indian cultivators characteristically have had access to their markets for cash crops only through a layering of middlemen, some of them full-time traders, others larger growers who have the income and credit resources to double as traders. These traders, who have had the financial staying power to speculate against seasonal fluctuations in farm prices, have accounted for the wide spreads between growers' and users' prices, often have reaped most of the advantage from seasonal upswings, and in general frequently have appeared to play a more exploitative role than a distributional one.

The traders' market power, moreover, has been heavily dependent upon the scarcity and usurious terms of the credit that traditional rural money lenders, often closely allied with the trading groups, have made available to the average cultivator. The latter, commonly unable to get credit for minor capital improvements or even production loans that would, for example, allow him to buy fertilizer, all too often has been trapped by his low productivity into seeking grievously burdensome consumption loans, especially for ceremonial purposes, from the local money lender. Once hooked, the farmer has been likely to stay permanently in debt to the money lender and perennially at the mercy of the trader, who stands ready to buy the marketable portion of his harvest at minimum prices.

The government of India's policy for breaking farm productivity free from the constraint imposed by these traditional

[8] See, for example, *All-India Rural Credit Survey*, Vol. II (Reserve Bank of India, 1954).

marketing and financial institutions is to spread an alternative
set of cooperative financial and marketing institutions through
the countryside. This, it would appear, is a perfectly sound, if
not the only possible, answer to the problem. Unfortunately,
the cooperative movement, for reasons that I shall try to sketch
below, urgently needs strengthening. But if this can be done,
the "service cooperative" solution to the farm marketing and
farm credit problems is probably the best one. It also is the
best vehicle for facilitating growers' access to fertilizer and
other essential supplies and for providing adequate local crop
warehousing that is not subject to the control of exploitative
traders.

The service cooperative is also an appropriate instrument
for building another vital link in the system of expansive forces
needed in the countryside: It can be the vehicle for a vigorous
extension of retailing—not only of farm implements, spare
parts, supplies, and building materials, but of fabricated consumer goods—into the remote reaches of the rural economy.
There is no other means by which cultivators' appetites for
cash (which in many instances largely are limited to the needs
posed by rents, taxes, and indebtedness) can be so effectively
whetted, thereby stimulating them to produce more and market
more of what they produce. As argued in Chapters 3 and 4,
it would be a tragic miscalculation if fiscal conservatism caused
Indian policymakers to hang back during the sixties from the
vigorous promotion of such an expansion in rural retailing.
It would be equally tragic if inadequate coordination among
the elements of a comprehensive rural program caused a failure also to promote the local-industry development, the farm-
to-market road building, and the other factors needed, along
with more merchandising to farmers, for triggering a self-reinforcing advance in rural output.

There are other points that deserve development under the
general heading of agricultural market-building and incentive-
harnessing, with regard, for example, to the desirability (1) of
monetizing all rural transactions, (2) of culling from existing
administrative practices in agriculture such disincentive features as the now widespread practice of charging for irrigation
water by the acre rather than by volume, and (3) of raising

agricultural taxes in a manner that does not motivate farmers to consume more and market less of their output. Let me, instead, return to a theme already established and just now suggested again by the remarks on rural retailing:

If the market-building problem for agriculture is conceived as broadly as it should be, neither the problem nor its solution can possibly be confined to agriculture. The environment that is needed to actuate cultivators' production and marketing must entail not only more retailing but more progressive local industries. It must include better roads and other public facilities. It needs a rural works program to construct these and other facilities, not only for the expansive effects that such a program can have on productive (including farm) capacity but for the withdrawal of redundant farm labor from agriculture and the lift that thereby can be given to the productivity of those cultivators remaining on the farm. Most critically of all perhaps, the needed agricultural environment must include a system for vigorously developing local marketing, industrial, administrative, and training centers that can exert a variety of impacts on the surrounding countryside.

The nonagricultural elements in this complex are just as dependent on a thriving increase in farm output and incomes as the latter is dependent upon them. The point is that any adequate rural development program must provide for a closely intermeshing promotion of both agricultural and nonagricultural elements in the same local areas if it is to have much hope of meeting the needs of either.

Agriculture and Community Development

I am suggesting that the essential difficulty with rural policy in India is its failure adequately to grasp a few key organizational principles that loom up amid all of the puzzling complexity of the Indian countryside. One of these is the need for making optimum use of self-adjusting markets as organizational devices. A second has just been emphasized: the need for a balanced, administratively integrated attack on the agricultural and nonagricultural aspects of the rural development problem. A third set of key issues has to do with the size of the focal rural development unit, with the balance to be struck between centralization and decentralization in Indian rural administration, and with the appropriate relationship in the countryside between grass-roots institutions, on the one hand, and, on the other, leadership injected from the outside by government. These all are matters that are illuminated by the experience of the Community Development program, dating from 1951 and, experimentally, from before that time.

Adverse criticisms of the community development effort—after a period of excessive optimism about the program in the early fifties, such criticism latterly has become, if anything, excessively widespread and vehement[9]—ordinarily are not overtly expressed in the terms just used. The most familiar complaint instead is that, despite its announced determination to be well-rounded, community development in fact has lacked functional balance in that it has achieved too little with respect to agricultural expansion. The program, it is widely alleged, has gotten too much into the hands of partisans of social uplift and has lost track of its economic-base priorities.

The reason for this, agricultural specialists in the Indian administrative structure are apt to charge, is that, in the effort to achieve an integrated organization of the rural development effort, agricultural extension and promotion have slipped too much under the aegis of nonagricultural administrators. For the specialized agricultural services, although stemming from state food and agriculture departments and, through them, from the Ministry of Food and Agriculture at the Center, are actually channeled to cultivators at the local level through the

[9] See Government of India: Planning Commission, Committee on Planned Projects, *Report of the Team for the Study of Community Projects and National Extension Service* (1957), 3 vols.; K. Santhanam, *Planning and Plan Thinking* (Higginbothams, 1958), pp. 100-01; M. J. Coldwell and M. Read, *Report of a (United Nations) Community Development Evaluation Mission in India* (Government of India, 1959); Government of India, *Seventh Evaluation Report on Community Development and Some Allied Fields* (1960); Rajeshwar Dayal, *Community Development Programme in India* (Kitab Mahal, 1960); and M. B. Nanarati and J. J. Anjaria, *The Indian Rural Problem* (rev. ed.; The Indian Society of Agricultural Economics, 1960), pp. 499-504.

newly established framework of Community Development and National Extension Blocks (there being, on the average, about one hundred villages to the block and fifteen to twenty blocks to the district, of which latter there are some three hundred in the country as a whole). The Block Development Officer, the chief administrator at that level, not only is seldom an agricultural specialist himself; he reports, not to the agricultural, but to the general administrative and planning hierarchy at the district and state levels, which in turn reports on development policy issues, not to the central Ministry of Food and Agriculture, but to the central Ministry of Community Development. Moreover, the agents for most of the government's day-to-day contact with cultivators on agricultural matters are the Community Development program's multiplying legions of "multipurpose" Village Level Workers (or *gram sewaks*), who, it is charged, do not have the time, stature, or trained knowledge to be very effective in this role.

Another common complaint about the community development effort overlaps the first. There is, many observers allege, a certain looseness in the whole "texture of operations" (to use the phrase of the preceding chapter). The program's administrative structure is cumbersome, the morale of its personnel, particularly at lower echelons, frequently is low; too often a sense of ineptness pervades the operation, which seems bogged down in a web of bureaucratic routines; and in particular, the program's functionaries seem to be preoccupied with such a surfeit of detailed targeting, quota setting, and reporting that they have little time to get on with their work.

This sort of disenchantment with the Community Development program often is summed up in the judgment that, while several of the original community development pilot projects of the late forties and early fifties had an air of adventure, were staffed with exceptionally dedicated and gifted personnel, and were indeed successful, they were like pieces of fine embroidery; they could not readily be reproduced on a mass basis. The attempt to do so, this objection concludes, has blanketed the country with a ponderous administrative structure full of busy work but with a program that, in most places, is only a watered-down, routinized facsimile of the germinal projects from which the whole effort sprang.

While both of these commonly alleged failings of the Community Development program are, on balance, real weaknesses, they do not suggest their own remedies. This is because they are symptomatic conditions. The root difficulties lie a step deeper.

In the first place, in choosing its focal rural-development jurisdiction the program fixed automatically and uncritically on the individual village. From the very beginning it succumbed to what might be called the "village fetish" in Indian thought. By this I mean the unexamined assumption that the single village (average size, about 600 persons) must continue to be, because it always has been, the key social, political, and economic unit in Indian rural life. Community Development has proceeded on the hypothesis that all rural plans must be drawn, all action programs must be mounted, and all development scores must be kept on a village-by-village basis.

In the next chapter we shall be noting that this focus on the individual village becomes most economically anomalous when one considers questions of industrial location, scale, and technology. But it also has two damaging implications for the Community Development program and for the agricultural expansion efforts that are channeled through it. For one thing, it commits the whole scheme to excessive administrative fragmentation. The attempt to plan activities and measure results in 600,000 minuscule jurisdictions maximizes the volume of paper work and busy work within the system. The attempt to create this many centers of popular contact requires the quick recruitment and training of such a massive number of village-level functionaries that it is quite impossible, on average, for them to be persons of much status and experience, or even of high average intelligence and dedication. And the compulsion to have these lowest-level operatives engage in activities that are "balanced" or integrated on a village-by-village basis has forced them to become Jacks-of-all-trades. The average village-level worker, as one longtime observer of Indian rural affairs has said, winds up being a boy sent to do a man's job.

The excessive administrative fragmentation to which the village fetish leads contributes directly to the conditions about which critics of community development complain. The village-level worker's lowliness, youthfulness, and lack of professional authority, along with his divided responsibilities, make him least effective in the realm that villagers take most seriously and think they know best, namely, farming practices. And the effect of excessive fragmentation on both the quality of personnel and the organizational structure underlies Community Development's general appearance of massive superficiality.

A second implication of the program's choice of the individual village as its target jurisdiction involves a matter of political and social tactics: The individual Indian village is typically a most unpromising arena in which to center the rural transformation effort. The whole of that effort, it must be remembered, is meant to bring about radical economic change and therefore challenges the status quo of the traditional society. In the process of stimulating expanding income, generating new activities and opportunities, and increasing rural occupational mobility, it breaks down old status patterns. It threatens traditionally privileged groups with a loss of relative power and prestige at the same time that it offers them opportunities for absolute economic gains. Accordingly, it must expect to generate some vehement local opposition.

The ultimate tactical problem of Indian rural policy is posed by the fact that throughout much of the Indian countryside grass roots political leadership still is largely the prerogative of those traditional local social and economic elites that are instinctively resistant to change. The problem, of course, is how to achieve effective change in this context—and still keep the peace.

One can give the defeatist answer that nothing short of a violent upheaval can unleash the forces of productive opportunity latent in the countryside. This, I think, is an unnecessary conclusion. But it gains plausibility when the reform effort, by centering its focus upon the reconstruction of the individual village *qua* village, challenges the forces of rural reaction on their own terms and on their own ground at their points of greatest resistance. The fact that such is precisely what the Community Development program attempts accounts very considerably for the air of ineffectiveness that too widely characterizes it. Conversely, the whole enterprise of rural development becomes more promising to the extent that the venue of the effort can be shifted to a new, enlarged frame within which new activities and new institutions can be built in a fashion that minimizes the overt displacement of traditional village institutions and village leaders. Gradually, under such an approach, many of the latter can be persuaded to assume constructive roles in the new pattern; and the rest, without precipitous loss of face, can be left to subside into neighborhood anachronisms.

So much for the proposition that one of the Community Development's root organizational difficulties has been excessive village-mindedness. Another, I have implied, has been an unfortunate resolution of its centralization-decentralization problem. In part, the two points overlap, for one way to put the contention about villages is simply to urge that the Community Development effort requires some *centralizing upward* into still numerous and dispersed but substantially larger jurisdictions than that of the individual village.

In its pattern of "development blocks," newly established in most of India but following the lines of the traditional *taluks* in parts of the South, the Community Development movement already has the framework for such a centering process. But thus far the block has simply been conceived of as a collection of villages—as an administrative convenience for facilitating the transmission of messages, materials, and personnel from state and district headquarters, on the one hand, to the operating (village) level, on the other. In a "centralized upward" scheme the block itself would become the primary operating unit. Its specialized services and personnel, of course, would reach out to its constituent groups and persons, who would continue to reside in villages. But instead of being an aggregation of developing villages, the block per se, replete with a reinforced center, would be the community to be developed, of which traditional villages, insofar as they retained their identity, would become the neighborhood components.

But this is only one-half of the centralization-decentralization story. Equally urgent, to pick up a theme introduced near the end of the last chapter, is the Community Development program's need for *decentralization downward*. As we have seen, the traditional British-Indian administrative system, to which the Community Development program has been made fully to conform, doles out little discretionary authority to its lower echelons. Moreover, there is a deep status cleavage between Indian Administrative Service personnel, who usually have not been posted below the district level, and the rest of the government service, which has been left, among other things, to man local rural development posts. The result is an echelon of Block Development Officers who have little or no scope for practicing the imaginative, innovative local program development that their areas need; are busied too much with detailed accounting upward; are obsequious in their deference to district officers; are accorded little status by the traditional leaders of their own communities; and have very limited career horizons. Not surprisingly, the average caliber of these officers leaves something to be desired.

These last few sentences refer not only to the impersonal allocation of powers and responsibilities among different levels of the administrative structure but also, implicitly, to the vital question of how to supply adequate reform leadership to the countryside in a manner that pays adequate deference to the principle of local self-determination. This is another of the key organizational questions over which India's rural policies of the fifties have exhibited a disturbing fuzziness. On the one hand, overly centralized administration has combined with the village fetish to down-grade the newly created position of Block Development Officer, which represented the most hopeful vehicle for injecting a catalytic new leadership into many tradition-ridden localities. On the other hand, there has been elaborate deference, from the beginning of the community development effort, to the concept of grass-roots self-determination—understood to mean, of course, village-by-village self-determination. The result thus far of reviving village panchayats (or councils) and other traditional local-governing institutions too often has been to entrench village elites in their traditional power positions while the newly provided reform leadership has been managing, at best, a limited growth.

A clearer view of the dynamic of democratic rural development would suggest that the injection of the most vigorous possible new leadership—generously endowed with power, discretion, and resources for creating incentives—into an orbit other than, and larger than, the village is by all odds the most important contribution that government can make to the rural development process. This, and not agricultural separatism, is the single best answer to the Community Development program's problem of agricultural ineffectiveness, just as it is the best way of energizing the whole operation.

Moreover, the provision of strong leadership is entirely compatible with the evolution of the kind of local self-determination that will suit the transformed rural society. For not only would a new breed of greatly strengthened Block Development Officer be fully responsible to elected governments at the state and national levels; from the beginning, these officers would have to win the substantial consent of their local constituents to keep their programs viable; their work, inevitably, would stimulate the organization of new local interests and the emergence of new local leaders; and it would be their business, not to abdicate to traditional village authorities, but gradually to nurture the development of new representative bodies and home-grown administrators at the block level.

Happily, there seems to be this kind of intention, as far as the development of local representative government is concerned, in the experimental so-called "democratic decentralization" scheme that has been under way in Rajasthan and Andhra Pardish since 1959-60. For while journalistic reports of that endeavor have tended to treat it as simply a promotion of traditional village panchayats, its far more significant innovation is the institution of responsible legislative bodies at the block level, charged with working closely with the Block Development Officer and slated to receive a progressive transfer of development-policymaking power from him and from higher echelons in the administrative hierarchy. But this deals only with the passive, follow-up side of the local leadership problem. So far as the reinforcement of the leadership itself is concerned, nothing very decisive has been done.

The Errant Cooperative Movement

The principles just set forth with respect to the community development effort can be brought equally to bear on the rural Cooperative Movement. According to the present diagnosis—and according to the Third Five Year Plan's official analysis—service cooperatives have a crucial role to play in the agricultural development process. They are to provide much of the supplemental services and supplies necessary to make the single-family-farm system of productive organization a serviceable framework for a rapid expansion in production. They are to supply effective and equitable alternatives to the repressive tribute that traditional traders and money lenders levy from the average cultivator. More generally, the rural cooperative is to be the key instrumentality for activating the monetized market in and around agriculture.

Anyone familiar with the Indian cooperative movement might well be skeptical of its capacity for accepting such responsibilities. The movement already has been under way for more than a half century and, aside from a few strikingly exceptional components, has exhibited little of the dynamic now called for. Indeed, in many parts of India, cooperatives have a tired, routine quality about them that exceeds the worst performance of the Community Development program. In other sections of the country, previously innocent of cooperatives, state administrations in recent years intermittently, for the sake of "satisfying" plan targets, have engineered the nominal, formal creation of thousands of new cooperative societies with little or no attention to the quality of their programs. The egregious superficiality of some of these efforts has served further to discredit the movement as a whole.

As subscribers to the cult of the village, the organizers of the cooperative movement have let the mystique of local self-determination dull their appreciation of the cooperative as an instrument for inducing reform and injecting outside leadership into the local situation. The cooperative is a natural for the latter role, particularly because of the immediate, tangible

advantages it has to offer the cultivator. The latter has no
difficulty grasping and appreciating the concrete commodities
and services that an effective cooperative can bring him—the
fertilizer, the credit, and others. If these are made really accessible, he will be quick to reach for them, and if they are
conditioned upon his becoming a member, or even a nominal
shareholder, he will probably go along. But it may be a long
time before he appreciates the significance of these more abstract involvements.

Thus the cooperative should be recognized as the case *par
excellence* of the constructive new institution that can best
originate at the innovating, nuclear center of the local economic region and quickly spread out into the hinterland, creating new opportunities and undermining old rigidities. Where
there are cooperatives to be built, or to be revived, at block-
center there should be leadership resourceful enough to get a
vigorous, multipurpose, block-level cooperative started on the
right track—with as much of the support, participation, and
capital of leading villagers as can be had, but with the additional help of cooperative know-how, trained personnel, and
financing imported from outside. Then the central society
can quickly extend branches to serve multi-village clusters in
their own neighborhoods.

This is a straightforward way to proceed. It smacks of no
pretense. Villagers can be enrolled as members of the block
society as rapidly as they can be recruited; their participation
in the actual direction of the society can grow as they learn
its potentialities; and the branches can eventually be given
increasing, even complete, autonomy if the membership
wishes. But meanwhile the cooperative can become established in the aggressive role it must play in development.

There are a few cooperative operations in India that have
followed this pattern, and at times a national agricultural-
cooperative policy has even veered tentatively in this direction. But then it has backed off in deference to the ingrained
notions that each individual village needs its own primary
cooperative society and that the government should go
through the motions of making each of these tiny cooperatives

appear to spring up as a spontaneous, wholly indigenous village institution.

The result, typically and plainly, has been to lodge the village cooperative in the hands of the same privileged village cliques that have been doing most of the traditional money lending and trading. By insisting on the pretense of indigenous origin, the forces of reform have surrendered the cooperative instrument to management by the very groups most inclined to resist massive rural reconstruction. In the process, the primary cooperative society has tended to become simply another device for reinforcing the pattern of rural privilege—with the comfortable new feature of a direct line of credit on the Reserve Bank of India.

The Agricultural Puzzle: Conclusion

If careful observers of the Indian economy agree on one thing respecting agriculture, it is that the farm outlook is the most problematical element in the nation's whole nearer-term development prospect. If they agree on a second thing, it is that the problem of achieving an adequate expansion in farm output is exceptionally complex. Beyond this, the consensus begins to break down. Nevertheless, there is widespread assent to what have been the first two points in the present analysis:

1. Despite the rapid acceleration in agricultural expansion that is now required, the present situation, looked at in relative terms and judged on the record of the fifties, is basically hopeful, not hopeless. Gains in farm output have begun to gather momentum, and the ferment of rural reform—necessarily a slow process if it is to remain nonexplosive—has set in.

2. The situation is also technically hopeful. Because of its very backwardness, Indian agriculture has an enormous opportunity, within its existing production-unit pattern, sharply to increase its yield by wider adoption of known combinations of known technical improvements. And the

latter for the most part are not expensive in terms of foreign exchange. To put the same point differently and say that agriculture's present problem is essentially one of organization and communication is to understand that "technically hopeful" does not mean "easy," especially in a noncoercive political context. But at least it does mean that accelerated agricultural expansion need not be contingent upon the political upheaval that would have to attend extensive further land reform or a massive change-over to joint cooperative farming.

This much of the present diagnosis, as I understand it, corresponds with the current position of official Indian farm policy, although, for obvious tactical reasons, the latter mutes the point about land reform and joint cooperative farming. The policies that thus far have been mounted to seize India's opportunity for accelerated agricultural expansion, however, appear distressingly inadequate. On this score, one might content oneself with generalized explanations and excuses. It might be argued, for example, that, since peaceful rural change is inherently slow-moving, all criticisms of existing programs are premature. Or the difficulties in agriculture could be attributed simply to the general frailties of Indian administration. Or one could rely on the sweeping (but considered) assertion that farm policymakers have simply grown too politically circumspect; they have become so concerned to avoid ruffling the rural elite's feathers unduly that they have lost their stomach for the limited, purposeful disruption of the status quo to which their reform intentions commit them.

The present chapter, however, has tried to be a bit more specific about the sources of the present difficulties of farm policy in India. In so doing it has advanced these further propositions:

3. The program has been unbalanced in its inattention—at least, in the ineffectiveness of its attention—to the possibilities for inducing expanded farm production and marketing via environment-conditioning reforms. In particular, as evinced in matters of price policy, of marketing and credit

structure, and of rural retailing, the program has shown little resourcefulness in exploiting the market mechanism as an expansion-accelerating device.

4. The organization of the program's efforts both directly to dispense guidance and assistance to cultivators (especially through the agency of the community development scheme) and indirectly to recast the farmers' market environment (particularly through rural cooperatives) has been grossly inhibited by a cluster of interrelated misjudgments: (a) about the serviceability of the minute, economically obsolescent Indian village as the focal rural-development unit, (b) about the need to lodge abundant discretionary authority at a local but supra-village level in the planning and administrative hierarchy, and (c) about the necessity for, and the democratic appropriateness of, importing strong enterprising, unorthodox reform into the rural context at this level. Most of the farm program's administrative clutter, personnel problems, and tactical ineffectiveness can be traced to these sources.

These certainly are not brand new propositions. Variants of all of them exist, sometimes prominently, in the voluminous official and semi-official literature that has accumulated around the Indian development process. Many times, moreover, policymakers have taken steps that can be hopefully interpreted as being responsive to these propositions. The steps, however, have been partial, incomplete, often tentative. They never have begun to add up to the wholesale recasting of policy that the present analysis would indicate.

If they are valid, therefore, the foregoing points have rather profound redirectional implications, and they have these as much for the American advisers as they do for the Indian architects of existing programs. For the two, broadly speaking, have proceeded hand-in-hand down the path to the present situation. Moreover, if American assistance and advice continues to be active in such fields as agricultural extension, community development, and cooperatives, American advisers, obviously, will continue to be intimately concerned with the issues we have had under discussion.

Many agricultural specialists, Indian and American alike, already have become deeply impatient with the frustrations and futilities of existing rural development efforts. But the redirection they typically propose—namely, to be freed from the embrace of the general community development program and be turned loose on a go-it-alone, agriculture-only course —is just about 180 degrees off the mark. This is where a final proposition emerging from the chapter comes in:

5. The needed redirection of Indian agricultural policy cannot possibly be purely agricultural. On the contrary, the outlook for agriculture depends importantly upon the development of nonfarm employment opportunities; it depends in several ways on the nature of the rural public works effort; it depends upon the pattern and vigor of a whole system of markets; and it depends vitally upon the size, character, and functions of the population centers around which rural activity is oriented. Any sensibly redirected agricultural program, in short, can exist only as an integral component of a larger rural policy frame.

The purpose of the next chapter is to consider, briefly and tentatively, what the composite shape of this larger frame may be.

7 THE ROLE OF THE TOWN
IN INDUSTRIAL LOCATION

Any development plan has a spatial dimension in the sense that each newly established installation or activity requires a locational decision. The federal character of the Indian constitution, moreover, has assured a significant place for state-by-state planning in the national planning exercise, and recently this focus on the states as geographical planning entities has been reinforced by various studies of particular states' development capacities and requirements.[1] In any case, in a democracy as regionally diverse as India it would be politically suicidal for national planners to be entirely impervious to regional differences, alleged inequities, and differentiated demands. And in India the government has been sensitive enough to the need for providing special stimuli to particular backward areas and regions to be judged a leader among the governments of economically underdeveloped countries in the field of "regional development."[2]

It may seem paradoxical, therefore, to say that the Indian authorities have addressed relatively little concerted thought and effort to the spatial dimensions of their development design. Yet I am strongly persuaded that this is so with respect to one vital matter—namely, the size distribution of the demographic concentrations (and, therefore, of the economic, administrative, political, and social concentrations) into which the activities of the developing Indian economy are to be gathered. This issue has little to do with the formal structure of the Indian constitution or with interregional differences. The question rather is what the transformed Indian economy's

[1] Particularly noteworthy are the various state "techno-economic" surveys that the National Council of Applied Economic Research (New Delhi) has prepared and began publishing in 1959.

[2] See Stefan H. Robock, "Regional and National Economic Development in India," *Papers and Proceedings of the Regional Science Association,* Vol. 6 (1960), pp. 65-81.

general pattern of geographical sectoring and/or centering is to be.

Like virtually every other aspect of the development process, this is an issue that the Indian intelligentsia, from time to time, has had in mind and about which the government's archives would yield a sizable collection of relevant working papers. But anyone who lingered in those New Delhi offices where the Third Five Year Plan outlines were being fitted together in the last months of the 1950's could only judge that most of the key planners were relatively unexcited about the average geographical scale of development activities. They acted as though they thought either that they had other more important things to worry about, or that there was comparatively little, in any event, that they could do effectively to control this aspect of the development pattern.

In that same period, however, there were planners in some of the state secretariats vitally interested in what might be called the nation's centering policy; there were isolated individuals and groups within such central government agencies as the Planning Commission, the Ministries of Food and Agriculture and of Community Development and Cooperation, and the small industries section of the Ministry of Commerce and Industry similarly concerned; and it was my own impression during the first half of 1960 that the issue was edging higher on the planning agenda. Read hopefully, the final Third-Plan document confirms this impression. The separate-chapter treatment it gives to the subject of "Balanced Regional Development" is concerned not only with the narrowing of inter-regional differentials but with the needs for achieving an adequate dispersion of new industrial establishments (in both the public and private sectors), for promoting an integrated development of agriculture and industry in the same local economic regions, and for developing the Plan's large industrial-core projects as "nuclei of regional growth." Similar notes are struck at other points in the document.

Thus it is just possible that the problem highlighted in this chapter already is well on the way to solution. But it would be dangerous to assume so. For one thing, as we shall be noting, the combination of factors tending to obstruct and obscure a sensible solution to the centering problem is formidable; the obstacles have had their way in the past and are apt to again. Moreover, in the case of the geographic deployment of the Indian experiment, the stakes riding on the avoidance of bad policy are extremely high. Indeed, if I am not mistaken, they include the opportunity for making the most constructive and novel contribution to the world's fund of development alternatives that is within India's capacity to make. And yet this chance is a comparatively fleeting one; probably it will have been either seized or missed before this decade is over. These are the reasons why it seems to me to be the part of responsible commentary, if anything, to overemphasize the matters we now take up.

The Agro-Industrial, Rural-Urban Continuum

We have noted the critical bearing that the nature and size of local economic and administrative centers have upon agricultural development. But industry also, of course, is vitally involved in, and affected by, the pattern of centering the economy evolves. The obvious point that agricultural development, industrial development, and nonagricultural, nonindustrial development all interrelate with one another within the same set of geographical coordinates is somewhat obscured in India by the functional splintering that is so characteristic of Indian administration.

This deep cleavage between functions, with its emphasis on "vertical" chains of command rather than upon the "horizontal" integration of programs at particular geographic or administrative levels, is not limited to the relations between agricultural and industrial programs. Those in irrigation and power, transport and road-building, other public works, cooperatives, and community development also tend to be administratively remote from one another—except for some superficial patching together at the village and block levels.

In the case of industry itself, not only is there functional cleavage between major-industry development and the small-industries program; within the small and cottage industries field alone there are no less than six separate central government boards—for khadi, handlooms, handicrafts, coir, silk and "small-scale" (modern) industries—each with its own budget, its own program, and its own organizational extension into the field. To complicate matters further, the Community Development scheme also runs its own village industries program, and both the states and the central government can be found running uncoordinated small-scale industry promotional operations in the same localities. In one city I had the pleasure of introducing the heads of two such units to each other for the first time.

The result of this extraordinary functional fragmentation is that most senior officials in the government of India who are in one way or another concerned with the development of the Indian countryside see the problem in the half-lights of their own functional specialties. And for each of the dozen or so functional programs that stretch into the countryside, the government houses within itself an influential group disposed to look on any move toward more integrated local programing as a threat to the integrity of its own vertical chain of command.

The attempt to bring the whole development effort into correct spatial focus is likewise seriously obscured by a dichotomizing of development issues along rural-urban lines. This too produces an administrative hiatus. Because of the tendency to conform slavishly to the size limit of 2,500 persons that the census takers have adopted as a matter of convenience for defining "villages," for many official purposes any issue involving centers with more than this number falls, by definition, outside the scope and responsibility of the "rural" development effort.

The blame in this case lodges, however, not primarily with Indian administrators themselves, but with those scholars of recent years (conspicuously including Americans) who have elevated the rural-urban distinction into a principal device of social taxonomy and thereby have imposed it upon development thought the world over. In a recent conference on development research, for example, we in the Brookings Institution were wholly conventional in falling into this trap. Two concurrent, and, therefore, mutually exclusive, seminars were scheduled, one on "rural problems," the other on "urbanization." The result was predictable: people interested in agriculture and villages attended the first seminar; a different group anxious to talk about the problems of metropolitan agglomerates went to the second; and the thinking of the conference was falsely polarized.

Such a polarization is erroneous in principle because the centering alternatives open to a developing economy actually constitute a continuum that stretches from the smallest villages to the largest metropolis. Each center of whatever size defines a region that, although its periphery may be economically and socially ill-defined,[3] contains a central, relatively "urban," area (larger centers may also include lesser centers within their fields of influence) and outlying, relatively "rural," areas. All such regions, large or small, also include a fairly broad spectrum of agricultural, industrial, and nonagricultural, nonindustrial productive activities.

A developing economy's basic spatial or locational choice (which may or may not be recognized and may or may not be subject to much discretionary manipulation by the central authorities) concerns the distribution of population and activities that is to be made through the continuum of center sizes. Theoretically, this distribution might be spread uniformly across the whole span of sizes. Or conceivably it could be as skewed toward the smaller-sized centers, as it presently is in India, where 82 percent of the population still live and for the most part work in places with fewer than 2,500 inhabitants; or it could be skewed toward the opposite end of the spectrum, as it is in many of the developed economies; or, finally, it would be perfectly possible in principle for the concentration to peak in the center sizes lying somewhere between these extremes.

The rural-urban dichotomy conveys no sense of this continuum of alternatives. Nor does it readily accommodate the fact that any policy designed to favor the development of centers of a particular size range needs to attend to a region's

[3] It may or may not be precisely bounded for administrative and political purposes.

areas both of demographic concentration and a demographic dispersion and therefore to contain a well-blended mixture of "urban" and "rural" ingredients.

As a practical matter, moreover, an "urban-rural" polarization of the development effort ill comports with the existing size distribution of population centers in India. As Table 6

TABLE 6. *Distribution of the Indian Population by Place Sizes, 1961 Census*

Place size	Number of places	Percent of total population
Up to 2,500	558,088	82.16
2,500–19,999	2,509	4.27
20,000–49,999	375	3.22
50,000–99,999	110	2.47
100,000 and over	73	7.89

Source: Government of India, 1961 Census, Provisional Population Totals. (The provisional census estimates did not include an All-India tabulation of the percentage distribution of population by place sizes, and the state tabulations, which the present estimates summarize, are incomplete. Consequently, the present percentage figures, while close approximations, are not precisely accurate.)

shows, while population is still concentrated at the village level, the nonvillage minority is spread quite evenly across the balance of the size range. There is not, as casual discussions sometimes seem to suggest, any lack of medium-sized centers lying between the villages, on the one hand, and the larger cities, on the other. Instead, throughout the size-class distribution there presently are bases upon which further concentrations of activities and population could be built.

Industrialization and Migration

What makes the centering issue presently dramatic in India is that in this very decade the country is destined to pass through a locational revolution. Thanks to the projected surge of industrialization during the Third and Fourth Five Year Plans, the increments of new activity to be located are unprecedentedly large. Roughly estimated, the new industrial capacity to be put in place during the sixties, measured by output capabilities, will be four or five times that established during the fifties and more than twice as large as the total capacity of Indian industry operative at the start of the Third Plan.

The same point can be put in terms of migration. The nation is, in any event, committed to a rapid occupational migration out of agriculture—or, what amounts to the same thing, a shift of most of the "natural" increase in the farm labor force to nonfarm work. Indeed, as we have seen, the shifting of redundant farm labor into more productive nonfarm employment is a good part of the essence of the Indian development design. The Third-Plan document estimates that by the end of the Fifth-Plan period the farm share of the total labor force, which was 70 percent in 1961, will have been lowered to about 60 percent; this means that about two-thirds of the new jobs created during the next fifteen years will need to be nonagricultural. The question is whether, and to what extent and in what way, this occupational migration need involve a geographic migration.

The decisions made in the 1960's on this question will have a profound direct effect on India's centering pattern. Moreover, since locational patterns tend, for some time, to be self-reinforcing, the decisions of the sixties can be expected to determine subsequent locational decisions for several decades to come. The basic configuration that emerges during the sixties, I shall be assuming in the following paragraphs, may take any one of three forms:

1. The new or expanded enterprises and activities (public or private) that receive the out-migrants from agriculture may be (or, at least, some observers hope they will be) village-centered. In this case the occupational migration presumably would necessitate little or no geographic migration.

2. Newly locating activities may be metropolitan-centered. This alternative would entail the most extensive and radical movement of population.

3. Or the new activities may be "town-centered"—bunched, that is to say, somewhere in the 20,000-to-300,000 range of the scale. Obviously, this alternative would involve a substantial relative shift in the location of work places. But, depending upon the number of such town centers (and, therefore,

on their average distance from the villages) as well as upon incentives, the availability of transport, and other factors, it might be possible for many of those newly employed in non-agricultural work to continue residing in their villages.

As a representation of the actual continuum of alternatives, this three-way classification is, in one sense, only one degree better than the rural-urban dichotomy I have just been criticizing. However, the three-way classification does have the enormous advantage of explicitly recognizing a middle possibility. Moreover, the differences between this middle alternative and the extremes on either side are significant enough to warrant the sharpened contrasts the present formulation provides.

Village-Centered and Metropolitan-Centered Location

Despite Indian development policy's genuflections to the mystique of the village, village-centered industrialization is not, to any important degree, a realistic alternative for modern India. This conclusion has been abundantly anticipated in earlier chapters. Aside from the matter of political and social tactics discussed in Chapter 6, the basic obstacle to the development of a progressive village-centered economy is simply one of the scale of production.

The village of 600, or 1,000, or even of 2,500 persons cannot provide an adequate market to support moderately complex retailing or consumer service operations, let alone much technologically progressive consumer goods fabrication. Nor can a single village hope to supply the managerial and labor skills, the financial, professional, and business services, or the social overheads and amenities needed to serve any significant array of industrial activities. Indeed, the individual village cannot even meet the minimum-scale requirements of many modern agricultural processing operations. Moreover, across-the-board village electrification, which a predominantly village-centered industrialization would demand, would, at the present stage of the Indian expansion effort, entail an unconscionably heavy investment in the nerve endings of the electrical distribution network.

On a variety of counts, in short, it makes no sense technologically to claim that the individual village offers a feasible setting for very much of the new industrial activity that will be inaugurated during the 1960's.

Metropolitan-centered industrialization, on the other hand, is not only feasible but natural. It has been the pattern of other developing economies in the past; official pronouncements to the contrary, it has been the dominant pattern of Indian industrial location to date; and certainly it will be the predominant pattern for the sixties and beyond unless concerted efforts are made to check it.

The explanations of why activities and population tend to be drawn to a few large centers in a newly industrializing economy are familiar and persuasive—whether one invokes the conventional emphasis on "external economies" or adopts Gunnar Mydral's more colorful rendering of the same idea, in which he argues that earlier-starting centers, by generating centripetal flows of resources and exerting "backwash" effects on the hinterland, enjoy a cumulative advantage over other areas. Among the lures that the metropolis works on private entrepreneurs are those of a concentrated market, of an established business community, of financial and other facilities, services, and amenities, and of a skilled labor pool. Migratory labor is drawn by the apparent employment opportunities. Dissatisfied villagers first gravitate to nearby towns and then, failing to find adequate employment there, move in due course to the large cities. Once there, for the most part they remain. Even though many of them succeed only in joining the army of the metropolitan unemployed, the chances of employment continue to look relatively better in the metropolis.

The very naturalness of metropolitan-centered industrialization causes some of the more influential Indian planners to shy away from schemes designed to divert India from this locational pattern. These are planners who, concerned above all to see the economy make good its Third-Plan and Fourth-Plan total-output targets and rightly recognizing that the assault on these targets is, at best, going to be a very close thing, fear the drag that an effective industrial dispersion policy might place on total expansion. They reason that a dispersal policy might succeed only in frustrating, not diverting, some of the expansionist drives, especially in the private sector, and further that, even where the centripetal forces could be overcome, it would require substantial and tangible offsets to do so. It is contended that the provision of these offsets—whether in the form of subsidies, restraints on efficient metropolitan producers, promotional services, additional social overheads, or whatever—would claim resources that otherwise could support over-all expansion.

This argument, echoed by a number of Western economists who have been observing the Indian development effort, is a substantial one. Yet the social costs implicit in a perpetuation of metropolitan-centered industrial location in India are even more sobering.

There is, in the first place, the prospect of sheer numbers. It seldom occurs to people who have seen Bombay and Calcutta, or even New Delhi and Madras, that India's largest cities are still extremely small relative to the country's population. However, as Table 7 indicates, the five largest cities in 1960 accounted for only a little over 3 percent, and the ten

TABLE 7. *Large-City Shares of Total Population in Selected Countries, 1960*

Country	Percent of total population living in	
	the 5 largest cities	the 10 largest cities
India	3.2	4.4
United States	9.6	12.1
United Kingdom	13.7	17.8
West Germany	12.0	17.6
France	9.9	12.2
Italy	10.2	13.5
Japan	16.3	19.7

Source: UN Demographic Yearbook (1961).

largest, for only about 4½ percent of the total Indian population. It is not certain, of course, that continuing industrialization and continued metropolitan centering will cause any particular number of the largest Indian cities to claim the same percentage of the total population as does the same number of largest cities in other industrialized countries. However, there appears to be some evidence that the metropolitan shares of the population in such countries exhibit a common tendency and, further, that the absolute number of metropolises that such countries develop is not closely related to their geographic or demographic sizes. In any event, it is very easy to imagine, looking at Table 7, that, if India continues to follow the metropolitan-centering route, the share of the population accounted for by its five largest cities will rise to something like 10 percent. For a population of 600 million, which India is likely to have by 1975, this would mean a five-city population of 60 million or, if Bombay were to retain its 1960 share of the five-city total, a Bombay of 23 million persons.

It is interesting that the only other Asian country listed in the table is the most strongly metropolitan-centered. This is Japan, which is also the second most populous of the other countries as well as the one whose division of labor between agriculture and other sectors is least tilted toward the latter, and whose major industrialization is closest to India's in time. If India should follow the Japanese example, the five-city share of a population of 600 million would rise to nearly 100 million, and we would have (on the same assumptions) the prospect of 35 million people crowding into Bombay. All such estimates, of course, are the loosest kind of projections.[4] But they serve to make the point that a formidable degree of metropolitan agglomeration would be implicit in any uninhibited extension of metropolitan centering in a country as populous as India and with so much industrializing left to do.

In the second place, it is probable that a continuation of metropolitan-centered industrial location would, before long, generate considerably heavier social overhead requirements than would a more dispersed locational pattern. At first

[4] See the estimate by Richard Meier that Calcutta may reach a population of 66 million by the year 2000, noted in R. H. Turner, "India's Urban Future," *The Economic Weekly* (February 4, 1961), pp. 133-35.

glance, it might appear that the reverse would be true. For the marginal additions of public facilities and amenities that would be necessary for equipping metropolitan centers, on the one hand, and smaller dispersed centers, on the other, to handle particular small increments of activity and population are usually less mistakable and postponable in the case of the smaller centers. Thus, it always seems that Bombay, for example, can absorb another three manufacturing enterprises employing five hundred workers apiece without making any immediate adjustments in its public health, education, police, urban transport, water, or other public services and facilities, even including electric power. But immediate investments in social overhead *would* be unavoidable if the same three factories were to locate, instead, in most Indian towns of the 50,000-to-100,000 range.

This contrast, however, is a very misleading one on which to base long-term policy. For the industrial increments locating in Bombay do require social overhead services. And since there is certainly no appearance of excess capacity in the existing urban plant of the larger Indian cities, extensive accretions of new industrial activity like those in prospect for the sixties are going to require before long sizable accretions of new social overhead facilities and services wherever the activity is located. Moreover, it may be that the incremental social overhead requirements of the large urban concentrations will prove to be relatively greater than those of smaller complexes. Whether or not the needs for, and costs of, public facilities bear some kind of an exponential relationship to city size is still an unsettled issue, but something of the sort seems probable in the case of many facilities and services.

In any event, there is finally this very concrete consideration: the new housing needs posed by Indian industrialization are unmistakably highest when location follows a metropolitan-centered pattern. For one thing, the real cost of minimum-standard housing in India is substantially higher in the large cities than in smaller towns. For another, as noted already, sufficient industrial dispersion would enable a large share of the occupational migrants from agriculture to become commuters and continue to live in their native villages, thereby postponing indefinitely a good part of the urban residential construction and the attendant drain upon scarce resources that rapid industrialization otherwise would entail.

In the third place, metropolitan-centered industrialization threatens India with grave social and political disadvantages. Metropolitan unemployment, it seems to be generally agreed, is qualitatively worse—it is more absolute, more frustrating, more debilitating—than village or even town unemployment. And, quite plainly, it is more productive of social violence and political upheaval. Most disturbing of all, metropolitan-centering maximizes India's drift toward the condition of a polarized, "dual" society. I have emphasized that demographically and economically speaking, Indian life, rather than being literally dichotomized, is distributed through a spectrum of place sizes. But culturally, one cannot escape the dichotomy between the new and the old, the scientific and the traditional, the experimental and the fatalistic, the achievement-oriented and the status-dominated. Instead of narrowing and bridging this gap, metropolitan centering widens it by tending to polarize the demographic spectrum. Its effect is to gather the progressive elements in the society into metropolitan concentrations that, in terms of income and ideas, pull farther and farther away from the traditional rural mass.

The deepening internal contrasts and tensions implicit in the trend toward a dual society would not necessarily be anti-developmental in a country whose central authorities were prepared to make heavy use of calculated coercion as a technique of social change. The aggravation of such tensions might be a perfectly logical course, for example, for a nation that was prepared whenever necessary, to implement its industrial thrust by "declaring war on the peasants" in the manner of Stalin in the early thirties. But policies that encourage —or even passively tolerate—a widening breach between the modern and traditional sectors of the society are inherently incompatible with an attempt, such as India's, to achieve radical economic change peacefully, via processes that avoid arbitrary coercion and enlist popular consent.

The Town-Centered Alternative

Once the alternatives are understood, the idea of steering much of India's mass of industrial location decisions during the sixties toward some middle ground between the technological infeasibility of village-centered industrialization and the lurking dangers of metropolitan centering has a compelling appeal. Towns in the 20,000-to-300,000 range offer the most congenial physical setting for a synthesis between the traditional-rural and the Western-urban strands of contemporary Indian culture. Town-centering would, at the very least, yield a less feverish problem of urban unemployment and make it easier for frustrated geographic migrants to retreat to the relative congeniality of village unemployment. Moreover, town-centered industrialization's requirements for many social overheads might, in total, be less than would be posed by unrestrained metropolitan agglomeration. In any event, the need for much of the urban housing that would otherwise be required to serve the new nonagricultural workers would be replaced by a need for additional bicycles, buses, and village-to-market roads that would allow many of them to commute from their villages. By the same token, a most effective means for opening the windows of the village to the new society emerging around it would be provided.

Furthermore, by maximizing the average proximity of agriculture to concentrations of industrial and commercial activity, a pattern of comparatively (but not unrealistically) dispersed industrialization would help to provide the kind of market environment that, the previous chapter emphasized, agricultural development so urgently needs. Indeed, town-centered development would supply the necessary frame for the whole network of development sequences, linkages, and feed-backs upon which the successful transformation of the Indian countryside so largely depends. To a degree that would be quite impossible in larger cities, for example, town-centering could marshal many of the rural unemployed—part-time as well as full-time—to the tasks of urban construction without dislodging them from their villages. While metropolitan construction also employs idle labor, of course, it cannot do so until workers from villages already have been converted into geographic migrants, and its skill requirements, on average, may be somewhat higher. By contrast town-centered building would make a more direct attack on the problem of activating idle rural manpower, would do so at a lower social cost, and by putting a much larger number of less roundabout multiplier processes to work at once would be apt to have a greater expansive effect, especially on local industries not significantly dependent on imported and other scarce equipment and materials.

Nor need advocacy of town-centered rather than metro-politan-centered development be just a matter of wishful thinking. The point just made—that there are greater capacities for mobilizing idle rural manpower advantageously if industrialization is decentralized—suggests one basis for suspecting that effective resistance to metropolitan centering would not necessarily retard the economy's over-all advance. Several other considerations tend to support the economic feasibility of rather extensive industrial dispersal in India. In its development of electric power the country already has progressed far enough toward the establishment of large regional and inter-regional power grids to make it a matter of comparative indifference whether the delivery of electricity to the bulk of the nation's industrial users is made to a few very large centers or to several hundred, or even a few thousand, smaller centers. (As noted above, distribution of electricity in the near future to hundreds of thousands of individual villages would be another, and a very much more expensive proposition.)

Likewise in the case of transportation, the existing network constitutes a base that further development could as readily adapt to the needs of an economy with many centers as it could to one with few centers. In fact, it is possible that the total goods-transport requirements (as well as the total pas-senger-transport requirements) associated with a given volume of dispersed industrialization would be less than those implicit in an equivalent volume of concentrated industrialization. For

(1) those industries whose locations (for reasons of processing weight losses or otherwise) are materials-oriented would tend to be situated in the same places and probably to require roughly equivalent amounts of finished-product haulage in either a metropolitan-centered or a town-centered economy. And (2) industries whose locations tend to be market-oriented (and for whom, therefore, the per-mile unit costs of acquiring materials are generally less than those involved in distributing products) might well wind up, on average, with shorter product deliveries to make in a town-centered economy than in a metropolitan-centered economy—*if,* for a considerable variety of products, efficient operations could be conducted on a sufficiently small scale to find adequate markets within nearby areas.

It is quite possible, moreover, that indigenous innovation of efficient capital-saving techniques and processes (promoted by the kind of technological policy advocated in Chapter 3) will increase the feasibility of dispersed industrialization. This is not a self-evident connection. It rests on two implicit assumptions—first, that smaller-scale enterprises are better adapted than large-scale operations to dispersed location and, second, that efficient capital-saving processes are likely also to be smaller-scale than the capital-intensive alternatives with which they are designed to compete. The first of these assumptions, as I shall be saying directly, is not always so. Yet it does make sense in the case of industries that would be expected to find all or most of their demand within their own regional markets. The second assumption—that among the alternative, effectively competing techniques for making the same products there is a positive correlation between capital-intensity and size—is not necessarily true. In fact, one recent study has found that smaller-scale operations, while using more labor per unit of capital, use just as much capital per unit of output; that is, they employ their labor less efficiently and their capital no more efficiently than the organized industries.[5] This is a subject, however, that requires far more extensive investigation. The study cited, although most com-

[5] P. N. Dhar and H. F. Lydall, *The Role of Small Enterprises in Indian Economic Development* (Asia Publishing House, 1961).

petently done, is much too tentative and incomplete to establish definitively the relationship between capital-intensity and scale for competing units of existing Indian industries. In any event, no findings as to the existing situation would wholly shake my intuition that, in the case of future Indian innovation, capital-saving substitutes contrived for Western industrial processes will tend to be smaller-scale operations than the Western-style processes they displace.

It should be emphasized next, however, that the economic feasibility of dispersed industrialization is by no means contingent upon a conversion of Indian industry exclusively or even largely to small-scale operations. On the contrary, the Indian economy surely will have a large number of very large-scale manufacturing establishments; but not one of these will be so large, and scarcely any will be so technically sophisticated, that it could not be readily accommodated, along with all of its necessary service enterprises and a fair array of lesser industrial establishments, in a town of 100,000 to 200,000. The proof of this is the manner in which India's most massive public-sector enterprises, including the three Second-Plan steel mills, have been dropped into thoroughly rustic areas, for reasons of proximity to raw materials, and with remarkable speed are having complete, medium-sized, planned urban complexes built around them.

This matter of the pulls that an economy's natural resource endowments exert upon its industrial location sometimes provides the rationale for another objection to the industrial dispersal thesis. The latter, it is argued, proposes that a multiplicity of small industrial centers be sprinkled uniformly across the national map or among the rural population without regard to the location of natural resources. But this objection too largely breaks down in the Indian case, though it might not in a smaller, more highly specialized economy with a less diversified set of resources. For India has a diversified, geographically widely distributed collection of resources; the country is seeking to build an exceedingly diverse industrial structure; and its market is so enormous that, even at this early, low-income stage of industrialization, it can accommodate a goodly number of (regionally dispersed) suppliers of most fabricated products. All of this means that the natural-resource-oriented, and most of the larger-scale market-oriented, enterprises can fall quite naturally into a pattern that is sufficiently dispersed so that it should not take a great deal of steering of additional locational decisions to supply the populated countryside with a fairly even distribution of industrial centers.

More generally, these last few paragraphs suggest the image of a town-centered mode of development that, in the Indian context, could be flexible enough to be practicable. In some instances town centers would have clusters of quite small enterprises that would either process local primary products or make finished goods for the local market. More usually, the center would house at least a few organized enterprises that would distribute to somewhat larger areas and perhaps even to the national and/or international markets. Not uncommonly, a center would be occupied very largely by a giant enterprise with its ancillaries. Any of these enterprises could be public or private, and their locations could be either natural-resource- or market-oriented. But in all instances the centers would have the spatial characteristics, the public facilities and amenities, the proximity to, and interrelations with, agriculture, the market-building functions, the public works program, the training facilities, and the local administrative leadership necessary to their mission as generators of local regional development.

I find one further point on the economic feasibility of town-centering particularly persuasive. The strongest centripetal force operating in behalf of metropolitan-centered location commonly is said to be the pull exerted by the already concentrated markets that exist in the largest cities. But, in the case of a country at as early a stage of industrialization as India now is, it actually begs the whole longer-run locational question to put much stock in this argument. For so much of the total locational outcome is yet to be settled that the question at issue virtually comes down to this: What will the territorial disposition of demand be in the Indian economy of 1970 and 1980? At this stage, the planners still are modeling with wet clay, as it were, most of which has not yet been put in place. The locational structure, to be sure, already has gone far enough in the direction of a metropolitan-centered pattern that a determined effort now to reorient its evolving contours is bound to encounter temporary difficulties. But so much of the modeling remains to be done that very soon the emergence of a new pattern would begin to be reinforced and facilitated by the very centripetal and inertial forces that are now alleged to obstruct it. Each new plant added to a town would strengthen the local market's pull on other enterprises. The same general point can be made about the local labor market's attractiveness to occupational migrants and about the self-reinforcing growth that would be experienced, beyond a point, by smaller but expanding business communities, concentrations of business services, and pools of skilled labor.

One has to be careful not to over-state this argument, of course. Certain specialized commercial, financial, and other service establishments obviously would continue to find metropolitan locations advantageous. More generally, different degrees of centralization would continue to be technically appropriate for different activities; thus the economy would continue always to have a broad spectrum of place sizes. But none of this refutes the key argument, as far as the distribution of activities across the spectrum is concerned: While any existing locational pattern tends within limits to be self-reinforcing, this need be only a transitory, not a massive, stubborn obstacle to a government intent upon altering the economy's existing locational vectors—*provided* the decision is made and implemented early enough in the industrialization process.

I have indicated my impression that in India's case the present still is just barely "early enough" for such a locational reorientation, whereas ten years from now will be too late. In those economies whose locational paths India seems presently to be following there is accumulating evidence that the long phase of superurbanization, during which metropolitan agglomerates grow in relative as well as absolute size as the economy approaches, then enters, its era of mature industrialization, is eventually succeeded by a phase of "de-superurbanization." During the latter period the metropolitan population moves from suburbs to "exurbs," manufacturing industries increasingly flee the mounting congestion of the metropolitan centers, and new plants, especially the branch factories of major private enterprises, seek decentralized locations in smaller hinterland towns. But this process of undoing what, in the first place, has been overdone is slow, costly, and painful. It must be triggered by, then itself aggravate, the peculiarly intractable problem of "center city blight," must overcome deep accretions of vested interests, ordinarily struggle to break loose from obsolescent public administrative structures, waste a great deal of capital, and subject millions of people to distressing dislocations.

Thus if the government of India allows the economy's presently emerging locational contours to form and jell as much as they will during this decade under the passive locational policies now in force, India not only will be committed to the emergence of metropolitan agglomerates far more enormous than anything the world has yet seen; it will have missed its opportunity to short-circuit the "superurbanization-de-superurbanization cycle." The country will have passed up its chance to head directly for the centering pattern that it may, in any case, eventually approximate by the far more circuitous and costly least-resistance route. Moreover, this pattern that for the moment is directly accessible is not just one that may suit Indian conditions at some future date; it is better fitted to India's political and social needs, and probably to its factor proportions, than is metropolitan centering right now. Thus the immediate opportunity for waging a successful campaign in behalf of town-centered industrialization is, beyond doubt, one of the most strategic that Indian economic policymakers ever will encounter. But it is, as I say, a short-lived opportunity, and it appears to be going by default.

The Lack of Focus in Current Locational Policies

As implied at the start of this chapter, an apologist for present policy might be able to cite enough language in the Third Five Year Plan document and to point to enough allegedly supporting programs to contend plausibly that the government already is doing "everything it possibly can" to implement town centering. Yet I strongly suspect that the situation has not altered materially from that which I last saw in mid-1960. At that time a great many influential Indians in and out of the government were inclined, in principle, enthusiastically to endorse medium-sized demographic centers as developmental nuclei. Yet there were no procedures for systematically screening specific locational decisions and seeing that they conformed to criteria calculated effectively to implement this preference. There was no evident provision in the organization or principal-staff assignments of the Planning Commission for any comprehensive effort at spatial planning. The diversity of agricultural, industrial, electric power, community-development, cooperative, and other quasi-autonomous functional programs extending into the countryside reflected no common centering policy. And specific policies often appeared to ricochet aimlessly from one center size extreme to another, in a manner that could only suggest little real grasp of what technologically feasible decentralized industrialization might offer and entail.

The early record of the industrial estate scheme was a case in point. The idea, developed in Britain and elsewhere, was that the government should undertake to provide integrated complexes of plant facilities and of electric-power, machine-shop, and other common services, at modest rents and fees, for clusters of moderate-sized manufacturers. It made, and continues to make, good sense in the Indian context as a device for facilitating the establishment of new manufacturing firms in desired locations. It was taken up in the Second Five Year Plan. However, besides failing to supply their clientele with much more than just rental space, most of the initial industrial estates were located in the immediate environs of large, including the very largest, cities. By 1959 authorities had developed guilt feelings about the way the program was compounding metropolitan-centered industrial location, and orders then went out from New Delhi to the state small industries commissioners that each should get busy and inaugurate at least one "rural industrial estate." But now unfortunately doctrine went to the other extreme and specified that in no event should one of these new "rural industrial estates" be established in a place of more than 2,500 persons. That is to say, rural developers were to do things the hard way; the new industrial estates were necessarily to be village-centered; they were deliberately to defy any tendency toward natural centering that a local economic region had begun to exhibit for fear that the program might not qualify as being sufficiently "rural."

A similar fuzziness about centering policies can be observed in the environs of those few thriving medium-sized towns, such as Ludhiana in the Punjab, where a vigorous array of small and medium-sized enterprises, manned to a considerable extent by bicycle and bus commuters from villages within ten to fifteen miles of the town, is energizing the emergence of a local regional center of just the sort I have been touting. Typically, around the periphery of such a center one finds village industry extension officers earnestly engaged in trying to lure workers away from the small manufacturing establishments in town (which, with their several machines and with their labor forces of a dozen or two, engage in some internal specialization and have the promise of competitive viability) back to tiny metal-working and other machine-powered shops in their own villages (which can practice little or no division of labor, have little capacity for nonsubsidized survival, and require the most expensive kind of power distribution). The same sort of indecisiveness over questions of scale was evident in the cooperative movement, which, after a (Reserve-Bank-inspired) feint in the direction of consolidated multi-village societies, reverted in early 1959 to the one-society-for-every-village formula deplored in the preceding chapter.

The confusion and ineffectuality that were observable in India's centering policies a couple of years ago were rooted in a remarkably perverse conjunction of contributing factors, and this is my reason for suspecting that the situation has not altered basically since. These included the "village fetish" and the reactionary inclinations of the rural elite; the anti-experimental disposition of British-Indian bureaucracy; the deep functional fragmentation of government programs; the lack of an aggressive, well-articulated technological policy; the metropolitan-centered orientation of established "organized" industry; the extent to which past cottage-industry and small-scale-industry programs had identified industrial decentralization with the protection of archaic and inefficient production processes; the preoccupation of the country's "main-line" central economic planners with the problem of scarce-resource allocation and their resulting bias in favor of centralized decision making; and the same planners' fears of locational choices that might retard the near-term pace of aggregative industrial expansion.

The joint effect of all of these circumstances comes down to this: In the developing Indian economy thus far no major party-in-interest has emerged, nor has any really effective alliance of lesser interests turned up, in behalf of the integrated, centered development of small economic regions. As a result, there is only one agency in India now—the nation's top political leadership acting on its own initiative—that can possibly supply the impulse necessary for a concerted drive toward town-centered industrialization during the short time that remains for such a move.

To ask for such a drive from a leadership that has been so long at the helm is to demand a great deal. For the Prime Minister and his Cabinet would need not only quickly to recast their major development priorities, but to press the town-centering cause against a formidable array of opponents and skeptics, inside as well as outside the governmental structure. They would have to recapture all of the zeal of a youthful regime, particularly in their effort to recruit, train, and, despite the inhibitions of the civil service tradition, adequately empower gifted and dynamic leaders for regional development programs. And for all of these pains they could expect little in the way of quick political reward.

Moreover, aside from near-term political hazards, it might be felt that the injection of a strong town-centered cast into the next phase of the development effort would aggravate what the Nehru government has rightly feared as the greatest fundamental danger threatening the viability of the Indian polity—that of sectional and communal divisiveness. On this score my own expectations would be the opposite. For regional divisiveness and discontent with central authority are very much a function of the number of specific irritations that localities encounter in their dealings with the Center, and this in turn depends considerably upon the extensiveness of the latter's direct, overt interventions into local affairs. Therefore, the more the Center can assign development decision making to local and regional levels without compromising the basic development strategy, the less chance there will be, it seems to me, for national unity to become tattered by petty irritations.

But this last is an arguable point, and its very uncertainty, when combined with the fact that a really determined push in behalf of dispersed centering would surely be an arduous, politically thankless undertaking in the short run, probably will deter the present leadership from seizing its fleeting opportunity for deploying Indian development along predominantly town-centered lines. Yet it also seems plain to me that the present leadership does still have a choice in this matter; it still has the capacity, the courage, and the charismatic authority to adopt and make good an effective redirection of locational policies during the sixties if it should become sufficiently persuaded of the urgency of so doing. This assumption is a necessary one if the questions to which we now turn—concerning the content of a town-centered locational program—are to have any practical relevance.

Needed Locational Staffing and Research

If the government of India were suddenly to commit itself to the energetic implementation of its announced preference for decentralized industrialization and dispersed urbanization, it would encounter a dilemma characteristic of reform efforts: It would lack much of the information needed for a definitive policy design; at the same time, it would have to begin to act long before all of the missing information could be gathered and digested. The sensible course would be to launch the staff and research aspect and the operational aspect of the effort simultaneously. The former should be placed organizationally so that there would be a ready opportunity for using the new data and new considerations it brought to light for advising and informing current locational decisions. And it should adjust its research priorities and timetable to fit the necessary dates for future decisions. Meanwhile, although beginning to act at once, those making operational decisions should confine them, where possible, to actions whose informational base was comparatively secure or to forms sufficiently experimental to facilitate modification as new experience and/or research findings came to hand. In this general way, waste of time and waste from error could be jointly minimized.

Organizationally it would seem essential that a central office of locational research be established at once as a distinct but integral unit within the Planning Commission staff. Such an office, besides gathering and analyzing data in its own right, would coordinate and cross-reference location-related studies by other public and private research organizations. It would develop, for the guidance of public and private decision makers, progressively more explicit formulations of the government's locational policies and of criteria implementing those policies. And it would review the locational aspects of the specific public investment projects and the agricultural, small-industry, and other development programs that would, as a matter of planning routine, be referred to it.

During the Second-Plan period no unit or senior official within the Planning Commission was specifically and primarily charged, as the proposed office would be, with concentrating on the spatial aspects of over-all plan design. Indeed in 1959-60 the only officially supported group that I could find specializing in this subject was a little "regional survey" unit working (with Planning Commission funds) within the Indian Statistical Institute in Calcutta. But this was too limited an effort, it was too remote from decision making in New Delhi, it had fallen too exclusively into the hands of India's small, otherwise neglected contingent of professional geographers, and it had been too inept, both administratively and substantively, in certain aspects of its performance, to have a significant impact on plan design. Until a locational research and advisory unit, well staffed with economists, technologists, and sociologists, as well as geographers, is assigned a key role near the center of the planning process and commands the active interest of the nation's top leaders, it will be hard to believe the government is serious about its alleged locational aspirations.

From the moment of its establishment such a central analytical and research unit would not lack an agenda. The following are illustrations, not a catalogue, of the topics to which it could usefully give concerted study.

1. *An inventory of town characteristics.* A variety of Indian decision makers, including those making private and public industrial investment decisions, those trying to attract industry to particular regions or to centers of particular sizes, and those deciding which social-overhead gaps in which localities should be filled first, could be greatly assisted by ready access to a comprehensive tabulation of the salient characteristics of towns in the 20,000-to-300,000 range. Such an array of information, organized by region and size class, should show each town's demographic characteristics; its present administrative, educational, training, health, water, sanitation, and police facilities; the extent and type of its power supply and transport connections; the number, size, and types of its present industrial establishments; estimates of its supplies of major labor skills; its financial institutions and business services; the scope of its retail facilities, hotels, and other related amenities; the composition of its housing stock; the size and character of local produce markets and wholesalers; its proximity to what kinds of cash-crop farm production; its region's rural cooperative facilities; the kinds, quantities, and proximities of its natural resources; and the sizes of the consumer markets that lie within specified radii from the central town.

Many bits and pieces of such information have been assembled in India. In 1959 one office within the Planning Commission tabulated a few of the characteristics of towns in the 20,000-to-50,000 range. The Indian Statistical Institute's

Regional Survey Unit made a somewhat fuller tabulation for towns in the state of Mysore. Such information has been included to varying degrees in some "techno-economic surveys" of particular states by the National Council of Applied Economic Research. And there are, no doubt, many other instances of partial accumulations of such information. But no adequately comprehensive and detailed inventory of town characteristics, to my knowledge, ever has been made readily accessible. Such information easily could be culled from the 1961 census and from regular reports, or if need be, from special reports received from the states and, indirectly, from their local administrators. Plainly a comprehensive compilation of town characteristics should be made immediately, be released along with appropriate summaries, and then be periodically updated.

2. *Studies of the industrial-scale and market-size implications of technological choices.* As noted already, we have much to learn yet about what, in the Indian context, the interrelationships are and may tend to become between optimal (that is, factor-cost minimizing) technological choices and efficient scales of production for different manufactured products, let alone for many consumer and business services. Particularly is this true of the new indigenous capital-saving innovations that we can hope an explicit and aggressive technological policy will promote. While there is a ferment of generalized interest in these matters in India as well as in such non-Indian quarters as university economics departments in the West and the United Nations' Bureau of Economic Affairs, there is an urgent need, as emphasized in Chapter 3, for a high-priority, organizationally pinpointed effort within the Indian planning process to bring all of this theorizing about technological desiderata concretely to bear on the Indian situation. Presumably the specialized staff that would serve such a newly sharpened and galvanized technological policy should be primarily responsible for analyzing technological alternatives. However, the staff supporting a newly galvanized locational policy should collaborate closely in this effort, especially with regard to the scalar dimensions of the alternatives. In

particular, the latter group would be concerned to study what size and density of markets would, in the light of the technological possibilities, serve to support efficient scales of production for different products.

3. *Studies of competitive structure in the context of dispersed industrial location.* The tenor of the present discussion has been that the government of India ought actively to promote the maximum decentralization of industrial activity that is consistent with technological progressiveness and efficiency of production. However, if one's speculations remain sufficiently abstract, it is easy to imagine that a single-minded pursuit of this locational policy could inflict India with a rash of localized monopolies. Such, it appears, might tend to be the case if the government were assiduously to promote centering so dispersed as to generate local markets that could support only one efficient unit of many manufacturing processes and if, at the same time, industrial promoters succeeded in establishing, product by product, one such unit in every center in which the local market had room for it.

Actually, this hypothesis may be too unrealistic to warrant concern. It imputes, to say the least, an improbable rigor to locational policy. It may underestimate the number of product lines in which very small productive units will be able to hold their own competitively, and it probably underestimates, in any case, the extent to which variously scaled processes for producing the same products will survive and thereby continue to compete in the same local markets. Implicitly, moreover, the fear that an all-out industrial dispersion policy could lead India into a market-structure trap may exaggerate, in the case of many products, the value of a local producer's locational advantage in his own market. Similar suppliers in neighboring centers might offer enough competition so that all that would be needed for guarding against the excesses and inefficiencies of local "monopolists" would be to keep the channels of inter-town trade freely open.

All the same, this is not a time to accept blindly such summary reassurances. As I shall be noting in succeeding chapters, there already is some evidence that private enterprise in India stands in need of a more effective anti-monopoly program. Particular pains should be taken to see that a new locational policy does not compound the problem. Thus a locational research unit might very appropriately explore the market structures that seem likely to emerge in different industries under different centering assumptions; consider carefully the feasibility of formulating standards as to the minimum numbers of alternative suppliers that would be needed to maintain effective competition in critical product lines; examine accordingly the desirability of reducing the average degree of dispersion in the centering pattern that locational policy promotes enough to accommodate such competition; study whether, in promoting industrial dispersion, the government should, on market-structure grounds, adopt a favorable, neutral, or adverse posture toward the spread of branch factories in lieu of independent local establishments (an issue that is by no means clear); and consider how policies in such other areas as credit, government procurement, cooperatives, and government enterprise might facilitate constructive competition in a dispersed industrial setting.

4. *Studies of the "company town" problem.* A town-centered scheme of industrial location, by locating most of India's largest manufacturing establishments in comparatively small population centers, would tend, unless effective counter-steps are taken, to produce a lot of what Americans call "company towns"—that is, communities not only whose labor market, but whose public administration, commercial and service establishments, housing supply, educational and cultural affairs, and even politics tend to be dominated by a single large industrial establishment. India long has had a few such towns. There is, for example, the classic case of Tata hegemony in Jamshedpur (now a city of 300,000), where, according to local testimony, the effective control of most aspects of municipal life still rests with the Tata Iron and Steel Company. Lately the list has been growing rapidly with the establishment of large public-sector enterprises at places like Sindri, Rourkela, Bhilai, Durgapur, and Naya Nangal.

At the start of a new factory-*cum*-township project it may facilitate planning and initial construction to have both the industrial and the municipal social-overheads aspects of the endeavor under a single, authoritative administration. But as soon as the factory begins to get into operation, collateral responsibility for township administration tends to make the management of the enterprise cumbersome and potentially inefficient. More serious: the managements of new company towns because of their impulse to develop "model townships" are strongly disposed, in view of the wide economic and cultural gaps that typically exist between the new community and its environs, to create enclaves that are isolated administratively and even tend to be cut off economically from their immediately surrounding regions. This of course, minimizes the new towns' effectiveness as nuclei for local development. Still more serious: the company town, if it survives as such for very long, is a fundamentally unhealthy political phenomenon. On this count, it makes little difference whether the dominating enterprise is public or private. In either event, company domination forecloses the emergence of effective and responsible local self-government.

In one or two of the public-sector company towns I have visited in India the resident managers have exhibited at least some awareness of, and concern about, this problem, but elsewhere they have seemed almost entirely insensitive to it. The subject is one on which a locational research unit would have a good deal of fresh ground to break. It should investigate the various patterns of local administration and of town-country relations now emerging in population centers that presently are dominated by single enterprises; it should consider the extent to which, and the circumstances under which, the deliberate addition of a second sizable enterprise to a company town might loosen the dominant company's grip on local affairs; it should examine the desirability, even during the period when local administration needs mainly to be imported from the outside, of providing such administration through a line of governmental command that is entirely or largely independent of the resident company; and it should devise suggested programs for developing responsible representative local government in one-company towns as soon as possible.

5. *Other locational studies.* In addition to some of the less obvious subjects just noted, a locational research staff within the Planning Commission should also, of course, join the power and transport planners in re-examining the centering implications of programs in those fields. In conjunction with manpower, industrial, and educational planners, it should devise a strategy for the spacing of training and educational activities. It should undertake continuing studies of the changes in general public and rural administration that would facilitate town-centered development. And, as a reflection of all of its other studies, it should be trying to identify more and more precisely just what relative distribution of population and activities through the nation's center-size spectrum would best serve India's long-term interests. Meanwhile, however, decision makers will have to be answering this last and ultimate locational question experimentally.

Immediate Policies for Town-Centered Development

With time for an effective redirection of India's industrial location rapidly running out, one can plead that the government of India push in the direction of town-centered development quickly and aggressively—but not recklessly. While it seems clear that most of India's increments of industry and of nonagricultural jobs during the sixties should be situated in places larger than villages and smaller than metropolises, it is altogether improbable, as we have seen, that most of the new activity can or should be fitted into centers that fall in one narrow size range. In particular, it is likely that many of the smaller centers in and around which it is desirable to organize agricultural and small-enterprise development will be too small quickly to attract much organized industry. Under these circumstances, the sensible course for the government in the exploratory stages of an intensified town-centering effort would be to stick to what is feasible, working, as it were, from both ends of the center-size spectrum.

On the one hand, many of the larger and medium-sized newly locating manufacturers who could be induced to select a district town in the 100,000-to-300,000 range instead of a metropolitan site would adamantly refuse, at present, to try a town in the 20,000-to-50,000 range. In such cases it would be foolish policy to insist on the smaller-town choice and very probably wind up with no new factory at all. Instead, the realistic course with respect to larger enterprises would be to focus initially upon diverting new industry from metropolitan to larger-town locations, at the same time taking advantage of a willingness to locate in still smaller centers whenever it arises and recognizing that, in time, a further dispersion of organized industry may be in order. Not only might such further dispersion become increasingly attractive to the enterprises themselves as incomes and population in the smaller centers continued to expand; the same factors would make such dispersion increasingly consistent with the maintenance of a competitive market structure.

On the other hand, in the preceding chapter, where we were concerned with agricultural development, with the collateral, integrated development of small local processing and fabricating enterprises, with the promotion of vigorous agro-industrial markets, and with the organization of rural public works activity, we saw the manifold advantages of centering that lies as close to (although above) the village level as is technologically and administratively feasible. That next higher level consists at present of the nation's approximately 5,000 development blocks whose total populations fall mostly into the 60,000-to-100,000 range and whose potential centers mostly are market (*mandi*) towns or larger villages that either now are of the 20,000-to-50,000 class or might shortly grow to that size as a result of a center-building effort. It is a fair inference from our earlier discussion that India's whole rural outlook depends crucially upon the degree to which a sizable portion of the nation's development energies and imagination now can be focused at this block-center level.

What is now needed, therefore, is a double-pronged attack that centralizes agricultural, village-industry, cooperative, and other village programs upward to block-center towns at the same time that it decentralizes new major-industrial location downward at least to the district-town level. One could not expect both aims to point to the same optimum center size immediately or, very possibly, ever. But it would be essential, were such a town-centering strategy adopted, that the two be recognized as divisions of the same strategy and (contrary to Indian administration's functional fragmentation tradition) be thoroughly coordinated. For the latter purpose, as well as that of coming to terms with the operational impossibility of effectively introducing a new program simultaneously in either 300 district towns or 5,000 block centers it would be appropriate to undertake both branches of the effort at the same time on a selected-district basis. Whenever a district town was taken up for promotion as a major industrial site, a scheme for integrated agro-industrial development would then be launched, with new and/or reinforced leadership and broadened powers, at each of the district's block centers.

The Indian authorities, were they to adopt such an approach, would know far better than I how to work out an appropriate articulation between the district-centered and block-centered elements in such a joint program. The trick would be to keep the two branches of the joint program adequately coordinated without at the same time encroaching upon the broad delegation of discretion that, according to the present analysis, should be made to the block level. The Indian authorities also, were they determined to implement the kind of town-centered development philosophy suggested here, would know well enough what substantive content should be injected into the district-centered and block-centered branches of their program. Partly to save the present discussion from the appearance of inconclusiveness, however, I want to sketch very briefly (and, in part, repetitiously) some tentative impressions.

Much of the decentralizing-downward effect that the government of India presumably wishes to work upon major industrial location could be accomplished in the ordinary exercise of its power to license new industrial establishments. The government would simply deny permission to locate factories of more than a specified size in population centers of more than a specified size—or to locate near enough to such population centers that their labor forces reasonably could be expected to commute from city to factory. Any such policy, it can be readily agreed, should be formulated as a set of clear-cut, readily interpretable standards; it should be applied even-handedly, and to public as well as private enterprises; and it should make some, although limited, provision for clearly justified exceptions—such as, perhaps, the metropolitan enterprise that wished to add facilities to retain its share of its metropolitan market.

However, it only beclouds the issue to damn the use of the licensing power to deny metropolitan location on the grounds that it is simply a "negative" approach to the problem. Of course it is. It is also a politically hazardous approach. But, in view of the centripetal pulls upon industrial location, it likewise is a virtually indispensable tactic if the locational authorities mean business. As for breadth of application, such a foreclosure policy should be rigorously applied, it seems to me, to the five largest Indian cities and their immediate environs—Bombay, Calcutta, Madras, Delhi-New Delhi, and Hyderabad. I should be inclined myself to apply nearly as rigorous standards to India's next seven cities (Ahmedabad, Bangalore, Kanpur, Lucknow, Poona, Benares, and Nagpur), the population of all of which exceeded a half-million in 1961.

The next cities—those that in 1961 fell into the 300,000-to-500,000 range present a more difficult choice. A number of these latterly have been gathering an industrial momentum relative to the largest cities that it would be unfortunate to arrest; there may be growing demands upon them to provide specialized services and products to their regions; and probably "they should be aided . . . to mature, to round out their complement of economic activities, and—particularly—to become bastions of 'terminal defense' against further migration to the eleven large cities."[6] Yet it seems to me there should be

[6] The quotation is from an unpublished paper, "India's Case for Industrial Dispersion" by William S. Royce, member of the Stanford Research Institute and from 1958 to 1960 a consultant with the National Council of Applied Economic Research, New Delhi. Mr. Royce's analysis of the dispersion issue is one that I largely

little positive promotion of new industrial location in this size range. Where particular locational decisions could be readily tilted toward smaller towns, this should be done, other things being equal.

Proceeding downward from the 300,000 mark, we quickly encounter most of the district towns that, I have suggested, probably should constitute the primary target area of industrial-dispersal policy. Thus far I have been saying that "negative" inducements toward location in this area are essential. But now it becomes equally important to emphasize that they are not enough. There is need also for positive facilitation. However, given the help of the "negative" policies, the governmental facilitation that is needed for wedding sizable enterprises to sizable towns can take the form, less of subsidies or other specific financial and promotional inducements, than of measures that fill the town's social-overhead gaps and augment its range of training, financial, and other business services. It is to such matters that those pressing district-town industrialization should primarily attend.

Block centers, on the other hand, are the points at which the government's full capacities for instigating and structuring, not just for facilitating, an interrelated set of development activities need to be brought most decisively to bear. This chapter and its predecessor have mentioned a variety of steps that would need to be taken as parts, or in support, of an intensified program of block-centered development, including effective consolidation of cottage- and small-scale industrial promotion efforts; strengthening of agricultural and industrial extension; provision of appropriate training programs; attraction, wherever possible, of units of organized industry; and establishment of strong block-centered cooperatives that would provide cultivators and small processors with improved supplies, marketing, and credit facilities, would extend retailing into the countryside, and would help, along with other measures, to activate local markets. All of these elements and more

share and to which I am greatly indebted. Mr. Royce left Benares out of his list, not anticipating that it would have exceeded 500,000 by 1961. Hence his mention of "eleven large cities" rather than twelve.

would belong in the effort. Yet there are two steps above all, that should be taken first and that, if taken, would most clearly signal a new departure in Indian rural policy.

The first is the provision, at the block level, of a wholly new order of administrative leadership endowed with increased resources and greatly expanded powers. This is not the place for an extended discussion of the recruitment, training, and responsibilities of this new breed of Block Development Officer—to whom, for purposes of differentiation, I should give some other title, such as Block Development Executive. Let me say only that I believe that this new group of block leaders should be regarded, quite literally, as the most critical class of development personnel in the whole government service; that members of the group should in salary and grade outrank certainly the Assistant District Collectors, and perhaps the District Collectors, through whom they would report upward; that, in response to a sufficiently resourceful recruitment effort, Indian society in a short space of time easily could produce 5,000 exceptionally gifted, forceful, and perceptive Block Development Executives; but that to find enough of them, recruitment probably would need to range well beyond the established civil service framework; that the positions should be of sufficient status, however, to attract many of the best I.A.S. personnel as applicants; that the powers of the position should accord with its status; and that specific training for the position, which, despite the exigencies of time, should not be hurried, should seek, among other objectives, to imbue the trainees with a vision of a progressive town-centered Indian society and an awareness of their calling to play a catalytic role in its emergence.

The second point concerns the initial and, to begin with, the foremost step in the program that this new block leadership would undertake: It would organize and, for an extended period, maintain a greatly expanded public works effort—less inhibited than in the past by official anti-inflationary anxieties and very possibly assisted, as to "financing," by P.L. 480 surplus foods from the United States. Such an effort, as we have seen, would augment farm productivity, supply social overheads for local industry, begin the retraining of occupational out-migrants from agriculture, and help to trigger an interacting expansion of farm and nonfarm incomes. The block development effort would move on quickly and logically to reinforce these ramifying consequences of a public works program. But the initial point of focus would be that program itself.

Conclusion

The locational decision making that India will be doing during the balance of the sixties will largely determine the spatial configuration of the economy for many decades to come. At the moment that decision making rather reminds one of an automobile rolling downhill in a fairly deeply rutted track, gathering momentum toward a destination that many regard as foreordained. But in many respects full-blown metropolitan agglomeration is an appalling destination for India, and it also is an unnecessary one. For a wrench on the wheel and some determined steering can break the vehicle free from the ruts and, without more than passing discomfort, set it on a different track toward a different destination—if all of this can be done before the car gathers further momentum.

This other destination—that of a technologically progressive, politically integrated, but geographically decentralized society organized along town-centered lines—would be something comparatively new in the world. Some of the earlier developing economies may now be working their way around to it by a painful, circuitous route. But passing, as they did, through their economically formative stages before their scientific knowledge was far advanced, the older industrial economies never really encountered in their early growth periods an opportunity for anticipatory escape from metropolitan agglomeration.

The sort of town-centering toward which India still has an opportunity to make a direct run may well be peculiarly fitted to the needs of heavily populated, capital-poor countries whose development problem, in effect, is to make the technological adaptations necessary for applying late-twentieth-century science to what is, by Western standards, a pre-nineteenth-century set of factor proportions. In any event, the town-centered pattern seems uniquely suited to the achievement in traditional, village-oriented societies of a rural transformation by largely noncoercive political and administrative techniques.

The destination, therefore, has an unmistakable appeal, not only for India but for many other nations watching the Indian experiment. The track to the destination, to be sure, has the typical disadvantages of a short cut. Although more direct, it is imperfectly defined and, at points may be a bit bumpy. However, its general outlines, both administratively and in terms of program content, are quite visible; it appears to contain no grave hazards. And there is reason to believe that, once turned onto this new course, the economy could proceed along it with no significant loss of momentum. Indeed, before long there might be a gain in momentum.

The real question is simply whether the turn will be made and made in time—while it is still possible to escape the ruts. Everything now is up to the driver. The passengers at this point, are no help; while generally holding a felicitous view of the alternative destination, many have mixed feelings about the feasibility and/or wisdom of veering off the beaten track, and some of the loudest have vested interests in sticking with it.

The most urgent, least comprehended major development decision facing the Indian government is whether now—on its own initiative and without further delay—it is going to swing the wheel hard over and, despite the initial bumps and the protests from the back seat, start heading directly for a spatial pattern of development that suits India's own times and conditions.

8 THE OUTLOOK FOR ORGANIZED PRIVATE ENTERPRISE—DOMESTIC AND FOREIGN

Next to India's "neutralism," Americans are most bothered about the role envisaged for private enterprise in its present development scheme. Actually their anxieties are considerably exaggerated. Yet the projected division of labor in India between the private and public sectors is, after all, significantly different from that in the United States, and it is natural for Americans—as indeed it is for Indians—to be concerned about the outlook for private, including foreign private, enterprise in the Indian development process.

The limitations of my discussion of this subject must be emphasized. It does not penetrate many detailed issues that merit examination, attempts little in the way of quantitative analysis, and rests on a smaller base of first-hand investigation than do some of the other chapters in this book.[1] Nonetheless,

[1] Even though the present subject claimed less than the one-fifth portion of my year in India that I had planned to devote to it, the following discussion does reflect interviews with about forty Indian private industrialists (including a half dozen of the highest-level private-sector executives) whom I met individually, in pairs, or in small groups, in Bombay, Calcutta, Madras, Bangalore, Mangalore, Jamshedpur, and Ludhiana; similar interviews with about a dozen executives of major American and British firms operating in India (and subsequently with several executives of parent firms in the United States); visits to major public-sector enterprises and their managements at Sindri, Alwaye, Naya Nangal, Durgapur, Rourkela, and Bhilai; extended exchanges with the principal staff personnel of the Federation of Indian Chambers of Commerce and Industry, the Bombay Merchants Chamber of Commerce, and the Bengal Chamber of Commerce (Calcutta); discussion of the private sector with officials of the Planning Commission and of the central Ministries of Commerce and Industry and of Finance, with the responsible officials in three state governments, with officers of the the Reserve Bank of India, the State Bank of India, and the Industrial Credit and Investment Corporation of India, with United States aid and embassy personnel, and with representatives in New Delhi of the World Bank and the U. S. Export-Import Bank; exchanges with other Western economists, in some instances

I feel fairly confident of most of the generalized observations the chapter ventures. Compared with other aspects of the Indian development problem, the private enterprise question is relatively easy to take a position on.

In focussing on "organized" industry, especially in the mining, processing, and fabricating fields, we shall be considering, according to the usual Indian definition, enterprises without electric-powered machinery having as few as one hundred employees and mechanized enterprises with as few as fifty employees. However, most of the output of private organized industry is produced by firms employing hundreds and, in many instances, thousands of workers.

Private Enterprise and the Government's Industrial Policy: The Rhetoric

The American business executive or congressman who, without briefing or forewarning, tunes in on public dialogue in India on industrial policy is apt to find the debate exceedingly bitter and may assume that the issue is whether private enterprise is going to be, if not entirely extinguished, at least confined within exceedingly narrow limits. For several reasons, however, this rhetoric does not mean all that it appears to say to the Western ear.

In the first place, the Western observer has an intercultural semantic gap to cross. In India "capitalism" is a bad word; capitalism historically has been linked to colonialism; and Indian like other Asian intellectuals, whether or not generally Marxian in their thought, have been deeply infected with the Marxian doctrine of economic imperialism. "Socialism," on the other hand, is a good word, somewhat as "democracy" now is the world over. Everyone appropriates it as a word of art, injecting whatever content he chooses. In its least formidable, and very probably most common, Indian meaning, "socialism" connotes simply a society that offers growing eco-

---

more actively engaged along the same lines; and some discussion with specialists in Indian universities and private research organizations.

nomic security and improving, increasingly equal, opportunity to all of its citizens. Thus the Congress Party's official adoption of first a "socialistic," and then a "socialist," pattern of society as a long-run policy goal involves no necessary commitment to a predominantly nationalized pattern of productive activity.

Second, much of the private-sector attack on the government's industrial policy in India, especially as propounded by the leaders of the Swatantra Party and by certain interests within the Bombay business community, is misleadingly shrill. The facts are that the Bombay and Calcutta stock markets have remained notably buoyant in recent years; that frequently they have spurted upward, for example, in response to the same new government budgets that the business federations concurrently have been officially condemning; that most Indian industrialists have continued to support the Congress; and that the few major industrialists who have been issuing blanket public indictments of government economic policy have usually at the same time been investing heavily in private industrial expansion.

In the third place, the rhetoric on the government's side of the debate also has been exaggerated. A variety of factors have motivated the present leadership to show a far more hostile attitude toward private industry in its formal political pronouncements than could be inferred from day-to-day decisions of the same leaders. For one thing, the stereotypes of the independence struggle still are powerful, and there is still a linkage, as I have said, between industrial capitalism and colonialism in the Indian mind. Moreover, the image that major private enterprise created for itself in India during the first half of this century was not one with which a mass political movement could easily ally. The earlier British enterprises producing for the Indian market tended to be rather hard-bitten, high-margin, low-volume operations that catered to the economic elite. And the businessmen of the traditional Indian commercial communities, whence much of India's early indigenous entrepreneurship came, have engaged altogether too much in sharp practices. Their enterprises, too often characterized by a management selected for reasons of family, caste, and status, by discriminatory employment policies, by radical inequalities among the incomes they distribute, and by conspicuous entrepreneurial affluence, thus far have developed a much less socially responsible cast, on average, than American business has acquired during the past generation.

Furthermore, the Congress often has needed to forestall attacks from the Communist Party on its extreme left flank. In addition, some of the senior members of the government, evidently including Jawaharlal Nehru himself, individually have had a genuine philosophical preference for the progressive emergence of a non-acquisitive society that would be far more rigorously "socialistic" than that term usually suggests in India.[2] Still further, the whole neo-Gandhian, cottage-industry, small-enterprise complex of interests has required some accommodation, and this typically has been at the overt expense of organized industry. And finally, some of the present leadership has had a long-standing fear that concentrations of private economic power will emerge that are not held sufficiently and formally accountable to the public interest.

This last concern led the Nehru government to adopt the principle that where concentrated power could not be avoided, for reasons of efficient scale or because of the strategic character of the products, the usual remedy would be public ownership and management. Such is the underlying rationale of the government's formal Industrial Policy Resolution, first issued in 1948 and then, in revised form, in April 1956 at the start of the Second Five Year Plan. The latter, still officially in effect at this time, specifies three groups of industries: "A" (including munitions, atomic energy, iron and steel, heavy engineering and heavy electrical plants, coal, oil, most mining, aircraft, air transport, railways, shipbuilding, communications, and electrical generation and distribution), "the future development of which will be the exclusive responsibility of the state"; "B" (including some mining, aluminum, machine tools, ferroalloys and tool steels, heavy chemicals, essential drugs,

[2] In this connection the rumor that the Prime Minister took a personal hand in drafting the introductory chapter of the Third Five Year Plan document (which extolls the virtues of socialism in a way that rather belies the pragmatic tone of the bulk of the document) is an interesting one.

fertilizers, synthetic rubber, and road and sea transport) "which will be progressively state-owned and in which the state will therefore generally take the initiative in establishing new undertakings, but in which private enterprise will also be expected to supplement the effort of the state"; and "C" the residual category, whose "future development will, in general, be left to the initiative and enterprise of the private sector."

The 1956 Industrial Policy Resolution naturally caused a great deal of consternation among Western observers. It was a policy prescription that scarcely any American would have written. Even if it still were the effective policy of the government, however, it would be only fair to recognize it as a legitimate attempt to answer in advance a problem—that of how reliably to assure the social responsibility of large aggregations of private economic power—with which the United States and other Western countries are visibly still struggling. The latter, most Westerners think, are gradually working out a series of partial, rather subtle, sometimes paradoxical answers that probably will serve their needs. But these are not the simple, forthright, readily discernible solutions that are likely to appeal to the architects of a new economy who want their new institutional constructions to be "logical." Westerners can well criticize India's Industrial Policy Resolution as being too simple and too doctrinaire an answer to the problem it addressed. But they should be slow to disparage it as being insincere or anti-democratic.

The Private-Sector—Public-Sector Split in Practice

The fact is, however, that the rigid categories and austere phrases of the Industrial Policy Resolution of 1956 in no sense adequately indicate the present disposition of the Indian government toward organized private enterprise. In practice the scope for private expansion is subject to compromise. Not only is the private sector presently faring far better than the laissez-faire publicists indicate, it does not by any means necessarily face the long-run relative shrinkage that the Industrial Policy Resolution seems to promise. In practice, indeed, the whole private-sector issue is far less controversial than the rhetoric suggests.

Even in 1956 the government showed no consistent hostility to private industry. In the Lok Sabha on May 25th of that year, for example, just a month after the passage of the Industrial Policy Resolution, the Prime Minister said:

> I have no shadow of doubt that, if we say "lop off the private sector" we cannot replace it adequately. We have not got the resources to replace it, and the result would be that our productive apparatus will suffer. And why should we do it? I don't understand. We have our industries, there is a vast sector, and we have to work it. Let the State go on building up its plants and industries as far as its resources permit. Why should we fritter away our energy in pushing out somebody who is doing it in the private sector?

> There is no reason except that the private sector might build up monopoly, might be building economic power to come in the way of our growth. I can understand "Prevent that, control that, plan for that"; but when there is such a vast field to cover, it is foolish to take charge of the whole field when you are totally incapable of using that huge area yourself. Therefore, you must not only permit the private sector, but I say, encourage it in its own field.

And since 1956 the government has been growing increasingly "pragmatic," to use its own term, in its attitude toward the private sector. It has taken pains to augment the credit facilities available to private industrial borrowers, has apparently abandoned any idea of nationalizing existing private firms extensively, and latterly has been granting permission for private ventures without close attention to the Industrial Policy Resolution's formal definition of sector boundaries. The Third-Plan document, while saying that "the expansion of industry will continue to be governed by the Industrial Policy Resolution of April, 1956," immediately goes on to adopt a conciliatory tone:

> As in the Second Plan the roles of the public and private sectors are conceived of as supplementary and complementary

to one another. For example, in the case of nitrogenous fertilizers where the public sector has already assumed a dominant role, it is envisaged that during the Third Plan the private sector will enter this field in a bigger way than in the past and supplement the efforts of the public sector. In the case of pig iron, the policy has been relaxed to allow the establishment of plants in the private sector with a maximum capacity of 100,000 tons per year as compared to units of 15,000 tons permitted so far. Programs for the manufacture of dyestuffs, plastics and drugs in the private sector will be largely complementary to the program for the manufacture of primary aromatic compounds as by-products at the steel works and of organic intermediates to be undertaken in the public sector. Similarly, whereas the manufacture of bulk drugs will be organized in a big way in the public sector, the further processing of bulk drugs will also be undertaken in the private sector.

Part of this new "pragmatism" simply re-states the fact that the private business community, whatever the rhetoric of the moment, always has been substantially represented within the Nehru government and the Congress Party. The party continues to be dependent financially upon major industrial contributors, and the government numbers among its ministers and senior officials many with strong sympathies for the private sector. In addition the government's recent shift away from doctrinaire restraint of private enterprise reflects certain lessons learned during the course of the Second Five Year Plan.

It is true that one of these lessons—one that became operative only as the planners began to get down to the task of operating a really integrated, closely calculated program of industrial expansion—would (standing alone) tend to tilt marginal choices in the direction of the public sector. This is a phasing problem. Even though Indian planners have some distance yet to go in this regard, as Chapter 5 suggests, they have been growing increasingly mindful of lead-times, of the fact that if an internally consistent import-minimizing pattern of production is to be built, some projects have got to be started far in advance of the time when the targeted volume of end products is due to emerge. Often awakening rather belatedly to the urgency of this lead-time consideration, the programmers frequently have felt that the only way for the government to make certain that these long-lead projects get started on time is to start them itself. Such is part of the explanation at least of the degree to which the Third Plan assigns expansion in such Category "B" industries as machinery and machine-tool manufacture to the public sector. However, the net impact of this pro-public-sector consideration on the government's operative industrial policy has been more than offset by three other lessons learned during the Second-Plan years.

First, government officials were surprised by the buoyancy of private industrial investment during that planning period. As we saw earlier, the vigor of the private sector's appetite for growth, catching the planners by surprise, precipitated a foreign-exchange crisis and so injected some serious discontinuities into the phasing of the over-all expansion. But one net effect of the episode was substantially to increase the government's appreciation of the private sector's capacity for making and implementing expansion decisions.

Second, there was a growing official appreciation during the Second-Plan years of the fact that entry of foreign private enterprise, especially into joint ventures with Indian firms, provides access to a type and quantity, not only of foreign exchange, but of technical assistance that can scarcely be secured by other means.

Third, the government acquired a far greater appreciation of the complexities of public-enterprise management during the latter fifties. There was also a mounting appreciation of the need to free public enterprises from detailed ministerial direction in the interests of efficiency. But this view also generated a corollary doubt—that the problem of assuring socially responsible behavior on the part of the large quasi-autonomous public enterprise might not, after all, be notably easier or different than it is in the case of the large private enterprise. The same experience that has generated such reflections has also, as we shall be noting, led to constructive reform in public-enterprise management. But in the process the public-sector "solution" to the problem of concentrations of economic power has lost a good bit of its attraction.

Organized private industry also has had a hand in improving business-government relations since the middle fifties. The period, as we shall have occasion to note later, has witnessed a substantial initial spread of professionalized management concepts and practices among major private-sector enterprises. Progressive elements in the business community, urged on and reinforced by the staffs of some of the major business organizations (notably that of the Federation of Indian Chambers of Commerce and Industry), have been urging private industry's responsibility to support the nation's long-term expansion objectives and to make its own efforts conform with the government's development scheme. Nor have these attitudes been wholly a matter of self-effacing business statesmanship. Rather, most of the country's more flexible, enterprising (and "pragmatic") corporate managers have been quick to appreciate (a) the necessary social overheads, (b) the relatively reliable framework of expanding demand, and (c) the protected domestic markets that comprehensive national economic planning of the Second-Plan and Third-Plan variety supply to new and expanding private ventures.

It would be nonsense, of course, to suggest that there is no longer any friction between the government of India and the private sector or that the latter's prospects are, in all respects, either evident or bright. Later I shall be underscoring certain problems, some of which presently confront the sector, others of which it poses to the economy at large. Nevertheless, it is a fair generalization that Indian private organized enterprise as a whole never before has thrived or enjoyed such effective opportunities for expansion as it has since the start of the Second Plan. Moreover, as became clear in Chapter 4, the sector's prospect for continued absolute growth during the Third-Plan period is secure and its chance of maintaining, or even of increasing, its share of total productive activity as the economy continues to grow after this decade is by no means yet foreclosed. The latter is an issue over which India's government leadership presently is divided. The outcome will depend partly on the political realignments that occur as the sixties proceed. But also it is apt to depend considerably on the performance of private enterprise during the next few years.

The Situation and Prospects of Foreign Private Enterprise

Americans are concerned about the outlook for the Indian private sector partly because they are favorably disposed toward private enterprise as such. But many of them also are greatly interested in the opportunities that foreign and, especially American, enterprise will have in the expanding Indian economy.

From the beginning of its tenure in 1947 the Nehru government has been officially receptive to investments by foreign enterprises that can further India's development objectives and are prepared to conform to the government's standards of business conduct. In support of this position the government has been consistently careful, for example, to subject foreign firms, once they are licensed to operate in India, to the same taxes that apply to domestic firms, and it has adhered to the principle that foreign investors are free to obtain the foreign exchange for withdrawing their earnings from Indian operations whenever they choose.

However, while formally correct, the welcome held out to foreign enterprises during the first ten years of independence was far from warm. The government's nationalist bias caused it to take a dim view of majority, let alone of exclusive, foreign ownership of industrial enterprises operating in India and to demand that the local managements and the technical staffing of foreign firms be rapidly "Indianized." Moreover, the government instituted an exceedingly slow, uncertain set of procedures for the case-by-case processing of applications by foreign enterprises for business licenses.

Given the state of mind of most potential Western investors, such deterrents were enough effectively to put them off—especially the American investors, with whom I am here chiefly concerned. American firms historically had had very little interest in the Indian market; they were finding abundant investment opportunities at home or in Canada and such more familiar overseas locations as Western Europe; they questioned India's political stability and strategic insulation from Communist take-over; fearing wholesale nationalization, they doubted that major private enterprise of any sort had much of a future in the "socialistic" Indian economy; and they often found their initial negotiations with Indian authorities difficult and unrewarding. The result was that, until the late fifties, the total inflow of foreign private capital into India was sluggish. The inflow of American private capital amounted to little more than a trickle.

During the past five years the mood of the relationship between the government of India and prospective private investors has undergone a marked shift as both parties have been overtaken by a new sense of urgency. As noted, the government has developed keener appreciation of both the foreign exchange and the technical and managerial expertise that foreign firms can supply to the development effort. For their part, foreign, including American, firms have been awakening to the potentials of the Indian market—and not just the distant potentials. Not only have they begun to appreciate the rapid, comparatively firm expansion in the domestic demand for producers' goods that the Five Year Plans project; foreign businessmen have begun to realize the potential size of consumer markets. In a country of more than 400 million people even a market that, to begin with, is limited to a small percentage of the total population can have great absolute size. If only five Indians out of a hundred use toothpaste, for example, that already is a toothpaste market half as large as the whole United Kingdom. Moreover, now that they have started to take India's development plans seriously and recognize the import-displacement strategy the plans embrace, foreign firms have been recognizing the long-run advantages of getting in early on the industrialization and market-development processes.

This confluence of Indian and foreign interests has been reflected at the practical policy level. The government, as noted, recently has been licensing new foreign and semi-foreign ventures without rigid adherence to its formal sectoring policies.

Foreign enterprises, including American ones, on the other hand, have been demonstrating an increasing willingness to participate in various mixed forms of enterprise. The government has become less doctrinaire in its insistence on majority Indian ownership. And many American and other foreign firms have become less rigid on the same issue. Some, like National Carbon, Ltd. (the Indian subsidiary of Union Carbide, which has become a major supplier of flashlights and other consumer goods and now is venturing into plastics), have taken the initiative by distributing sizable portions of their equity on the Indian shares markets. More firms have entered into joint ventures with Indian entrepreneurial partners. And some of the American participants in this most popular of cooperating arrangements have been willing to accept minority roles. Several Kaiser enterprises, for example, have settled for only 26 percent of the voting shares in their respective joint ventures (this being the minimum holding that, under Indian company law, retains a veto power over major changes in corporate policy).

Indian managements and Indian authorities have recognized the reasonableness of the desire of foreign partners in certain instances to fortify their investments with contracts that give them control over the management and/or the technical processes of a joint industrial venture for a specified period. Conversely, the managements of many of the newer American and European undertakings argue the desirability of a fairly rapid turnover of technical and managerial posts to Indian personnel—and have been practicing what they preach. (In this regard they differ almost comically from the managers of some of the old-line, pre-independence British business houses, who soberly assure their interviewers that Indians, while capable of good routine management, simply lack the capacity for handling breakdowns and other stress situations in the industrial process.)

The government's recent formal moves to stimulate foreign private investment—such steps as the completion of a tax-reciprocity treaty with the United States and agreement (despite its distaste for the procedure) to "Cooley Amendment" loans of P.L. 480 rupee-sales proceeds to American firms operating in India[3]—have been less important than the generally more agreeable mood in which it has been approaching the negotiation of arrangements with foreign business applicants. The cumbersome, case-by-case aspect of these negotiations remains, but the need for more expeditious processing has been recognized. And within the past couple of years the government has sponsored the establishment—in New Delhi, with a branch in New York—of an "Investment Centre" that, besides propagandizing private investment opportunities and introducing potential Indian and foreign business collaborators to each other and helping them arrange financing, is designed to assist would-be private foreign investors and their Indian counterparts in preparing project prospectuses for submission to the government. Meanwhile many Western firms have been learning how useful an Indian partner can be for facilitating the clearance of joint-venture proposals through the government's screening routines, among other things.

All of this rapprochement has begun to yield significant results. During the past five years private enterprises from Great Britain, the United States, West Germany, Italy, Switzerland, Japan, France, Canada, Austria, the Netherlands, and Sweden all have entered into joint ventures with Indian firms.

. . . The number of approved schemes of foreign technical collaboration and financial participation were 24 in 1957, 109 in 1958, 162 in 1959 and 388 in 1960. During the first half of (1961), 206 such schemes were approved by the Government. Of the agreements approved in 1960, 62 were with firms in the USA, 128 with firms in the United Kingdom, 73 with firms in the Federal Republic of Germany, 43 with firms in Japan, 82 with firms in other countries. About two-thirds of the agreements in 1960 related to the engineering industry including manufacture of industrial machinery, machine tools, precision and industrial instruments, electrical equipment and accessories and transport equipment. In 1948, in the private sector, foreign business investments amounted to Rs. 2,588 million. By the end of

3 See Chapter 12 below.

1959, the total foreign business investments in India's private sector were valued at Rs. 6,107 million ($1,286 million) showing an increase of about 139 per cent in 11 years.[4]

The surge of American private investment in India has been particularly noteworthy. In 1957 the United States for the first time outstripped the United Kingdom as the largest single supplier of new private foreign capital, and it has maintained the lead since. American firms have moved actively into such industries as aluminum, rubber, pharmaceuticals, chemicals, plastics, fertilizers, cement, and diesel engines, and American enterprises have been exploring a great variety of other fields. As both Indian and American government authorities remark, not only have many more American firms been looking into possibilities in India; those doing the looking commonly have stayed longer and have made more careful investigations than were typical five years ago.

Furthermore, the ferment of interest in Indian operations, although first evident among large American manufacturers, has begun to spread to smaller American firms, partly as a result of small-business visitations to India arranged by the U.S. Departments of Commerce and State. I admit to some fear, after observing the apparent naiveté over inter-cultural differences that some members of these American small-business delegations displayed, that this contrivance of face-to-face encounters between Indian and American small enterprises might do more harm than good. But, according to the unanimous judgment of those Indian businessmen and the Indian and United States authorities that I queried on the subject, the confrontations have been eminently successful. Indeed, the only complaint was that, when they have been brought together, Indian and American small enterprisers sometimes have been so infected with initial enthusiasm for each other that they have made unrealistically ambitious oral commitments. Nevertheless, the attempt to promote collaboration among smaller firms has been enjoying some net success.

[4] G. L. Mehta (Chairman, Governing Body), speech on the occasion of the inauguration of the New York branch office of the Indian Investment Centre, October 2, 1961.

The recent acceleration of private foreign investment already has begun to generate some new Indian anxieties. At least two of these are so prevalent in high policy circles that they warrant careful consideration by the partisans of foreign private enterprise. First, there is the fear that Western firms, by continuing to ally with the biggest and best-known Indian firms, may accelerate the concentration of private economic power. Second, some officials fear that, as private foreign investments grow and prosper, the remittance of foreign earnings may eventually create a dangerous strain on the precarious Indian balance of payments in the long run.

One can enter a strong rebuttal against both of these contentions. On the first count, for one thing, the factual premise underlying the charge is dubious; the fact is that in many instances Western firms have chosen small and medium-sized Indian enterprises as their partners. Furthermore, insofar as Western enterprises do ally with the largest Indian firms, they only reflect—they do not invent—tendencies that are inherent in any early-industrializing situation. Thus private foreign investment does not basically alter the problem of concentration of economic power with which a responsible government must, in any event, sooner or later come to grips.

On the second count—regarding the withdrawal of earnings —the counter-arguments are: (1) The principal alternative to private equity capital as a source of foreign exchange is loans, and these (either private or public) can create far more inflexible claims on the country's future exchange than does equity capital. (2) Private foreign investment, by generating domestic output of goods that are either exportable or of the import-displacing kind, can augment the nation's long-term foreign-exchange position far more than the investor's remittance of earnings depletes it. (3) The foreign investor's capacity to withdraw his earnings freely is a strong stimulus to new foreign investment. Thus the net impact of free withdrawals on the balance of payments may not be adverse at all. Finally, (4) a great part of the foreign earnings that accrue in an expanding market like India will, at any rate, be re-invested locally as long as the climate for foreign investment remains good.

These are sound arguments of which the Indian authorities need to remind themselves whenever a bad case of nerves about power concentrations or profit withdrawals threatens to induce them to retreat from the constructive policy toward foreign private investment they have been developing lately. At the same time, it is not enough for the foreign private business communities and their national governments, such as the United States government, to argue their cases on these points. They need also to work hard to build their cases through their behavior—making a conscious effort, whenever there is the opportunity, to choose Indian partners in a way that helps disperse rather than aggravate indigenous concentration; timing their remittances of earnings to avoid periods of particular stress on the Indian balance of payments; investing and reinvesting with an eye to the long-term potential of the Indian market; and, in general, practicing good business citizenship in the country they have adopted.

All things considered, the prognosis for those foreign firms that are prepared to undertake sustained and, in the terms just discussed, responsible, participation in the Indian development effort was never better than it is presently. The future Indian market has for some time been one of the world's most challenging; in the past three or four years it has become, as a practical matter, increasingly accessible. The long-run outlook for foreign, like domestic, private enterprise remains in doubt. But here too the outcome will depend heavily on the performance that is demonstrated in the meantime. One of the more eloquent but also measured and sensible statements of this net appraisal was that made by G. L. Mehta, Chairman of the Industrial Credit and Investment Corporation of India and former Ambassador to the United States, at the conclusion of a speech to the Far East-American Council of Commerce and Industry of New York in October 1959.

I think the general prospect can be briefly described as follows. In the short run good, but subject to continued regulation of investment, prices, imports, foreign exchange, allocation of raw materials (mostly intended to conserve scarce resources); and one must be prepared to put up with the dilatoriness and irritations of government machinery, some of which is unavoidable in any country. In the longer run, too, the prospect is good but there is a possibility of successive incursions of the public sector and of expanded controls. This danger will be held in check, not by debate but by private enterprise showing its capacity, of which I have no doubt, to do a better job. For foreign investment, the prospects are as good as or better than in the rest of Asia, thanks to better administration, financial and political stability of Government, an unblemished record of fulfillment of commitments and the large size of the market.

It would be tempting to conclude by saying, bluntly, that economic self-interest should lead you to invest in India; that you should be driven in the same direction by the humanitarian considerations which are so splendidly reflected in America's open-hearted generosity to the world since the war; that investment in India would make an important contribution towards strengthening those regions where freedom is weakest and the threats to it are greatest. I think, however, that you are better able than I to calculate the risks of and returns from alternative investments; that it would not be appropriate for an outsider—even the friendliest one—to lecture you on your duties as citizens and men; and that one should clearly distinguish business from purely ethical and political considerations.

I must, however, ask you carefully to weigh, not simply the risks of investment in India, but also the risks of the alternative of not investing. A decision *not* to invest involves risks no less great, and perhaps greater, than a decision to invest—and may be even more costly in the long run. In many fields of industry, a decision not to invest may mean the loss of the Indian market for many products in the not too distant future. A decision to abandon a place in that market carries with it a heavy responsibility: not simply the loss of prospective profit, but a denial of the contribution business can make towards building the more prosperous and harmonious world which is the keystone of American policy.

In the last paragraph of his speech, however—immediately following these heady words—Ambassador Mehta felt compelled to sound what must have been a very flat note for his audience, and we shall do well to follow his example. "From our point of view, from India's," he said, "it is only fair to say that I see little prospect that foreign private investment can make a large quantitative contribution to India's economic growth." In their enthusiasm American partisans of private overseas investment often seem to think of it as an alternative to government-to-government capital assistance. This is plainly nonsense in the Indian case if one accepts the approximate dimensions of the present development scheme. The Third Plan's total requirements for foreign credits amount to Rs. 2,730 crores, or more than $5.7 billion; and even this, as we saw in Chapter 4, is probably an understatement. Yet the Indian planners, though assuming active efforts to promote private foreign investment, have felt they could project only Rs. 300 crores, or $630 million, of this amount as coming through private channels. Even if these anticipations should be too low by one-half (and I know of no reason to believe they are unrealistically low at all), private sources could supply only slightly more than one-fifth of the Third Plan's net foreign-exchange requirements.

Nevertheless, this fraction, whatever its size turns out to be, will constitute a significant contribution to the development program's total foreign-exchange needs. And, as I have said, the contributions of technical and managerial skill that can be packaged with this particular form of foreign exchange, can be even more important than the foreign exchange itself.

Mixed Industries, Mixed Enterprises, and the Emergence of Modern Management

On at least two counts, the dichotomy between the private sector and the public sector is an unsatisfactory framework for analyzing the prospects for Indian industrial organization. For one thing, the trend in India more and more is to various admixtures of public and private components, both in the organization of particular firms and in the composite organization of whole industries. In the second place, in public, private, and mixed enterprises the overriding problem—how to develop effective management—is essentially the same. The problem arises from different backgrounds in the private and public cases, but the management needs and the responses to those needs that are presently emerging are not primarily a function of the type of ownership.

In principle, of course, there is nothing startling about the admixture of private and public enterprises in the same industry. Indeed, such a mixture is inevitable in any industry like coal, steel, or locomotive manufacture where, with private enterprise already operating, the government decides also to become a producer without nationalizing the existing private operations. The present trend seems to be toward more rather than less of this. In a number of instances new or newly-expanded private operations have been approved in the same industries in which new government enterprises are being started. Such, for example, is the case in fertilizer, pharmaceuticals, machine-building, steel, and coal.

One sometimes hears the complaint from private, including foreign private, operators that such private-public competition in the same industry is inherently unhealthy on the grounds, first, that governments, when the chips are down, usually are inclined to do their buying and regulating in a fashion that favors their own enterprises and, second, that the public enterprises compete unfairly since they are not trying to maximize profits. Plainly, if the Indian government is to encourage a viable joint private-public tenancy in the same industries, it must take pains to put these fears at rest. But this, for as so-phisticated a government as the Indian, should not be impossible.

What is needed to allay the first fear is simply what the government must do, in any event, in the interests of efficient management of public enterprise. It must abandon a monolithic image of itself and instead accord a very considerable degree of autonomy and detachment to government enterprises. Given such an arm's-length relationship within the government, it should not be excessively difficult for general government officials to give even-handed treatment to public and private enterprises within the same industry.

The answer to the second fear is that, far from being indifferent to profits, government enterprises should make it their business to make and retain profits—good profits—for purposes of reinvestment. As J. Kenneth Galbraith put it several years ago, there is no place in an economy so urgently in need of assembling development resources as India is for the kind of "post-office socialism" that contents itself with the static goal of rendering a current service at a price that just covers costs.[5]

If the Indian government and its enterprises can adhere to ground rules of the sort just indicated, the coexistence of private and public enterprises in the same industry, far from being deplorable, should serve only to reinforce intra-industry competition in a socially desirable manner. Instead of shrinking from it, private managements, if they are confident of their claims concerning the greater efficiency and flexibility of private enterprise, should look to such rivalry with enthusiasm. So should those public-enterprise managers who claim that private enterprise typically pays more for capital and management than is needed for effective industrial operation and expansion. As the public benefits from such rivalry, it may well find that in practice (as I shall be saying shortly) it becomes increasingly difficult to tell the public managers from the private managers.

Intermixtures of private and public components within the same firm are somewhat stranger than intra-industry mixtures to American eyes. Yet in the cases, for example, of private firms operating government factories, of government agencies operating in facilities constructed and leased by private corporations, of local utilities of mixed public-private ownership, and of a central banking system that is owned by the private member banks but is run by an agency of the federal government, Americans have seen a variety of mixed enterprises in their own country. West Europeans have seen many more. In any event, such mixed enterprises are now multiplying in num-

---

[5] "Some Notes on the Rationale of Indian Economic Organization," paper prepared for the Indian Statistical Institute, New Delhi, April 1959 (mimeo.).

ber and variety in India. They include, for example, "government" enterprises, some of whose equity is sold on the open market or is owned by private corporations, government enterprises whose chairmen and other principal directors are major private industrialists, private enterprises operating in government plants, private enterprises with terminal contracts to provide the initial management and technical supervision to government factories, private enterprises with government-appointed directors, and joint ventures wherein one partner is a public and the other a private enterprise. They constitute a broadening middle zone between "purely private" and "purely public" enterprise, from which anyone concerned with the practical affairs of the Indian economy can ill afford to stand aloof.

Foreign private enterprises, in particular, if they wish to explore the full potentials of the Indian market and in doing so, maximize the Western contribution to the Indian development process, must be prepared to experiment with what may be, by their home-country standards, rather novel mixed alliances. Thus STANVAC, for example, found it expedient to enter into a joint oil exploration venture with the government of India; American firms have held the general design and initial management contracts of the earlier public-sector fertilizer factories; and Merck, Sharpe and Dohme on one occasion negotiated an agreement under which it simultaneously (1) undertook to provide the engineering and technical assistance for the central government's new Hindustan Antibiotics factory and (2) entered into a joint venture with Tata's (the largest private Indian business house) to produce a number of Merck's own branded products.

Some may question whether such behavior by American firms is adequately faithful to "private enterprise principles." By my own lights, it is at any rate eminently faithful to "American-interest principles." The Merck contract, for example, clearly forestalled a greater Indian dependency upon the Soviet drug industry and its technology. Indeed, there is need, it will be argued in Chapter 11, for the United States government to persuade many more American firms of the importance of undertaking technical-assistance and initial-manage-

ment contracts with enterprises the government of India has
firmly decided to commit to the public sector. The important
point for our present purposes, however, is that a trend toward
a progressive blending of private-sector and public-sector activity is apparent, and that this serves only to underscore the
fact that India's urgent need for management development is
neither an exclusively private-sector problem nor a public-
sector one. It is, rather, a problem to which Indian industry as
a whole must seek a common solution.

The circumstances of two particularly effective Indian business managers whom I met in the course of my 1959-60 travels
illustrate what the nature of this solution may be. One, a chemical engineer with considerable experience in Western private
enterprise, was the manager of a fertilizer factory that is
jointly owned by two state governments, the central government, and the Industrial Credit and Investment Corporation of
India. Thanks to the divided public ownership, the resident
management had acquired an unusual degree of autonomy and
was enthusiastically introducing progressive organizational,
technical, and financial procedures for the profitable manufacture of fertilizers. The other manager, having emerged from a
background of long public service in the Railway Ministry, was
general manager of a large engineering subsidiary of one of
India's largest private business houses. The latter had accorded
him a good bit of autonomy somewhat inadvertently, as the
by-product of undertaking the largest (automotive-producing)
part of the enterprise as a joint venture with an experienced
European producer, who had the initial management of that
majority part of the operation. Instead of staying idly in the
background, however, the Indian general manager appeared
to be doing an admirable job of "handling" his European
managers (who required mediation in their interactions with
the Indian environment more than they themselves realized), of
learning from them, and of reorganizing and readjusting the
balance of his operation to fit external supply and market conditions, on the one hand, and to complement his automotive
production, on the other.

The points to be made are two. First, these men, despite differing backgrounds and the different formal and legal circum-

stances of their organizational situations, were essentially similar: they were first-class professional business managers who (as far as I could tell) had won and retained their positions wholly on the basis of professional competence. Second, both happened to have been accorded sufficient autonomy to make full use of their professional managerial talents. Whether one looks to Western or to Soviet examples, these two characteristics—the development of a trained body of professional managers chosen on the basis of merit, and the delegation to such managers of broad discretion in choosing the means for achieving their few assigned objectives (including the making of profits)—seem to be essential features of any dynamic modern industrial system. In India both privately organized enterprises and publicly organized ones have encumbering traditions that obstruct the emergence of progressive management of this sort. The encumbrances are different, but the need to surmount them is the same.

In the case of the private sector, the managerial disabilities are those that go with family-and-caste-dominated enterprise, nepotism, and the traditions of sharp practice and/or "Scotch-banker" conservatism that characterize some of the commercial communities. In the case of the public sector, the disabilities, to revert to Galbraith's phrase, are those of "post-office socialism": standpatism; excessively cautious, centralized, time-consuming decision making; fear of error; and interference by political authorities who confound aggressive management and worry too much about the economy and probity of the current performance of government enterprises and too little about their contribution to long-term development.

India's eventual escape from this tradition of mismanagement is, I should suppose, assured. But the speed of the escape will bear heavily on the pace of industrial development achieved. In the case of the private sector, the pattern of reform already is established. The most successful great family houses are choosing middle-level managers on a merit basis and are slowly but surely moving in this direction in selecting top managers. And the full-time managers are being accorded enlarged zones of discretion. Professional management organi-

zations, with specialized staffs, are growing rapidly in membership and in some metropolitan areas are showing great vitality
in their programs. Many business leaders are avidly interested
in new managerial systems and techniques imported from the
West.

The Indian private "managerial revolution," to be sure, is
not a precipitous one. For example, while caste evidently is a
diminishing criterion for preference, the change is grudging.
And while the Indian business community's acceptance of the
usefulness of university-level management education now has
carried to the point of creating a moderate clamor for the services of American university schools of business, there is not yet
adequate demand and support for similar services on the part
of Indian universities. Nevertheless, the vectors of change are
set, and the pace is accelerating.

Somewhat paradoxically, public enterprise by comparison
may turn out to be the reactionary segment of Indian industry,
at least in the area of managerial reform that is ideologically
neutral and motivated by concern for efficiency. For here (although I must particularly emphasize my lack of close study of
public-sector management) the management-inhibiting traditions appear particularly stubborn. Nevertheless, here too reform forces are at work—in some of the enterprises themselves, at points of enlightenment within the central and state
government ministries, and in such organizations as the Indian
Institute of Public Administration. Moreover, there is every
prospect of a contagion of improved managerial practices
across sector boundaries, from private operations to public,
and vice versa where the situation warrants. This will be
achieved by various mechanisms: competition in mixed industries, collaboration in mixed enterprises, and common profes-
sionalization throughout Indian industry.

To revert finally to the role of foreign private enterprises in
India, it is apparent that foreign companies can serve as principal carriers—into public enterprises as well as private—of this
contagion of managerial development that is still in the beginning stages in Indian industry. It is this, more than guidance of
the split between the public sector and the private sector, it
would seem to me, that is their real mission in India.

Some Other Industrial Organization Problems

To summarize the argument thus far: the outlook for participation by both domestic and foreign private enterprise in India's present industrialization scheme is generally favorable. At any rate, the long-run fate of private enterprise is very much in its own hands; politically speaking, it has a fair chance to demonstrate its merit as a vehicle for development. In responding to this opportunity, the greatest single challenge facing private enterprise (like public enterprise) is to develop more progressive and effective management; and it is in this area that foreign private enterprise can render its greatest service and, at the same time, exploit its greatest comparative advantage.

While these broad and (from the private-enterprise viewpoint) generally optimistic points seem to me to deserve principal emphasis in a brief treatment of private-sector prospects, it would be misleading to suggest that the outlook for industrial enterprise is not beset by a variety of perplexing problems. I want to call particular attention to four of these: (1) the adequacy of financing for private industrial development, (2) the question of management's relations with organized industrial labor, (3) the need to guard against the spawning of inefficiencies in production behind import barriers, and (4) the issue of economic concentration.

Each of these problems deserves more extensive exploration than it can be given here. The first two already have received considerable attention in the official and unofficial literature dealing with Indian development, but the latter two have been too much neglected.

1. *Finance and taxation.* The financing problem of private development projects, like public projects, subdivides into the questions of foreign exchange and of domestic resources. The first of the sweeping (and fallible) judgments I would venture here is that—remembering always the severity of the foreign-exchange problem—private organized industry's *relative* access

to foreign exchange is probably by now roughly comparable with that of public investment. Private enterprise now has gained access to World Bank credits dispensed through the Industrial Credit and Investment Corporation of India, to U.S. Export-Import Bank loans, to a new line of credit supplied by the United States that has been made available to private borrowers through the (government of India's) Industrial Finance Corporation, and to the selective foreign-exchange loans being experimented with by foreign banks. Above all, Indian businessmen have been learning the advantages of the joint venture as a means for acquiring foreign exchange.

As expansion proceeds, some of these resources will need replenishing. But a workable pattern of foreign-exchange credits seems to have been established. Likewise, with the establishment of the Industrial Finance Corporation, the Industrial Credit and Investment Corporation of India and the Refinance Corporation serving large-scale enterprise, state industrial credit institutions serving medium-sized firms, and special government agencies and cooperative credit institutions serving small-scale enterprises, the worst institutional gaps in the domestic industrial credit structure appear also to have been closed.

Two other private-sector financing problems for the sixties may well prove more difficult. One concerns the over-all adequacy of the private sector's internal financing of investment. The most disturbing trend to which private-sector spokesmen have pointed in registering their objections to the Third Five Year Plan is the recent decline in the fraction of private industrial investment being financed out of the firms' own gross savings. This attrition of internal financing, I should hasten to emphasize, by no means necessarily proves, as some private-sector people would have one believe, that the level of company taxation is excessive. Business taxation is a rather more intricately complex subject in India even than it is in most countries, and I shall not pretend to deal with it adequately.[6]

[6] Two comprehensive and responsible treatments, as of their dates of publication, were contained in National Council of Applied Economic Research, New Delhi, *Taxation and Foreign Investment,* 2nd ed. (Asia Publishing House, 1958), and W. Fried-

Yet I would hazard these impressions: (1) In its recent annual budgets the government has been eliminating some of the grosser inequities from the company revenue code. (2) The accelerated depreciation and investment-credit features of Indian tax law are among the world's most liberal. (3) It is hard to believe that the average level of company income taxes, which is substantially lower than in the United States, is too high for a nation with India's need for revenue for development—especially when protection against competitive imports so reduces the risks and enhances the profits of domestic production.

Thus the shrinkage of the self-financed portion of private industrial investment constitutes no self-evident case against the appropriateness of the corporate tax structure. The whole matter, however, deserves comprehensive study. For, quite plainly, if the economy's expansion is to be served by a smoothly functioning financing mechanism, the fraction of industry's gross receipts that is directly reinvested should, if anything, be rising, not falling.

The other object for concern in the field of private domestic finance may well be the organization and operation of India's securities and, in particular, its shares markets. These are active but, at least to the casual eye, exceedingly erratic in their behavior. The way that new issues immediately after their introduction typically are bid up to several times their value at issue, so that someone other than the issuing enterprise gets the bulk of the subscription of resources that the issue elicits, seems particularly objectionable. The whole securities-markets situation warrants a long, hard, dispassionate look by outside specialists.

2. *Labor.* This discussion makes no attempt to treat such vital issues as the political orientation of the Indian labor federations and the domination of the process of settling labor disputes by arbitration rather than by collective-bargaining procedures. Instead, within the broad field of labor organiza-

mann (ed.), *Joint International Business Ventures in India*, Columbia University, May 1959 (mimeo.). However, these should be supplemented by current periodical sources for recent changes.

tion and industrial relations, I want to focus momentarily upon the cost pressures and the inhibitions to production expansion that comparatively strong unionization and strong labor-welfare legislation may create in so underdeveloped an economy as India's.

I choose this emphasis not out of any reactionary bias against the rights or welfare of industrial labor. However, it does appear that in India—as one by-product of the lead that democratic political development has gained over economic development—institutions for the benefit and protection of workers have achieved an advanced stage of development at a much earlier stage of industrialization than has been usual in other industrialization processes. From a humanitarian point of view, this is all to the good. But it tempts organized labor, encouraged by its parliamentary and other political affiliates, to press for higher levels of, and higher rates of improvement in, compensation than the levels of, and gains in, productivity in novice industries may justify.

Manufacturers who occupy a protected quasi-monopoly position in a market whose consistent expansion is practically assured are not disposed to resist such demands very strongly and may not appear to be seriously injured by them. However, in the process, receipts that should be reinvested may be diverted into personal incomes and—what is far more serious—India's capacity to export at competitive prices may be gravely undermined. Equally serious is the fact that labor's elaborate protections, particularly in a period when some entrepreneurs have not yet fully embraced an expansionist view of the future, may deter private manufacturers from pressing production to the limits of their capacity. Thus in late 1959, for example, spot studies of selected industries made by government industrial planners revealed many instances where producers, despite ample demand, were hanging back from adding an extra shift to their operations because of their reluctance to assume the long-term obligations (including severance pay) to additional workers that would be incurred under existing law if they added to their permanent work forces.

I am not suggesting any formal change in existing labor legislation and wage-determining procedures. For one thing, it would be politically unthinkable. But I do suggest that the welfare-minded leadership of the Congress Party may need to remind itself afresh of the importance to the national interest of restraint upon labor costs and of the minimization of obstacles to decisions to expand; that the political authorities should encourage the managers of public enterprise to bargain vigorously with their labor and then assure them of reasonable insulation from political repercussions when they do so; that Indian private managers need to develop a quickened concern for cost and price restraints; and that there is a continuing need for Indian labor leaders themselves to formulate their specific demands with a full awareness of their broad implications for the development program.

3. *Avoidance of protection-induced inefficiency.* The point here is similar to that with respect to labor costs, and it can be put briefly. It is, if I am not mistaken, extremely important. It is the nature of an import-displacing development strategy, of the sort India has adopted, to create by means of import-restrictions a quasi-monopolistic, hothouse environment for the protected indigenous industries. Such an environment probably is essential for getting the local industrial growth to take root. But it is also precisely the environment most likely to nurture inattention to production costs, slack scheduling and controls, inefficient, unimaginative marketing, and general managerial slovenliness in the new enterprises. To the extent that the environment is allowed to work these effects, it tends to weaken domestic industry's chance for survival should it ever be re-exposed to the rigors of foreign competition, and, even more surely, it dangerously limits the economy's development of an effective ability to export.

One of the most critical, if less conspicuous of India's industrialization problems, therefore, is to contrive effective substitutes for international competition as a stimulator of operational efficiency in the newer industrial enterprises. Although government regulation may not be an entirely fruitless avenue to explore in this regard, compulsory controls generally are very clumsy instruments for inducing efficiency. Much of the answer probably lies in the development of a professional managerial class that accords operational efficiency a high place among its professional standards. Another part can be supplied by making Indian industrialists much more broadly export-minded and by creating inducements to export which do not, at the same time, exempt exporters from meeting the rigors of foreign competition. Another part of the substitute for international competition may be provided by the promotion of domestic competition—both among public, private, and mixed enterprises and within markets supplied entirely by private producers. Hence the linkage of this issue to the one that follows. At least standing alone, however, none of these partial answers entirely meets the problem. The problem is one that warrants continuing close examination and, very probably, continuing policy experimentation.

4. *Economic concentration.* Many private industrialists and business-federation spokesmen in India display great annoyance when the few intellectuals who seem really agitated about the matter raise protests about monopolistic tendencies and the concentration of private economic power. On the other hand, I have heard one particularly gifted head of an American firm that is conducting a major manufacturing operation in India say that there are few things India needs more than a strong anti-monopoly law. In this case I think the American businessman is right.

It is true, of course, that in any newly industrializing economy the first producer of any product is in some degree a monopolist—and that this does not necessarily mean much as far as the long-term prospects for the industrial structure are concerned. However, the Indian problem of economic-power concentration is not, by any means, as superficial as that. In the past two chapters we have mentioned two counts on which India needs to be particularly alert against market-power problems—one, the need to avoid localized monopolies if the economy should shift to a town-centered pattern of industrialization, and, the other, the loss of international competitive discipline that attends an import-displacing strategy of industrial development. Moreover, the Indian private sector's propensities for economic-power concentrations are unusually strong. The tradition of pre-independence British business was in this direction. The British-invented system of industrial organization known as the managing agency was, like the American holding company, a device precisely for the purpose of broadening the span of control of particular managements over various productive activities. And, having learned the potentialities of this device, the great Indian business houses already have two- and three-generation histories of building up industrial empires.

The degree of private industrial concentration that already has been attained in India is, at least by some standards, formidable. A series of articles in the *Economic Weekly* (Bombay) in November and December 1960, for example, concluded that five of the largest business houses, each of family origin—the Tatas, the Birlas, the Mafitlals, the Walchands, and the Mahindras—control 539 companies, 444 through sole or majority ownership and the rest through minority holdings. Of the 539 companies, which are mostly industrial and trading companies, the Tata and Birla complexes alone contain some 471 constituent firms.[7] There is, to be sure, enormous diversity in the holdings of most of these control groups, so that the possibility of domination of particular industries by single corporate collectives is reduced. However, there are instances of this; there are ample opportunities for market dominance through the collusion of a very few major houses; and, in any event, the political dangers inherent in concentrations of private economic power exist quite as much in industrially diverse ones as they do in those that are industrially specialized.

Emerging as it does from a nineteenth- and early twentieth-century British background, moreover, Indian law provides no really effective restraints on industrial concentration and anticompetitive practices. The dream of post-independence policymakers, as we have seen, was that a complete answer to the dangers of private concentration would be supplied by public enterprise—either as a socially accountable substitute for private monopolies where a high degree of concentration could

[7] R. K. Hazari, "Ownership and Control: A Study of Inter-Corporate Investment," *Economic Weekly* (Bombay, November 26, 1960, p. 1713; December 3, 1960, p. 1755; December 10, 1960, p. 1801).

not be avoided, or as a yardstick regulator of large private operations in markets where the two types of operation would coexist. In practice, however, the average performance of public enterprises in operation has scarcely served as a "yardstick"; and the machinery for rendering them politically accountable is proving so cumbersome that the reform needed for operational efficiency, if I am not mistaken, is in the direction of much greater autonomy for professional public-enterprise managers. But to the extent that such reforms are indeed effected, they will leave the large public enterprise in nearly as anomalous a position as is the large private enterprise so far as the social accountability of major corporate decision makers is concerned. It may, therefore, be virtually as important for public enterprises as for private to be subject to the rigors of an actively competitive environment.

Thus my impression is that India has a great deal of research, of rethinking, and of policy innovating yet to do in the field of market structures and competitive practices. I myself have not begun to study this exceedingly complex subject enough to know what the appropriate answer is. My hunch is that American antitrust law may have more relevance to the Indian situation than most Indian lawyers, political scientists, and economic policymakers suspect; that, nevertheless, the appropriate prescription in the last analysis will have to be very largely indigenous. I am firmly convinced, however, that the whole issue is being dangerously neglected at present.

Conclusion: The Implications for American Policy

The inferences that United States government policymakers and American firms might draw from this limited review of Indian private-sector prospects and problems are fairly obvious.

The private-sector *vs.* public-sector issue as such has been greatly overplayed. The recent drift of Indian government policy has been markedly toward a rapprochement with major private enterprise, and the private sector's effective opportunity for expansion is secure, at least for the time being. The question of the private sector's long-term share of productive activity is due to become increasingly blurred as private and public enterprises overlap one another in the form of mixed enterprises. But to the extent that the question retains meaning, there is nothing sufficiently rigid about present government policies to upset the view that the private sector's long-run fate will turn largely upon its own long-run performance.

In this situation it is perfectly appropriate for American interests—both government and private—to urge, and even to induce, the government of India to make private-sector choices where the choice is still open, where the private alternative is economically and managerially sound and ready to go, and where the niceties of intergovernmental intercourse permit. But it would be fatal to the over-all effectiveness of the Indo-American relationship for the United States government to become so doctrinaire in this regard that its private-sector preference appeared to be the overriding influence shaping its economic policies toward India. And it would greatly reduce the impact that American enterprise can have on Indian development if American private firms refused under any circumstances to associate themselves with Indian public-sector undertakings.

For private American firms, the procedure for entering the Indian market, although still somewhat cumbersome, has improved, particularly for those undertaking ventures jointly with Indian partners. The hazards of investment have been considerably curtailed. The prospects for returns are good in the near term and in the longer run, very good, particularly if foreign enterprises as a whole build a constructive record of encouraging local participation in their investments, of developing and employing Indian managers and technicians, of reinvesting their earnings, of timing their profit withdrawals with some attention to the Indian balance of payments, and of forming their local connections in conformity with Indian market-structure policy. It is the business of the United States government to do what it can to promote such behavior by the American firms operating in India.

The focal industrial issue in India, both for the administrators of the United States foreign aid program and for American firms with Indian operations, is, by all odds, that of management development. Every industrial project undertaken should be designed and implemented with an eye to the contribution it can make in this sphere. Additionally, United States foreign aid policy especially should be shaped with some sensitivity to other key industrial organizational problems India faces. In particular, United States projects to promote the development of progressive labor-management relations should be designed with a self-conscious awareness of their possible near-term economic impact on an economy in the early stages of industrialization; and United States aid programmers might well take the initiative in encouraging increased investigation of India's market-structure needs and prospects, offering the government of India technical assistance to this end.

India's export problem is not particularly complex. But it is going to be an enormously difficult problem to solve—and an extremely critical one. Especially for those formulating American policies toward Indian economic development, it is as important an issue as any we touch. For probably it is in the field of international trade policy, more than in its foreign aid programs or in its policies toward American private overseas investment, that the United States is most apt to fall short of supporting and facilitating Indian economic development in the manner that this country's own best interests dictate.

The Problem

The outlines of the Indian export problem already have been sketched in Chapters 2 to 4. The realization of India's development scheme depends critically on raising the volume of the nation's exports (which totaled Rs. 632 crores in 1960-61) to about Rs. 830 crores in 1965-66, the last year of the Third Plan, and to Rs. 1,300 to 1,400 crores by 1970-71. Thus the feasibility of the production and income targets programmed for the sixties, the adequacy of the projected foreign-assistance budget, and the prospects for making the approach toward self-support that, it is planned, should be well under way by 1970 all hinge on the feasibility of doubling—indeed, of substantially more than doubling—Indian exports during the course of this decade.

As India confronts these formidable export goals for the sixties, it cannot draw much reassurance from its recent experience. On the contrary, as the Third-Plan document flatly states, "Over the past decade, on the whole India's exports have been stagnant." They averaged Rs. 614 crores annually in the Second Plan as against Rs. 609 crores during the First

Plan. Admittedly, export markets were exceptionally stimulated by the Korean War during part of the First-Plan period and adversely affected by recessions in the United States and, to a lesser degree, in Western Europe during part of the Second-Plan period. Nevertheless, the irregular rise throughout the fifties extended only from a level of Rs. 578 crores in 1950-51 (before the Korean War demands had registered their full impact) to Rs. 632 crores in 1960-61. This was an average annual gain of less than 1 percent. The average annual gain projected for the sixties is 8 percent. Obviously, if the development scheme is to be made good, India must engineer a radical change of pace in its export expansion—and must do so very abruptly.

The problem looks even worse when one examines the prospects in terms of commodity groupings. India's foreign marketings commonly are divided into "traditional" exports, composed of agricultural products and related manufactures (notably cotton textiles), on the one hand, and newer exports, on the other. As I first suggested in outlining the basic rationale for an import-displacement development strategy in Chapter 2, the prospects for expanding traditional exports, which still accounted for three-fourths of India's total exports in the final year of the Second Plan, are, over-all, rather narrowly limited. This point many Indian analysts have been at pains to make[1]—I believe correctly. At the same time, other commentators caution, also soundly, that Indian decision makers must guard carefully against becoming defeatist on this point. It is true, as Professor J. B. Condliffe pointed out in a seminar in New Delhi in late 1959, that traditional exports face particular adversity when they are "unstandardized, of variable quality, badly packaged, and marketed in a rather haphazard fashion."[2] It is also true that India can greatly reduce her *share* of the world market for traditional exports,

[1] See, for example, S. J. Patel, "The Capacity to Import and Economic Development: India," *The Economic Journal* (September 1959).

[2] "Exports in the Third Plan," paper delivered at Seminar on Planning, Federation of Indian Chambers of Commerce and Industry, New Delhi, November 26-28, 1959 (mimeo).

however constricted or expansive the latter may be, by acquiescing in the emergence of an inflationary internal cost-price structure or by allowing an undisciplined growth in domestic demand to divert marketable output away from the export market.[3] And it is probable, as Condliffe argues, that the country must continue throughout most, if not all, of the sixties to rely on traditional exports for the majority of its export earnings.[4]

Thus some expansion of traditional exports is essential, however limited their outlook may be, and India can afford to leave no stone unturned to this end. Additional sales of farm commodities and related manufactures to the Communist-bloc countries, whose share of Indian exports rose from 1.3 percent to 8.0 percent from 1952 to 1960, must be sought; sales to other developing economies in Asia and Africa, as well as to the major industrialized markets in Western Europe, Japan, and North America must be pressed; and in particular, as indicated below, India must negotiate insistently with Western Europe for the international trade-policy adjustments needed for facilitating a higher degree of processing for some of its agricultural exports. Yet, after all of these specifics have been conceded and the general need for intensifying the promotion of traditional exports has been granted, the prospect for expansion in this quarter remains limited.

The fact is that the stagnation of Indian exports during the fifties cannot be explained, over-all, by a shrinkage of India's share of the world export market. On the contrary, in the case of several major commodities such as tea and cotton textiles, Indian market shares rose.[5] And yet total exports of agricultural products and related manufactures decreased from nearly Rs. 500 crores in 1950-51 to less than Rs. 475 crores in 1960-61, and jute and cotton textile exports alone, which had

---

[3] See Anne Kruger, "Capacity to Import and Economic Development: India: A Comment," and P. T. Bauer, "A Note on the Capacity to Import and Economic Development," *The Economic Journal* (June 1961).

[4] *Op. cit.*

[5] See, S. J. Patel, "A Rejoinder to Comments on Export Prospects and Economic Growth: India," *The Economic Journal* (June 1961).

totaled Rs. 250 crores in 1950-51, a decade later were only Rs. 180 crores, despite some recovery from a low in 1958-59.

Moreover, the commodity-by-commodity prospects are discouraging. Historically jute, tea, and cotton textiles have been among India's principal exports. But today jute faces growing competition not only from synthetics but from expanding production in Africa, the USSR, and elsewhere of such natural substitutes as kenaf; world demand for tea rather plainly is income-inelastic; and while there is room for improved Indian policies with respect to cotton-textile exports, as will be discussed below, their outlook is very adversely affected by the rapid multiplication of textile industries, especially in the Asian and African markets, in which India traditionally has sold most of its exports, as well as by the emergence of Pakistan, Hong Kong, and China as aggressive low-cost exporters.

In its chapter on "Europe and the Trade Needs of the Less Developed Countries" in the *Economic Survey of Europe in 1960,* the United Nations Economic Commission for Europe estimates that for the non-Communist underdeveloped world as a whole minimum import requirements are apt to rise to about $60 billion by 1980. (Here and in the rest of this section the value estimates are in constant 1960 prices.) ECE calculates that by 1980 the same underdeveloped economies' traditional exports (as defined above) can, at most, be expected to double, rising from a level of $17 billion in 1960 to about $35 billion in 1980. In the ECE projection most of this gain would be in exports of agricultural and related commodities from one underdeveloped economy to others and to the Communist trading area—categories that together it is estimated will rise from a value of $5 billion in 1960 to $15 billion in 1980. During the same period the traditional exports to developed non-Communist countries are projected as growing from $12 billion to about $20 billion. This probably is as careful and reasonable an estimate of the over-all trade prospects of the underdeveloped economies as has been made. Whether India, even with maximum effort, can manage to stay abreast of such a pattern of traditional-export expansion is highly uncertain, since the composition of Indian agricultural exports is not weighted heavily toward the kinds of tropical fruits and foods which, among the traditional exports, have the best growth prospects in the developed-economy markets.

Let us assume, however, that the relative growth of Indian traditional exports will manage to match the expansion that ECE projects for underdeveloped countries as a whole and, further, that their percentage growth in the first of the two decades the ECE estimates cover will be as great as that in the second decade. This would suggest a 1970-71 level of traditional exports for India of Rs. 670 crores, or 142 percent of the 1960-61 figure. Almost surely this is as optimistic an estimate as anyone could seriously make. Yet it means that if India is going to make good an export need of, say, Rs. 1,350 crores in 1970-71 its "nontraditional" exports, which stood at a level of Rs. 158 crores in 1960-61 (85 percent of which was accounted for by nonagricultural manufactures and minerals) will need to rise to an annual value of Rs. 680 crores by the end of the Fourth Plan.

There is, at least, some basis for encouragement about the possibilities for expansion in this category, since during the fifties, while traditional Indian exports were losing ground, other exports nearly doubled, from Rs. 82 crores in 1950-51 to Rs. 158 crores in 1960-61. However, during the sixties such a two-fold expansion in nontraditional exports will not begin to do the job; what is needed, according to the foregoing estimates, is a more than four-fold increase in ten years. Such is the sobering nature of the real export problem that is implicit in the present development scheme. It is, to say the least, a problem that merits the most earnest attention—first of the Indians themselves, and second of such friends of Indian development as the government of the United States.

India's Own Efforts in Behalf of Exports

Professor Condliffe and others rightly have taken the government of India to task for not making export promotion, especially during the Second-Plan period, a sufficiently integral and important part of its total development planning. Under the Indian development scheme a smaller portion of the total adjustments required for achieving national self-support at rising income levels is to be supplied by export expansion than by import displacement. This does not mean that the former is any less critical or difficult an aspect of the program than the latter, but for a time the planners fell into the error of acting as if it were. This error has been admitted and, so far as statements of intent are concerned, reversed in the Third-Plan document. Emphasizing the urgency of the objective, the new Five Year Plan asserts the government's determination to promote exports by limiting the growth of domestic demand for exportable commodities, by increasing the comparative profitability of selling abroad as against selling at home, by encouraging the competitive capacity of export industries, and by arousing public concern over the export problem.

Between the exposition of export policy contained in the chapter on "The Development of Foreign Trade" in the Third-Plan document itself and the list of specific measures that has been developed both in formal reports and in internal ministerial discussions during the past few years, Indian officials have in hand a wide assortment of concrete policy proposals for stimulating export expansion. One class of these measures would strengthen the incentives of Indian producers to export, both by restricting their alternative incentives to market domestically and by adding positive inducements to market abroad. Under the first subheading, although there is repeated emphasis in the Third-Plan document and elsewhere on the need to restrain domestic consumption in the interests of expanding exports, there is little evidence that the government in providing such restraints intends to go much beyond prescribing the general fiscal policy that it deems appropriate, in any case, for achieving the minimum degree of inflation that is consistent with maximum sustained domestic output expansion. The temperate character of this particular kind of export-promotion policy is very commendable. For extensive resort to consumer-goods rationing would overburden India's public-administrative capacity; and similarly if the nation's designers of fiscal and monetary policies were to adopt a highly austere stance because of a fear of domestic inflation, the resulting restraint on the activation of idle manpower could be unconscionably costly.

The better course, while allowing consumer demand a comparatively loose rein for stimulating the expansion of labor-intensive, mostly non-exportable consumer goods production, is to create positive incentives for the export of exportable goods and, at the same time, where feasible, to adopt specific controls limiting the flow of such exportable commodities into the domestic market.

On this last count, for the broad range of industrial products whose manufacture requires imported materials, components, spare parts, or productive equipment, the allocation of import licenses provides the government with a ready-made and reasonably manageable control mechanism for favoring export production. So used already, it may be more aggressively employed to this end in the future. The point about which there can be no mistake, however, is the need to strengthen the positive inducement to export. The government must do what it can to see that the economy's exceptional interest in foreign exchange is reflected in exceptional yields for export production. The simplest means for accomplishing this is probably through the extension of tax concessions to export production —not only in the case of excises, which already have been virtually eliminated from exports, but with respect to corporate income taxes on export earnings. The boldness with which the Indian government moves on the latter will be one major indicator of the vigor of Third-Plan export policy.

A second class of available export-promoting measures bears upon the ability of Indian exporters to supply foreign buyers with goods of competitive quality at competitive prices. To reiterate a point made above, there is need for sufficient fiscal and monetary restraint to check general demand-induced inflation without inhibiting idle-resource activation. With respect to cost control, in addition to whatever can be accomplished by sheer exhortation or by the government's publicizing of the results of the comparative-cost studies that the Third Plan promises, there are two primary needs whose importance was emphasized in the preceding chapter: first, the development of professionalized, efficiency-minded industrial management; and second, promotion by the government of a more competitive market structure.

Giving an adequate priority to export expansion may require some displacement of other desired features in the development design. Export promotion may, in certain instances, dictate a more capital-intensive brand of industrialization than would otherwise be indicated by the economy's factor proportions. For instance, expensive automatic looms would appear, at first glance, to be about the last kind of textile machinery that capital-poor, labor-rich India needs, and during the first half of the Second-Plan period the authorities took this view; no licenses were granted for the importation of automatic looms. However, such looms are essential to the manufacture of the high-grade fabrics that India has not traditionally exported but in which her best chance, within the textile field, presently lies of recouping some of the secular losses of custom that have been afflicting her bulk trade in coarser fabrics. Thus in 1959 the government licensers wisely began allowing a substantial import of automatic looms by establishments that indicated their intent to use them exclusively or largely to produce for export.

In a somewhat similar vein, the Third-Plan document remarks:

It is visualized that in industries which are significant for developing exports, licensing policies should take account of the economies of scale. This factor should also be given weight in determining the location of individual units. In these industries the level of costs has overriding importance and national interest requires that this consideration should receive precedence over certain other considerations which have normally to be kept in view in the scheme of planned development.[6]

[6] Government of India: Planning Commission, *The Third Five Year Plan* (1961), p. 140. Cited hereinafter as Third-Plan document. The language closely parallels that used by the British economist, Sir Donald MacDougall in *Economic Weekly* (Bombay, April 29, 1961), p. 673.

In view of my own strong persuasion of the need for dispersed industrial centering, I would plead that the export-promotion rationale not be allowed to become a blanket excuse for a slack locational policy. Any locational decisions in favor of cities that are justified on export-promotion grounds should be based on penetrating comparative-cost studies, not on stereotyped assumptions about the advantages of such location. For such assumptions, it was emphasized in Chapter 7, commonly claim altogether too much. Nevertheless, it is apparent certainly that export considerations should place a tight constraint on policies that would promote the traditional cottage-industry manufacture of nonexportable products in a manner that would inhibit the international competitiveness of organized industries producing exportable versions of similar or substitutable products.

One final method of assisting exporters to engage in international price competition should, in India's circumstances, by no means be foresworn. That is resort, by one means or another, to a double pricing system, wherein foreign buyers of Indian products are charged lower prices than are domestic buyers, and suppliers, nevertheless, are motivated to sell abroad at these lower prices. Such differential pricing, practiced by many countries in many guises, does not, to be sure, measure up to the standards of the ideal system of freely flowing international exchange, toward which most governments of good will, including the Indian, aspire. But it is a foible that a country in India's straits certainly should be permitted. Indeed, if a government chooses the right means, it can make differential export pricing advantageous to its exporters in a manner that, as I understand it, does not even violate the formal conventions of the General Agreement on Trade and Tariffs. That method, which also avoids most of the cumbersomeness of other double-pricing systems, is one already mentioned—namely, to grant corporate income-tax concessions or exemptions to earnings from export.

Earlier I argued that such tax concessions would strengthen the incentive to export. Now I am saying that they would also tend to lower India's export prices. The implicit assumption necessary to make these two propositions consistent is that exporters would in fact be likely to split their tax savings, retaining some as increased profits but passing the rest along to their customers in the form of lower prices in the course of competing with other international suppliers. Such concessions, in other words, are needed both to make international competition attractive to Indian manufacturers and to sharpen their competitive weapons.

A third, possibly the most important, class of export-promoting measures that India can undertake relates to export marketing. In the first place, there is need for much more intensive and systematic efforts to redesign and adapt Indian manufactured products to fit the wants of foreign buyers. Oddly enough, the Indian organization that is most progressive in this regard, as far as I know, is a cooperatively organized portion of the handicrafts industry. Under the aegis of the Indian Cooperative Union of New Delhi (in some cases with Ford Foundation support) styling and merchandising experts from Europe and the United States have been brought in for brief visits in recent years to study the craft and handloom products of traditional village industries and suggest to the Indian Cooperative Union feasible design and product innovations that would appeal to Western buyers. The Union then has performed the training and other functions necessary to adapt the work of the members of its constituent handicraft cooperatives to these new specifications. Measured by the resulting increase in export earnings, these efforts have been strikingly successful. Industries that could apply the same technique to far larger segments of the nation's export potential might well follow the ICU's lead.

A related need of would-be exporters is for much higher standards of quality control. More government support of the propagation of quality control techniques is indicated and possibly the formation of exporters' associations that, as in Japan, can certify products meeting minimum quality standards. As far as the general organization of the industrial export function is concerned, the industry-by-industry Export Promotion Councils that the government organized during the Second-

Plan period are better than nothing, but they too often have served as little more than discussion clubs. More aggressive and operational forms of promotional organization are in order.

There is a place for the development of strong specialized export houses, as has been recognized both by government and by private enterprise for some time. By serving the pooled marketing needs of many manufacturers, they can establish overseas organizations and develop concentrations of specialized market knowledge and marketing skills that no single manufacturer could afford. Probably there is a need for a few such export houses with product-line specializations. In view of the importance of building markets for Indian industrial products in many of the other newly developing economies, there is also a place for a few such houses with regional specializations—so that, for example, one could build up a strong field organization for marketing a broad line of Indian industrial products in West Africa. The state trading organization requires similar strengthening as the country's marketing agency with Communist-bloc countries. And there is also need for reinforcing India's general commercial representation overseas, both within its diplomatic missions and through the touring of private delegations.

The final set of measures that the government of India can be expected to undertake as part of an intensive export-promotion campaign will consist of international negotiations. What can be accomplished at international conference tables to reduce the obstacles that external tariff barriers, quota systems, and ocean freight rate structures currently present to Indian exports—particularly manufactured exports—can be quite as essential as all of the marketing development, cost restraint, and export incentives that can be achieved internally. India's delegates will need to negotiate with all the shrewdness of which they are capable. However, since this aspect of Indian export promotion is one that the American public will tend to view vicariously from the other side of the bargaining table, it may as well be considered from the American perspective.

The Responsibilities of American Policy

The United States government cannot serve as the particular agent of any other nation's export drive. Some American importers have developed a special interest in Indian exports, and more might appropriately do so. But a great many of the world's developing economies face export problems that, in varying degrees, are analogous to India's, and in devising its own international commercial policies the United States government can ill afford to play favorites.

This does not mean, however, that the United States must remain officially uninterested in India's export difficulties. Indeed, for sensible American policymakers, this would be an impossibility. For, as we have seen, the success of the Indian development scheme as a venture in the attainment of international self-support hinges upon the achievement of the country's export objectives for the sixties. If the United States government is interested in protecting the multi-billion-dollar public investment in Indian economic development that the American people will be making in the course of the first four of India's Five Year Plans, it must be most vitally concerned with the expansion of Indian exports. However, it is important to remember that, because of the nature of international commercial policy, the United States, rather than assisting India uniquely, must deal even-handedly with all countries in a similar situation.

Developing and maintaining a constructive American trade policy toward the exports of underdeveloped economies is bound, in terms of United States domestic politics, to be one of the more difficult and unrewarding ventures a Washington administration could presently undertake. The substantial mandate that the Kennedy Administration has won in the Congress for its program of trade liberalization vis-à-vis Europe may seem to signal a metamorphosis in the historic resistance of American legislators and of their more articulate interest-group constituents to freer international trade. However, this is much the easier phase of the needed trade-liberalization ef-

fort. For it can be sold primarily as a matter of direct commercial self-interest. The United States must act quickly, it is
argued, to avoid being frozen out of a buoyantly expanding
European Common Market. The tariff reductions to be effected are strictly reciprocal, and the net near-term effect of
the offsetting reductions, it can be confidently predicted, will
be to ease, not aggravate the United States' balance-of-payments difficulties.

By contrast, such export-hungry developing countries as India cannot offer reciprocity when they seek trade concessions
from the advanced economies. For the time being their need
is radically to expand their exports while permitting no more
than the programmed expansion in their imports. Thus what
they ask of the United States and other developed economies
—at a time when this country's balance of payments already is
in some trouble—is, in effect, unilateral tariff reductions whose
near-term impact on our balance of payments would certainly be somewhat adverse. In other words, countries in
India's position ask the United States Congress and other
Western authorities to accept a double standard—one that recognizes that most early industrializing nations face balance-of-
payments problems that, relatively speaking, are so much more
extreme than those of the United States or any advanced economy that they deserve a distinctly more liberal trade-policy
treatment than those countries can afford to grant in return.
Perhaps worst of all for purposes of winning acceptance with
the American public and Congress, the exports that such countries must expand most rapidly and for which trade-barrier
reduction is most urgently needed are the very "cheap-labor"
manufactures that agitate American protectionists the most.
If admitted in substantial volume, such imports unquestionably
would displace some traditional American manufacturing.

In order that the picture not appear too forbidding, it must
be emphasized that the level of economic activity is so very
much higher in the developed than in the underdeveloped
economies that these desired trade adjustments would need to
have only a small quantitative impact on the former in order
to work the desired effect on the latter. Thus the analysis of
the Economic Commission for Europe, mentioned earlier, esti-

mated that the non-Communist underdeveloped world as a whole needs to expand its industrial exports by $15 billion between 1960 and 1980 and that, of this increase, Western Europe should absorb about $5 billion worth and the other developed non-Communist economies, including the United States, another $5 billion worth. The ECE analysts then go on to calculate that, in the light of the probable economic growth of Western Europe during the next two decades, all that is actually needed is that 1½ to 2 percent of the increment in European domestic demand be met by manufactured imports from the developing economies.[7] Any reasonable estimate of the United States' "share" of the needed expansion of the developing economies' exports would fall in the same low range.

However, as I have emphasized, achieving an adjustment in United States commercial policies that will actually meet the needs of the underdeveloped countries will be a delicate, politically sticky business. To generalize from the Indian case, action on three trade fronts will be needed. In the first place, as was suggested above, moves to stimulate United States imports of Indian manufactures are in order. From the first two fiscal years of the fifties to the last two years of that decade, because of the stagnation of exports in the traditional category, India's total exports to the United States fell from an annual average of Rs. 144 crores to an average of Rs. 91 crores, or about 37 percent.[8] This trend plainly must be reversed, and while much can be accomplished by according a friendly reception (and perhaps even providing some technical assistance) to the intensified marketing efforts that the Indians should be making in their own behalf, there is need also for selective United States tariff reduction.

[7] *Op. cit.*, Chapter 5, pp. 47-48.
[8] *India's Balance of Payments, 1948-9—1955-6* (Reserve Bank of India, 1957), Table 21, p. 76, and *Reserve Bank of India Bulletin* (December 1961), Table 51, p. 2100. U.S. Department of Commerce data, roughly comparable, but valuing Indian exports at their landed value in the United States, show exports falling from an annual average of Rs. 127 crores in calendar 1950 and 1951 to Rs. 95 crores in 1959, or by 25 percent.

In the second place, India, like most of the other countries in Asia and Latin America and some in Africa, presently can use the help of the United States on the European trade front. Here the issue, of course, is whether the upheaval in trade policies and trading patterns that is being caused by the swift growth of the European Common Market can have the effect, not only of preserving the underdeveloped countries' past degree of effective access to the European market, but of opening this newly integrated and expanding market more widely than before to the manufactures of the newly industrializing countries. India's special anxieties over Europe are the fear, which it shares with its other Commonwealth partners, of a loss of preference in the United Kingdom; concern that tariff equalization on the continent may cause it to lose more business than it gains; and particular unhappiness with European tariff structures that greatly favor unprocessed over processed imports in the cases of such agricultural commodities as groundnuts and jute. The European trade authorities are generally aware of the underdeveloped countries' export problems and presumably are sympathetic to them. But responsible United States policymakers at every opportunity—in their own trade and negotiations with the Common Market, in OECD, and in their other dealings with their European allies—should use this country's bargaining leverage to champion easier access to European markets for the developing economies' industrial as well as agricultural products.

Finally, it is the business of a concerned American government to do all it reasonably can to facilitate the expansion of the exports—again, particularly, the industrial exports—of countries like India to other developing economies. Such assistance may appropriately include support in multilateral trade-policy negotiations. Occasionally and informally, it may entail moves that help bring buyers from underdeveloped countries together with sellers from those countries. If and as the United States' balance-of-payments position permits, such assistance may include offering United States government credits for use in procuring industrial aid goods from third (developing) countries. Most important of all is a willingness on the part of the United States to have its financial assistance used for the development of industrial capacity, not just for supplying the recipient countries' domestic markets, but for producing exports, even when these exports may compete with American exports in third markets. In the case of India, for example, there is every indication that, with proper cost control and invigorated marketing, the country should become a major exporter of steel and of a great variety of lighter engineering goods to the Southeast Asian, Middle Eastern, and African markets.

Far from deploring this prospect, as some elements within the American steel industry have, the responsible course for the United States government is to do all it reasonably can to speed its realization. For if India is to have any real chance of quadrupling her nontraditional exports in this decade, her Western friends must do more than wish her well. If the West cannot overcome its own political inhibitions enough to extend India some solid assistance on the trade front, the rest of the help it is supplying will lose much of its importance.

Government-to-government economic assistance is not the only aspect of American foreign economic policy that is relevant to India, as I have been emphasizing. But it is the most expensive and will continue for some time yet to claim the most attention.

We have seen in Chapter 4 that India's aid need for the sixties is massive. The Third Five Year Plan (if one adds in the Rs. 130-crore figure for which, it will be remembered, the Plan document makes no explicit provision) forecasts a net-import requirement of Rs. 2,180 crores in addition to the surplus foods to be received from the United States. However, a figure two hundred-odd crores higher, nearer the mid-point of the range of net-import estimates implicit in the aggregative model underlying the Third Plan, looks much more realistic. Adding the necessary amount for debt repayment, this brings the requirement for 1961-62 through 1965-66 for new foreign capital (net of surplus foods) to about Rs. 2,900 crores. Allowing for a Rs. 300-crore inflow of private foreign investment, this indicates a need for government-to-government assistance of about Rs. 2,600 crores, or $5.5 billion, exclusive of aid under P.L. 480.

The Third-Plan document's preview of the Fourth Five Year Plan suggests rough equality between the two Plan periods' need for net imports and for new foreign capital, other than food surpluses; the requirement for the latter should decline somewhat in the late sixties. However, there is reason to hope for a rapid rise in private foreign investment from the Third- to the Fourth-Plan period. Thus the need for government (non-P.L. 480) external assistance during the Fourth-Plan years seems likely to be on the order of Rs. 2,300-2,400 crores or $4.8 to 5.0 billion, making the aid requirement for the whole decade 1961-62 through 1970-71 approximately Rs. 5,000 crores, or $10½ billion, net of surplus foods.

There is no indisputable basis for determining how much of this should be bilateral United States government assistance. In forming a judgment one must consider these factors among others: (1) the past American share of India's aid totals; (2) the extent, during the sixties, to which the West European nations, in view of the enormous expansion in the aid requirement in this decade, would have to increase their contributions before they began to encroach on the share of the burden left for the United States; and (3) the fact that India's limited capacity to undertake new obligations to repay conventional foreign-exchange loans (see Chapter 12) may curtail the relative contribution that World Bank loans can make to the country's expanded net import needs during the sixties. My own net conclusion is that, if the amount of aid needed for the sixties (in addition to the P.L. 480 assistance) is to be forthcoming, the United States will have to supply at least two-fifths of it, or between $4 and 4½ billion. The P.L. 480 foodgrains provided during the Third-Plan period will be valued at another $1½ billion, and an additional contribution, say half as large, may be indicated for the latter sixties. Adding these figures together, it appears that the need for United States government aid to India during the decade of India's Third and Fourth Five Year Plans will probably total between $6 and 7 billion.

Although these obviously are large amounts, I am not going to use the limited remaining space in this book further to justify them. At the "Aid-to-India Club" meeting of May 1961 the United States pledged more than $1 billion of grant and loan aid for the first two years of the Third Five Year Plan, and earlier it agreed to supply more than $1 billion worth of P.L. 480 foodgrains during the first four years of that Plan. Thus, at this time, the above estimates do not seem to be out of line with official United States plans. As the decade proceeds, in any event, new commitments will have to be appraised in the light of emerging conditions that cannot, at this time, be fully anticipated.

The important point is that extensive aid, including a large volume of American aid, during the sixties is absolutely essential to India's development strategy. Rather than lingering further over the matter of size, this and the two succeeding chapters will concentrate on the procedural aspects of the Indo-American aid relationship. For not only must the amount of aid be large; it must be of the right composition; its conditions must be reasonable; and the whole complex of procedures for designing, rendering, receiving, using, accounting for, and financing the assistance must be sensible. These procedural matters often are harder to manage than the simple (if painful) matter of size.

Strings, Bargaining, and Sovereignty

Despite denials the fact is that all foreign aid carries strings and every foreign aid relationship involves bargaining, however genteel, between the aiding and receiving parties. The question is, how acceptable are the strings and how constructive the bargaining.

Any rational donor or lender wants some prior satisfaction on the uses to which his contribution will be put, as well as typically some *ex-post* information about whether the recipient's intentions were made good. Moreover, in the case of democratic governments this natural impulse is fortified and formalized by the phenomenon of political accountability. The aiding parties of the first instance, the governments, are not legal principals but agents. Their discretion is constitutionally and politically limited, and they are held responsible to the superiors (legislatures and electorates) through elaborate, meticulously prescribed financial and other accounting procedures.

The specification of uses, the setting of conditions, the tying of strings to aid is a touchy business if the recipient is a sovereign nation. It is particularly so in a country like India, where the pale legal abstraction of sovereignty has been freshly animated by a struggle for independence. But the tying of mutually agreeable strings to aid is inevitable. In principle, it is feasible where the aiding and receiving parties have common or compatible objectives. In practice, it works best where the rendering and receiving of aid is recognized as a straightforward bargaining relationship between legal and moral equals, in which each party has something to gain from the transaction and is prepared to negotiate, but not beyond certain points.

Procedurally, United States aid to India now holds the promise of a constructive, healthy relationship in this sense. But the present relationship has emerged from a rather clouded, confused background; it is inhibited by some outdated attitudes; and it has acquired, or has not yet sufficiently shaken loose from, a number of organizational and procedural handicaps.

The Conditioning of the United States-Indian Aid Relationship

Each bilateral aid relationship, like every marriage, is in a measure unique. The organizational synthesis achieved by two particular governments is never quite the same as that of another pair, even if the latter includes one of the same parties. The texture of the United States aid relationship with India differs noticeably, for example, from those the United States has had with such smaller, "defense support" countries as South Korea and Vietnam and from those it had a decade ago with such Western nations as France, Italy, and the United Kingdom.

The personality trait, it seems to me, that has most differentiated the official American posture in India is that of diffidence. The United States government sometimes has acted as though it were treading on eggs in its aid transactions with India. A very high estimate has been placed on the government of India's sensitivity to its sovereign prerogatives. There has been a reluctance to share—indeed, to presume to share—responsibility for the development design. For a long time during the fifties there was, as a result, a certain standoffishness, a reticence in official communications, a passiveness in the American aid program, at least at the top levels.

The managers of United States economic programs in India have been keenly aware of various circumstances that in com-

bination differentiate India from other underdeveloped economies. For one thing, here was the rarity of a recipient government with a democratic political accountability almost as real
and exacting as that of the United States government itself.
Moreover, the very massiveness of the Indian economy made
outside assistance a lesser ingredient in the development formula than was the case in several of the other underdeveloped
economies the United States has assisted. And yet the United
States government was only one—albeit, the largest—among
many aid sources. The United States never has been prepared
to shoulder as large a fraction of the total aid burden in India
as it has in a number of smaller countries; and India has
evinced no desire to depend exclusively on any one source of
assistance.

In India, furthermore, United States aid authorities confronted an underdeveloped-economy government whose top
political, professional, and administrative cadres were highly
sophisticated in a Western sense. It was a government thoroughly nettled by United States military assistance to Pakistan. Above all, it was a government that, as the leader of the
Afro-Asian "neutralist" bloc, not only represented an outlook
on international affairs distinctly different from that of the
West, but confronted the United States more nearly as a *de
facto* equal in the realm of power politics than any other government it had assisted economically, at least since the Marshall Plan.

An Era of Cross-Purposes (1951-59)

This last circumstance made for an uneasy harmony as to
objectives in the United States-Indian aid venture, a difficulty
that was gravely aggravated by the erratic course of American
foreign assistance philosophy during the fifties. Ironically
enough, the program was started under the aegis of a philosophy that already had been virtually shelved in Washington before Chester Bowles, its apostle in India, began his
brief ambassadorship in mid-1951. Bowles, with his buoyant,
humanitarian liberalism, was the very personification of the

Point Four idea—never, perhaps, a completely realistic idea, in that it assumed that "bootstrap" development could be widely catalyzed simply by relatively inexpensive American exports of "knowhow," unaccompanied by any heavy export of capital by the United States government. But Point Four, at any rate, was a fresh, bold concept. It was the first direct, unqualified expression of broad American concern for the welfare of the newly developing nations. And it had little, if any, cold war overlay; it proposed to assist the underdeveloped peoples for their own sakes. It was an American policy highly compatible with Indian purposes.

However, before it ever really gathered organizational momentum in Washington, Point Four was shunted aside by the Korean outbreak in June 1950 and by the radical consequent shift in American foreign-aid policy to a preoccupation with (military) "mutual security." Thus the beginnings of the Indian program in 1951-52 under Ambassador Bowles, although temporarily animated and magnified by the infectious personality of its chief architect, were detached from the new mainstream of American foreign aid philosophy. In addition, of course, they represented a retiring Administration and a party about to lose power. Almost inevitably, Bowles left India at the beginning of 1953 having raised greater expectations of American support than his government was prepared to make good.

The resulting disillusionment only enhanced New Delhi's disenchantment with Washington's new view that foreign assistance should be regarded primarily as an instrument for reinforcing positions of allied military strength around the periphery of the Communist world—a policy in which the government of India saw, besides faults of principle, inflammatory local possibilities in its provision of American arms to Pakistan. This American aid posture, adopted largely by the Truman Administration, was consolidated and stiffened in the Dulles era. Most objectionable to Indian ears, was the Secretary's statement that neutrality as to the Western-Communist struggle was inherently immoral. Friction between the two governments also was compounded by the government of India's particularly voluble and doctrinaire advocacy of public enterprise during the middle fifties, a position that especially grated on the nerves of the Eisenhower Administration, which felt morally committed to the promotion of private enterprise overseas.

Despite this web of cross-purposes, the United States aid program survived and haltingly broadened as the fifties proceeded. That it did testifies partly to the sheer inertia of public programs, once they are begun, and to the fact that complex programs typically are more complex in their motivations than simplified accounts of grand strategies would suggest. The United States posted a series of highly competent ambassadors to New Delhi during the fifties—in addition to Bowles, George V. Allen, John Sherman Cooper, and Ellsworth Bunker. They helped keep the program alive. So did many talented American technicians, administrators, and other professionals who came to India under United States aid auspices and found specific useful projects for the employment of their own skills and of United States aid monies. Whatever the vagaries in the high policy line, the Indian program drew more than its share of the competent American professionals willing to accept under-developed-country assignment, and enough officials and members of the Congress in Washington remained alive to the importance of Indian economic development to give these field workers in India some effective backstopping. Finally, much of the credit for the survival of the aid program during the difficult middle fifties belongs to the pragmatic common sense that the Indian government, despite rhetorical differences, continued to display in its working relationships with the United States.

The number of projects and sub-programs continued to expand. The technical assistance effort started with a staff of 64 United States technicians in India during fiscal 1952 and gradually expanded to a peak of 207 program personnel during fiscal 1957. The annual rosters of the United States Technical Cooperation Mission (TCM) show that during its first eight years (fiscal 1952 through 1959) about 37 percent of its American technicians worked in the areas of agriculture and natural resources, 29 percent in industry, transportation, and labor, 26 percent in health, education, community development, social welfare, and housing, and 8 percent in other fields. These specialists—all of whom were attached to, or connected with, specific development projects—accounted for the great majority (for 85 percent in fiscal 1959, for example) of TCM's total American staff. In fiscal years 1958 and 1959 the number of American technicians being supplied in India declined by about one-quarter, but at the same time the number of Indian technicians being sent for advanced training overseas was radically increased (from a little over 100 to more than 350 in 1958 and double that in 1959). On both aspects of the technical assistance program, and on some supporting supplies and equipment for the American technicians, the United States government had spent a total of $70.3 million by the end of fiscal 1959.

Meanwhile TCM had gotten into the commodity (or capital) assistance business, supplying, in addition to United States farm surplus commodities, $270 million of grants and credits under the heading of "Development Assistance" by the end of fiscal 1957. These financed a wide array of Indian imports of semi-finished and finished capital goods and raw materials. Out of this total, some $215 million was assigned to various "projects" (though, in some instances, "projects" were defined broadly, as, for example, $35 million for "augmenting steel supply"), while $55 million was classified simply as "general commodity imports—non-project assistance." Of the $270 million, $140 million was in grants, $130 million, provided in fiscal years 1955-57, took the form of loans repayable in rupees (or in dollars in the unlikely event that India preferred) in 36 progressively rising annual installments starting four years after the credits were granted. In addition, after the expiration of TCM's "Development Assistance" appropriations in fiscal 1957, about $38 million was provided out of special funds that mutual security legislation had made disbursable at the President's discretion—$20 million as a loan to an iron ore project in Orissa, the rest in grants to India's malaria eradication program.

The accretion of United States government aid programs in India during the fifties, moreover, ranged well beyond those administered directly by TCM, the overt United States aid agency. In the first place, there was the 1951 Emergency Wheat Loan of $189.7 million, for which the Export-Import Bank acted as the United States government's agent.[1] Furthermore, the "sale" of American farm surpluses to the government of India for blocked rupees far outweighed the other forms of American commodity assistance thus far mentioned. A fragment of these surplus commodity "sales"—about $67 million by the end of fiscal 1959—was made under Section 402 of the Mutual Security Act of 1954 and did flow through TCM channels. But the great bulk—$658 million during the same period—was made under Title I of Public Law 480 by the United States Department of Agriculture, for which the American Embassy's Agricultural Attaché acts as the representative in India. In addition, under Titles II and III of P.L. 480, the United States government gave $5½ million worth of surplus foods[2] for Indian famine relief in 1955 and 1956 and, by the end of fiscal 1959, had granted $94 million of surplus foods for distribution in India by American voluntary agencies. Finally, after fiscal 1957, TCM's capital assistance activities were replaced by two other United States lending programs. The Export-Import Bank opened a $150 million line of credit for India (dollars repayable in dollars) in February 1958, and the new Development Loan Fund had extended $175 million of "soft loans" (dollars repayable in rupees) by the close of fiscal 1959. TCM was nominally designated as the DLF's field inspection agency in New Delhi; beginning in 1959 the Ex-Im Bank posted its own representative there. But, as will be emphasized below, both operations were heavily centered in Washington.

When all of the United States government aid programs to India during the eight fiscal years 1952 through 1959 are added together, it can be seen that total American bilateral assistance obligated during the period came to $1,725 million,

[1] By allocating to the support of Indian institutions of higher education the first $5 million of interest that India paid on the loan, this program gave rise to an "Indian Wheat Loan Educational Exchange Program" (administered by USIS), that had expended most of its resources by the end of fiscal 1959.

[2] Including $500,000 of ocean freight.

of which surplus farm commodities accounted for about $825 million. A breakdown of the financial forms that the assistance took, ranging from the least burdensome from the Indian viewpoint (grants) to the most burdensome (loans to be repaid in dollars) is shown in Table 8. Seen in one piece, this is a sub-

TABLE 8. *U. S. Government Aid Programs to India, Obligations, U. S. Fiscal Years 1952 through 1959*

(Dollar items in millions)

Program	Grants	Loans repayable in rupees	Blocked rupee sales	Loans repayable in dollars	Total
Technical cooperation	70.3				70.3
Development assistance[1]	140.1	130.0			270.1
Other TCM-administered[2]	18.9	20.0			38.9
1951 Wheat Loan				189.7	189.7
Wheat Loan Education	5.0				5.0
Export-Import Bank				151.9	151.9
Development Loan Fund		175.0			175.0
Subtotal					900.9
Farm surplus, MSA, Sec. 402			66.7		66.7
P.L. 480, Title I			658.2		658.2
P.L. 480, Titles II & III	99.5				99.5
Subtotal: Farm surplus					824.4
Totals	333.8	325.0	724.9	341.6	1725.3

[1] Excludes $66.7 million of surplus wheat and cotton rupee sales under MSA, Sec. 402 administered by TCM and classified by it as "Development Assistance."

[2] Includes $22.2 million from the Asian Development Fund ($20.0 million loan, $2.2 million grants) and $16.7 million of Special Assistance for Malaria Eradication.

Source: U. S. Technical Cooperation Mission Program Office, New Delhi.

stantial program. Indeed, if one imagines aid being given at the same rates throughout a ten-year period, the assistance given in other forms than surplus farm commodities would equal more than one-quarter of the total need for such United States assistance that has been estimated for the Third and Fourth Five Year Plan periods; and total aid, including surplus farm imports, would amount to about one-third the requirement that has been calculated for the decade beginning in fiscal 1962.

But the fact remains that during much of the fifties the program in India was something of an orphan. It seemed best,

under the circumstances, to concentrate on a number of discrete and manageable projects that minimized the American
involvement in the broad issues of Indian development planning. Accordingly, United States operations in New Delhi were
supplied with only a scant general programming staff. Moreover, because of the public-vs.-private-enterprise issue, the
United States program tended to shy away from heavy industrial projects, other than those in the electrical power field.
And the program's remoteness from Washington's dominant
foreign aid policies, as well as the Indian government's cool-
ness toward the latter, put American personnel in India on the
defensive in aid negotiations.

During the early and middle fifties, it seemed easiest and
wisest for the American official in New Delhi to create the least
possible disturbance and, so far as it was feasible, to do whatever the Indians asked. Thus the basic procedural agreement
on technical assistance that Chester Bowles negotiated in January 1952 provided scant guarantees of American participation
in development design. And the evolving United States program became an extraordinary accumulation of bits and
pieces. As of the end of fiscal 1959, TCM listed no less than
133 "projects," the largest of which (railway rehabilitation
and expansion) claimed only $53 million. The average obliga-
tion per project was less than $2.4 million. This diffuse pro-
gram was mostly what the Indians had asked for after sizing
up the posture, biases, and organization of the United States
effort and being anxious to cover a lot of odd items in their
own development budget. However, thus splintered and having
no effective defenses against a progressive, untidy proliferation of United States aid-rendering agencies, the program's effective impact on Indian development fell far short of its
potential.

A Mending Relationship Not Yet Mended (1959-61)

The present Indo-American aid relationship is far healthier
than it appeared three or four years ago, mainly because of a
re-ordering and broadening of American foreign policy objec-

tives. Beginning with the establishment of the Development Loan Fund in 1957, the United States government has been showing increasing concern for the successful noncoercive development of economically backward nations, regardless of their status or potential as military allies. While, as I shall be saying, the design and operation of DLF entailed some critical concessions to those who resisted the premise on which it was based, the premise was unmistakable: The supplying of substantial capital assistance to developing economies, over and above what they could accept in the form of normal hard-currency loans, was to be a major, continuing, self-justifying United States government function worthy of administration by a permanent agency specifically designed for the purpose.

From the beginning India was the favorite "case in point" of this new phase of American foreign aid policy. While her increased claim upon American attention was precipitated by the way she ran into Second-Plan foreign-exchange difficulties in 1957-58, the new focus upon India would have been predictable in any case for the reasons outlined in Chapter 1. The rapprochement of the parties to the Indo-American aid relationship also was assisted from the Indian side by the Nehru government's growing "pragmatism" toward private enterprise. Moreover, several developments in 1959, including India's difficulties on her northern borders, the deftly reticent way (greatly respected by perceptive Indians) in which the United States couched its reactions to those difficulties, and the extraordinary warmth of President Eisenhower's reception in New Delhi in December of that year, added to the fund of good will with which the Indo-American aid relationship began the 1960's.

Substantive aid developments during the two years leading up to the launching of India's Third Five Year Plan in April 1961 reflected the increased harmony over objectives. During United States government fiscal years 1960 and 1961 DLF approved some $350 million of new loans to India, thereby maintaining the latter's status as by far the largest claimant on DLF funds. The Ex-Im Bank, with its 1958 line of credit now fully committed, loaned an additional $14 million in fiscal 1960 and extended some $50 million of further credits in fiscal

1961. TCM's technical assistance outlays achieved somewhat higher levels during the final two Second-Plan years. Most striking of all, Indo-American agreements signed in the latter half of calendar 1959 provided for new deliveries of $269 billion worth of surplus farm commodities, and then in early 1960, as noted already, the United States agreed to supply an additional 17 million tons of foodgrains valued at $1.1 billion[3] by the end of the Third Plan's first four years.

Moreover, there were some encouraging changes in the procedural aspects of the relationship. For one thing, the setting up of DLF indicated an intent by Congress to inject more continuity into United States aid operations, even though the effort achieved little immediate success and, indeed (see below), may not have been well suited to the existing timetable of Indian aid requirements. During the course of fiscal 1960, delays in India's use of its line of Ex-Im Bank credit were straightened out; frictions concerning joint United States-Indian administration of the rupee proceeds of P.L. 480 sales were eased; and in the course of the extended deliberations within the Indian government concerning the design of the Third Five Year Plan, senior United States officials had opportunities for more extensive and penetrating exchanges about general development design than ever before. Furthermore, the arrival in New Delhi of C. Tyler Wood to assume the newly established joint post of Economic Minister in the United States Embassy and Director of TCM created, at the country level, the best organizational opportunity yet for the coordination of the disparate elements in the United States economic programs.

Indeed, the situation was so much better with the Indo-American aid relationship by mid-1960 that some officials on both sides, in their enthusiasm for the improvement, implied that it was practically perfect. This was certainly not so. In the two following chapters I shall not try to evaluate or even report changes in the New Delhi end of the United States aid program during Ambassador J. Kenneth Galbraith's tenure, since, unlike my analysis of the procedural situation as of mid-

---

[3] In addition, the United States undertook to provide one-half (valued at about $200 million) of the cost of transporting the grain to India in American bottoms.

1960, such comments would have to be based on hearsay evidence. In 1960, however, it was apparent that the Indo-American partnership still was burdened with severe—though remediable—procedural defects, which, unless they are corrected, could keep even an adequately large aid program from meeting the needs of this decade. Some of these defects were bad habits inherited from the difficult fifties. Others had more recent causes, some primarily Indian, some United States-centered, and some the joint responsibilities of both sides. Many of these defects had this in common: No automatic or effortless correction was to be expected; to put them right would require an explicit, in some cases difficult, set of reforms. While I have great confidence in the leadership that the United States aid program has been receiving in New Delhi recently, I fear that—particularly in view of the appalling disarray that afflicted the Washington end of the foreign-aid operation during the first year and more of the Kennedy Administration—many of these reforms have yet to be made.

The Qualities of Aid and the Qualities of Its Financing Vehicles

Foreign assistance is an acceptable label for any program of an external government or international authority that raises the receiving nation's wanted imports of goods and/or services (and/or raises its foreign-exchange balances) without comparably raising the current claims against its foreign-exchange position.

By this standard, all foreign-exchange grants or in-kind grants of any goods or services that a government wants enough to accept are "assistance." So, just as surely, are all sales of commodities or services for which payment is accepted in blocked local currency (that is, currency that can be neither converted nor exchanged for exports from the aided country). The same is the case with those "soft loans" where the loan is in foreign exchange but repayment and interest are accepted in blocked local currency. "Hard" loans, where interest and principal have to be paid in convertible currency, qualify as assistance if the claims that the loan creates on the recipient's foreign exchange are deferred long enough or are kept low enough to cause a significant import advantage while the borrower is building its capacity to produce and to generate export earnings or replace needed imports. Finally, the payment of foreign exchange or of desired goods or services to a country in exchange for commodities or services of which it has a ready supply for export, but for which it could not otherwise find an export market, must also be counted as a kind of "foreign assistance." The last of these varieties of external aid, in the case of India, is confined largely to its relationships with Soviet-bloc powers. There are examples of all of the others in its aid transactions with the United States.

The definition given above does not cover the granting or lending by an external government of blocked local-currency funds to a host government, or to anyone else, for use in the country whose currency it is. In India such disbursements of United States rupee holdings are by-products of foreign aid transactions, and, as such, they will be examined at some length in Chapter 12. But they add nothing to Indian resources and do not themselves deserve the foreign aid label.

Except for stipulating that "assistance" be something the recipient country wants enough to accept, the definition adopted includes aid of all qualities—whether it is badly wanted or is barely wanted, whether it is tied or is untied as to use or as to country of purchase, whether it does or does not generate complementary claims on local resources, whether it is well planned or poorly planned, timely or untimely, efficiently used or wasted. So understood, the qualities of a given amount of aid are what determine its effectiveness. The definition also, as was just noted, embraces assistance involving different types of financing arrangements—grants, soft loans, hard loans, and the rest.

This distinction, between the nature of the assistance and the nature of the financing arrangement that accompanies the assistance, is a useful device for classifying the characteristics of an aid relationship. Accordingly, in the next chapter we shall consider some of the aspects of the Indo-American relationship that concern the rendering and receipt of the assistance itself. Then, in Chapter 12, we shall go on to the financing arrangements, which determine the nature of the claims (if any) that acceptance of the aid generates against the recipient country. First, however, there is another preliminary matter to be disposed of.

Bilateral and Multilateral Assistance

The International Bank for Reconstruction and Development (the "World Bank") supplied India with about $590 million of loans, or about 23 percent of the foreign aid commitments (other than those involving American surplus farm commodities) the country received during the 1950's. United Nations agencies supplied small additional amounts. A very substantial expansion in these multilateral aid programs is envisaged in the Third-Plan projections that underlie the estimates of needed bilateral United States assistance made earlier in this chapter. It is true that India's limited ability to service additional "hard" World Bank loans makes it unlikely that expansion of the latter can or should be proportionate to the growth in her total aid requirements. Nevertheless, even if the ratio of multilateral to bilateral assistance does, for this reason, decline moderately, India's total net-import requirements for the sixties are so high that the Third and Fourth Plans invite a larger absolute increase in multilateral assistance than the international agencies will find easy or convenient to meet.

All the same, it is sometimes suggested that the expansion of the multilateral programs should be far greater; that the United States and other national governments should substantially reduce their individual aid programs and channel their resources, instead, through such international bodies as the UN, the World Bank, and the latter's new soft-loan satellite, the International Development Association. Such agencies, it is argued, would distribute their assistance even-handedly; they would have no national interest axes to grind; and, therefore, they could get away with giving stiffer, more cogent advice and with setting stricter standards for the use of assistance than the aided countries ever would accept from individual external governments.

If such a substitution of multilateral for bilateral aid were a real, as well as desirable, possibility in the Indian case, it would, of course, greatly downgrade the importance of many of the current procedural difficulties in the bilateral Indo-American relationship. Plainly, however, a substantial substitution of this sort is not possible. Nor, I suspect, is it even desirable, if one's prime concern is for the success of Indian development.

In the first place, while the attitude of the United States Congress toward multilateral aid arrangements has changed considerably in the post-World War II years, it will be a long time before it is willing to provide *as much* foreign assistance exclusively or mainly through international intermediaries as through bilateral arrangements, in which it retains more direct control over the purposes for which, and the conditions under which, aid is given. And it is doubtful, at least in the Indian context, that the advantages of multilateral over bilateral administration are worth much sacrifice of quantity.

For, in the second place, the comparative advantages of multilateral aid administration are, at best, highly mixed. Some of the benefits claimed are significant ones. One cannot fail to be impressed, for example, with the testimony of Mr. Paul Hoffman that, as director of the UN Special Fund, he has found recipient governments more responsive to requests for information and more receptive to technical guidance than he ever did as head of the Marshall Plan. One wonders, however, whether part of the reason for this may not be the small size of the Fund and the fact that, therefore, it could not conceivably interfere significantly with the pattern of national development policies anyway. At any rate, there are some distinct administrative *dis*advantages in multilateral operations. The very multi-national character of the personnel of an international agency may cause special kinds of inefficiencies and often a certain cumbersomeness. Where, as in the case of the World Bank, such agencies do achieve a clear institutional image and an efficient operation, it may be only by adherence to a rather rigid set of doctrines that limits their freedom to maneuver in specific situations.

In the third place—and this is decisive in the Indian case—a pronounced shift from bilateral to multilateral operations is one of the last things the government of India wants. With respect to United States assistance, Indian leaders are aware that a diversion into international-agency channels might reduce the world-wide volume of American assistance. But beyond this, they believe that they are likely to get more than their per-capita or pro-rata share of the total American outflow if they can continue to deal directly with the source government. The Indians do not want to be put into the same statistical category with two or three dozen other countries at a lower stage of development readiness; they fear the inappropriate egalitarianism that international politics injects into the parceling out of funds under multilateral operations.

The Indian government, moreover, wants to keep its foreign aid bargaining dispersed. Not only may the present arrangement occasionally allow India to play off one benefactor against another; it maximizes the autonomy of Indian development planning. And the latter a government of the independence and stature of the Indian is no readier to surrender to the World Bank or the United Nations than it is to the United States or the Soviet Union.

A massive shift toward multilateral assistance, therefore, does not appear to be in the cards, at least during India's period of greatest need. The difficulties of the bilateral Indo-American aid relationship cannot be by-passed by this device. They must be coped with directly.

11 AMERICAN PROCEDURES FOR RENDERING AID

The administration of a foreign aid program, of course, is a two-party process. The character of the operation is heavily conditioned by the nature of the recipient's development planning and public administration—particularly when the aided government is as completely in charge of the development program as it is in India. Thus the procedural problems that have beset the Indo-American aid program are to a considerable degree a function of the weaknesses in Indian planning and administration that were examined in Chapter 5. Nevertheless, the blame for some of the joint arrangement's difficulties rests on the United States, and it will be these difficulties that mainly occupy us in this chapter. Specifically, I shall comment on problems that arise in connection with (1) the organization of the American program, (2) the earmarking of aid as to use, (3) the tying of aid to country-of-origin purchases, (4) attempts to make longer-term aid commitments, (5) the rendering of technical assistance, (6) the quality of United States aid-program personnel, and (7) certain aspects of intergovernmental planning, coordination, and accountability.

U.S. Organizational Difficulties

Whatever the imperfections of the planning and administrative processes that determine India's requirements for foreign assistance and affect its ability to use the assistance once it has been received, the actual negotiation of foreign aid programs is highly coordinated within the government of India. A single office—that of the Additional Secretary for Foreign Assistance Operations in the Ministry of Finance's Department of Economic Affairs—serves as the point of formal contact with the New Delhi representatives of all official aiding bodies, governmental and international. It is entrusted with the continuing puzzle of how to match up the quantities, types, and timing of needed outside assistance, as determined by the planning and political authorities, with the quantities, types, and timing of the assistance being offered.

The senior civil servants who man this office have learned their jobs well. They are, of course, distinct individuals, and most of them specialize in dealings with particular governments or agencies, or in particular forms of financial assistance. But they have the air of a team. They are graceful people who typically succeed in maintaining cordial relations with all aiding parties. But they candidly approach each foreign aid arrangement with an eye to the contribution it can make to, and/or the problems it can create for, the total solution to India's net-imports problem.

By comparison, as we saw in the preceding chapter, the American side of the Indo-American aid relationship has been organizationally diffuse in New Delhi. Disconcerting as it has been, however, this splintering of the American operation at the field level has not been the key organizational problem on the United States side. For one thing, the appointment of a combined Economic Minister and Technical Cooperation Director seemed to supply the necessary structure for consolidating American government operations in India; in any event, this issue was bound to fall into place as fast as, and not much before, certain other problems were solved.

In the first place, in 1960 there was a fundamental need to consolidate and simplify the organizational structure of foreign assistance at the center of United States operations in Washington. It made very little sense for the International Cooperation Administration, the Development Loan Fund, and the Export-Import Bank all to be conducting aid programs in the same country and yet have the degree of autonomy vis-à-vis each other that they enjoyed. It made even less sense for the negotiation of P.L. 480 surplus food sales, one of our largest and most useful forms of economic assistance, to be in the hands of a Department of Agriculture that, actuated almost entirely by the interests of American agriculture and/or its own domestic farm policies, had little concern for the nuances of foreign policy.

Operating economic assistance programs of the scale and urgency of that to India demands a single comprehensive foreign aid agency. It was plain in 1960 that such an agency should have the aspects of permanence that had been accorded the Development Loan Fund but should enjoy much greater flexibility as to program than the Loan Fund had achieved. An adequately comprehensive aid agency could, perhaps, use a still-independent Export-Import Bank as its banker for hard loans, but the aid agency needed to coordinate the negotiation of such loans. Likewise such an agency should be able to procure such food surpluses as it wished and as were available from the Department of Agriculture, but should be solely responsible for negotiating their use as aid goods. After a painfully prolonged siege of backing and filling, the Kennedy Administration's establishment of the Agency for International Development in the fall of 1961 went a considerable distance toward meeting these needs. Yet the Administration also temporized alarmingly. It failed to make the P.L. 480 ("Food for Peace") Program an integral part of the AID operation, and it provided no effective means for integrating the Export-Import Bank into the comprehensive assistance effort.

AID evidently goes farther toward remedying a second basic difficulty of its predecessor organization in rendering aid to India—namely, the lack of a strong country focus. Until late 1961 United States assistance operations were organized on the tacit principle that foreign aid problems are essentially the same everywhere in the economically underdeveloped world. The structure was subdivided by broad categories of assistance or by the financial forms that assistance takes. Thus we had the soft-loan specialists, the hard-loan specialists, the surplus farm commodities people, and the technical assistance specialists. But as for concentrated staff groups with a comprehensive knowledge of the peculiarities of the Indian economy, its requirements, potentials, weaknesses, and strong points, there were none in the Export-Import Bank headquarters or in the Department of Agriculture, almost none in

DLF, and because of the inadequacy of ICA's budget relative to its responsibilities, there were surprisingly few even there. The India specialists in the State Department shared the special inhibitions of the Foreign Service and, at any rate, had no direct cognizance of aid programs. There was no point short of the Under Secretary of State at which all of our economic assistance programs to India could be brought into single focus. And that really was too high a level to serve the purpose of injecting a penetrating knowledge of country into the aid effort, for it was the same point, of course, at which all other country programs the world over were finally seen as totalities.

The lack of sufficient country focus in the organization of an assistance effort, beside raising, within the Executive Branch of the government, inherent obstacles to the formulation of comprehensive programs tailored to the needs and the capacities of particular countries, denied the United States Congress an adequately full and interpreted presentation of the situations and problems of countries it was being asked to assist heavily. During DLF's tenure as an independent agency, for example, its budgetary presentations typically dwelt far more on the evolving institutional characteristics of the Development Loan Fund than they did on the condition and requirements of economic development in India— or in any other particular part of the world. As a result, the Congress had little opportunity to follow the strategy of aid allocation that many leading legislators preferred: namely, in any given short period, to concentrate the bulk of United States assistance on those few countries whose needs seemed especially heavy and urgent.

The third basic organizational problem of the aid-to-India program, and one that may still persist in some degree, was that of vertical coordination—more specifically, of the delegation of adequate aid planning and bargaining authority to the United States agencies in New Delhi. If there is to be a true country focus in the organization of the foreign assistance effort, then the analytical and negotiational center of gravity in the United States Executive Branch's formulation and management of particular country programs must rest in the

American field missions resident in the aided countries. This is not to deny, of course, that all major decisions formulated by the field agencies must flow to and through the parent agencies in Washington for review and authentication. But if an aid program geared to the particular requirements of a developing country is desired, it can be best formulated in an adequate mission in that country; all the United States government's aid negotiations and other working aid relationships with the assisted government should be through that mission; and the mission alone should be responsible, on the American side, for the basic examination and recommendation of assistance projects.

The appropriate vertical relationship, in short, is that which was successfully adhered to in the original Marshall Plan organization. As some of the latter's veterans remember, at the inception of the Economic Cooperation Administration several of the recipient governments hastened to post their most astute negotiators to Washington on the theory that they could get more of what they wanted by going straight to the source. Invariably the initial proposals of these operatives were met by ECA officials in Washington with the polite response, "This is very interesting, but I assume that you have taken it up with our country mission. Our only formal dealings with your government, of course, are through it." It did not take long for the recipient countries to get the idea and bring their best negotiators back home, where they could do some good. The Marshall Plan program continued to be organized and to operate with a definite country focus.

The United States aid program to India has violated the principle of adequate delegation to the field on all fronts. P.L. 480 sales, Export-Import Bank loans, and DLF loans all have been negotiated in Washington, and the essential decisions concerning them have been made there. Even in technical assistance matters, the Technical Cooperation Mission in the past was highly circumscribed by ICA in Washington. Washington-centered aid negotiations sometimes have been carried on by officials who appeared to be comically ignorant of Indian conditions; sometimes they have resulted in United States' acceptance of projects whose design could have been distinctly improved by adequate joint Indo-American consultation in India; often they have left United States officials in New Delhi ill-informed and embarrassed vis-à-vis their opposite numbers in the government of India; and frequently they have failed to mesh sensibly with programs originating in the mission.

From 1958 to early 1961 the government of India bore part of the onus for this situation by maintaining Mr. B. K. Nehru in Washington, with the unique designation of "Economic Commissioner," the rank of ambassador, and the duty, in effect, of by-passing aid representatives in New Delhi and extracting any economic assistance he could from the United States government, the World Bank, and any other potential source. India made this move at the time of its Second-Plan foreign-exchange crisis, very possibly impatient with the weakness of United States aid agencies in New Delhi at that time, dissatisfied with the then still official United States aid philosophy, and prompted obviously by the same purpose which made some European countries post strong economic negotiators to Washington at the start of the Marshall Plan. But where the Europeans failed, Mr. Nehru—previously Secretary of the Ministry of Finance (senior civil service post in the Indian government) and an altogether personable, persuasive, and gifted official—succeeded. Having established close personal ties with the heads of the United States aid agencies, his practice was to drop in with a shopping list, as it were, and negotiate on the spot. And they, with their Washington-centered operations, generally acquiesced.

B. K. Nehru's special mission undoubtedly helped awaken American leaders to the importance and urgency of Indian needs and increased United States assistance in the short run. But once a reconciliation of Indian and American objectives had been largely accomplished, a perpetuation of his role would have been inconsistent with the development of the American aid-rendering structure that was in India's own long-term interests. It therefore augured well for the future of assistance procedures when his special assignment was discontinued and Mr. Nehru was shifted to his nation's regular ambassadorship to the United States in early 1961.

One other organizational reform on the American side of the Indo-American aid relationship was essential in 1960, but it followed so logically from the three already named that it may not deserve separate designation. The American aid mission in New Delhi needed to be strengthened, especially in its central programming staff, if it were to carry the expanded responsibilities that I have been suggesting. Fortunately, the strengthening needed was essentially only quantitative. TCM had no problem of quality in its central programming staff at the end of the fifties; it simply was shorthanded. Moreover, it appeared that, if the country mission were given the full measure of responsibility here suggested, along with a reasonably commodious budget, it should have no great difficulty in recruiting general administrative and programming personnel of the right experience and calibre. Yet the matter of personnel reinforcement did urgently need attention. (Special personnel difficulties in some specific technical assistance fields are mentioned below.) Furthermore, now that Washington has recognized that the need for more general programming experts in United States missions overseas is one of world-wide proportions, the problem of finding enough such people looks far more difficult than it did from just a New Delhi perspective a couple of years ago.

The Earmarking of Aid Uses: How Much Project Tying?

A developing economy such as India's in the sixties requires a great variety of commodity imports. These are frequently broken down, according to their ultimate destinations, as "consumer goods," "government purchases on current account," and "capital goods," with raw and semi-finished materials and components being somewhat fuzzily classified as inputs that may contribute to any one of these end uses. Moreover, "capital goods" often are further subdivided into those intended for maintenance or replacement uses and those to be used for new productive capacity. Despite its usefulness, this classification symbolizes one of the worst headaches of indigenous development planners. For external suppliers of foreign exchange are strongly inclined to restrict the use of their funds to the purchase of expansion-investment goods, especially capital goods imports destined for physical incorporation into specific development projects. "We'll provide the generators, the imported machinery, and perhaps the imported steel for the particular projects that we can size up and specifically endorse," aiding governments tend to say, "but we don't want to provide financing for all of your general-purpose imports that may or may not be put to good use."

This attitude is simply bad economics, say the Indian government's representatives in foreign assistance transactions. And they are quite right—if one's analysis is sufficiently broad and accepts one critical assumption, namely, that the Indians' over-all development scheme is sound and will be faithfully carried out. If this is so, then *all* of the imports the plan designates as necessary are quite as much "development" requirements as is the most productive-looking piece of equipment supplied to the most dramatic new industrial project.

Just as essential as the closely planned requirements of major projects are the import requirements of the many ancillary and complementary smaller enterprises that must be initiated or expanded to allow the big projects to produce effectively. The need for keeping existing capacity from contracting is quite as important as are the expansion requirements for new capacity. Moreover, "capital goods" is not a very meaningful description of the imports required for enlarging industrial output anyway. The imports really needed to swell the output of chemical manufacturing, for example, may be ones to augment the effective capacity of one of that industry's domestic suppliers, say machinery fabricating, or of one of *its* suppliers, say the domestic steel or coal industry. And the imports required for boosting output in these industries may not be "capital goods" but critically needed raw materials. Or, indeed, the development import need may, in just as strict a sense, be for additional "wage goods" that, by neutralizing inflationary pressures, will permit a higher rate of domestic investment than otherwise would be safe. It is in this sense that the provision of P.L. 480 foodgrains clearly can serve as "capital assistance."

Thus the Indians have general economic logic overwhelmingly on their side when they argue that all of the imports they need for development cannot possibly take the form of capital goods, let alone capital goods ticketed for individual development projects; that it therefore makes no sense to try to match up the country's requirements for "foreign capital" with particular batches of capital goods imports; and that the insistence of aiding parties on trying to maintain such linkages at least greatly complicates the development problem and may, if carried far enough, actually prevent its solution. At the same time, the Indian authorities know, of course, that the practice of earmarking assistance as to use will not, and cannot, be totally abandoned. From their viewpoint, therefore, the practical questions that determine how manageable the earmarking practice is likely to be in any planning period reduce to the following four:

1. *Where assistance is earmarked, how tightly is it to be tied to specific projects, and how narrow is the acceptable definition of a "project" to be?* The tighter the tying, the greater is the problem of keeping the inflow of earmarked aid funds, plus accruals of other foreign exchange, acceptably matched up with the schedule of commodity imports that the total development program requires, and the greater are the dislocations in the over-all effort that delays in particular projects can cause.

2. *How well do the project preferences of India's several benefactors complement each other within the framework of her own development scheme?* Project-tying obviously is far more awkward if all of the aiding parties want heavy industrial projects and nobody is interested in agriculture, or vice versa.

3. *Is all the foreign assistance to be project-tied or otherwise closely earmarked as to use, or will a sizable residual be left untied?* This can make a great difference. A recipient can submit gracefully to a lot of very strict aid-earmarking if some extra aid funds are available for picking up uncovered

bits and pieces of the program, buying essential raw materials, or quickly breaking unexpected bottlenecks.

4. *How much of the economy's total projected import requirements will have to be aid-financed?* This too, of course, can make a considerable difference. The larger the fraction of a developing economy's total import requirements that it can finance by expenditures of its own export earnings or foreign-exchange reserves, the more academic its objections to earmarked assistance become. The critical comparison is that between the net-import requirement and the aggregate of what can be called the project-assignable imports. If the former quantity begins to overtake the latter, the difficulty of administering exclusively project-tied assistance in a way that satisfactorily matches foreign-exchange sources with uses mounts, as it were, geometrically. And if the net-import requirement actually exceeds the requirements for project-assignable imports, the problem becomes literally insoluble if all assistance remains strictly project-tied.

We need, for the Third Five Year Plan period, some concrete answers to the questions just listed. First, however, it will be well to establish the central role of the United States in India's project-tying problem and to weigh the reasons that currently incline the United States government toward project-oriented aid in the face of the apparent burden of economic logic. For its reasons are by no means trivial.

The drift in the United States aid program to India during the latter fifties was in the direction of stricter use-earmarking. Earlier, as we have seen, although the American program was strongly project-oriented, many of the projects were minor ones, frequently picked up at Indian suggestion, that served to fill lacunae in the general development effort. Moreover, during the period ending in fiscal 1957, much of the TCM-administered "Development Assistance" was frankly of a "program" rather than a "project" type; it was earmarked only to the extent of supplying broad categories of materials (say, steel) to unspecified or only broadly specified categories of users. Furthermore, the Development Loan Fund's initial loans to India, made under the pressure of India's 1957-58 oreign-exchange crisis, were essentially of this same loosely armarked character. But during the last couple of years of he Second Five Year Plan, TCM, already shorn of "Develpment Assistance" funds, began (for independent good reaons) making moves to concentrate its technical assistance n fewer, larger projects more strictly of its own choosing, nd DLF began confining its loans to "project assistance," trictly construed. In 1959 sharp Congressional criticisms of he Indian aid program's past diffusiveness and poor suscepti-ility to end-use accounting tended to reinforce this shift in he American aid posture.

More recently American officials have been worrying about he possible consequences of excessive United States stiffness n this regard—with the tangible result that in fiscal 1961 DLF egan in a few instances once again to extend "program" oans to India. Nevertheless, project-tying still is significantly eavier than it was in 1957, and two factors make the timing f this shift in American policy particularly awkward from he Indian viewpoint.

In the first place, during the Second Plan India used up er surplus foreign-exchange reserves; she herself can no onger take care of nearly as many of the non-project residuals n her import requirements as she could during most of the ifties. Second, Indian aid negotiators fear that American roject-tying may be imitated by such other assisting govern-nents as the British, the West German, and the Japanese. Vhile American earmarking practice has been growing tricter on average, these other governments have continued o negotiate loan agreements that specify only broad categories f use—for instance, that so much sterling shall be devoted o the purchase of industrial machinery of one kind or an-ther, to be installed wherever the Indians choose. However, f the other Western governments now should shift to the American practice, with American assistance already tightly armarked,[1] Soviet-bloc assistance always completely so, and

---

[1] It is well to remember that all of the large volume of P.L. 480 ssistance is, by definition, essentially earmarked as to the com-nodities to be imported.

the World Bank fairly inclined to earmark its funds, there will be little leeway left in the situation.

But now as to the motives for earmarking: The Indians believe that the other Western governments have a strong political motivation at home for project-tying their assistance in that it gives them closer control over the distribution among their own industries of the patronage their aid programs create. In the course of considerable interrogation of American officials, however, I found no evidence that such patronage control was a major objective of the United States government's preference for project-tying.

A second reason for choosing project-oriented assistance undoubtedly is strong in the Soviet case and has been talked about a good deal in some American, especially Congressional, circles. This is the so-called "impact" argument—the claim that big, discrete projects that can be most dramatically linked with the name of a donor country are the type of assistance most likely to win the good will of the people in the recipient country. While this argument cannot be dismissed out of hand, especially when applied to the extreme diffusion of American project assistance in India, neither its assumption of fact nor its assumption of purpose is very persuasive in the Indian case. Public opinion polls, for what they are worth, repeatedly have shown that the majority of rank-and-file Indians who are aware of the issue at all know that their country has received more assistance from the United States than from the USSR, even though the former has no single project in India nearly as dramatic as the Bhilai steel mill. More to the point, the United States' principal purpose in offering aid to India is not, in any case, to be loved or appreciated. It is to help Indian economic development succeed well enough to secure the survival and strengthening of a constitutional, nonauthoritarian, peaceful social system. Americans need to be far more concerned with the economic and, thereby indirectly, the political, "impact" of their aid effort than with its psychological or public-relations effect.

A third, far more cogent, reason for preferring project-tied assistance in India may not even yet be sufficiently appreciated within United States official circles. This is first, that it is far easier to package together extensive, meaningful technical assistance with project-oriented commodity assistance than with general balance-of-payments support, and second, as will be discussed below, that the Indians are inclined to underestimate their needs for technical assistance. To the extent that the United States can effectively staff such arrangements, it would be greatly to the Indians' advantage for us to follow the Soviet example and press them into more such capital-*cum*-technical assistance package deals.

Quite plainly the strongest factor motivating United States aid earmarking in India, however, is simply the desire of the United States government, in the interests of adhering to its own procedural standards, to retain substantial accountability and control over United States expenditures. Such retention is constitutionally and politically required—the United States Congress being unwilling to make a larger delegation of its spending power to the government of India than it is to the government of the United States. Moreover, regardless of the legalities and politics of the matter, most conscientious United States aid officials are unwilling to make the initial assumption upon which the whole "overwhelming economic case" against strict aid earmarking rests. They are unwilling to make the blanket assumption that Indian planning is uniformly sound or, even less, that the planned development scheme will be faithfully executed in all of its particulars. They insist on retaining some right to participate in decisions made as to Indian uses of American funds and some right to review the results. And these impulses, combined with the mixture of American diffidence and Indian aloofness that has kept the United States government at arm's length from general development planning in India, have strongly inclined United States officials toward discrete, manageable, and measurable projects in which they can satisfy their own requirements for program and administrative review with a minimum of intergovernmental embarrassment.

No American who shares my mixed views of the quality of Indian planning and administration should make light of this last motive for aid earmarking. Moreover, the technical assistance argument for project-oriented aid is powerful. Thus the case for a strict, possibly even more selective, allocation of American assistance is an impressive one. But on the other hand—and now we come back to our listing of the practical questions that Indian aid administrators confront—the hard facts of Third-Plan aid administration appear to be these: (1) Judging from the recent practices and inclinations of the aiding parties, the use-earmarking of aid to India promises to be substantially stricter during the Third-Plan years than it was, on average, during the Second Plan. Fortunately, (2) the project preferences of the several donors remain reasonably complementary. But (3) the fraction of India's total foreign assistance that is not strictly earmarked may reach a new low in the early Third-Plan years. And (4) this will be the worst possible time for that to happen, for during the Third Plan the net-import requirement will not just closely approach the total of project-assignable imports; it will grossly exceed the latter. Indian aid authorities estimate that a quarter of the Third Plan's net-import requirement—say Rs. 600 crores, or $1.3 billion—cannot, by any stretch of the imagination, be ticketed for projects, and some Western observers fear that even this estimate is too low.

Where, in a period when project-tying is the vogue, are these funds to be found? Rather clearly, it seems to me, the answer will have to come from America, and it will need to contain three elements.

In the first place, in DLF operations, henceforth to be carried forward under AID auspices, the "project" concept will need to be loosened for certain purposes as much as legitimately can be done by administrative interpretation. As indicated above, there have been recent moves in this direction, and these are all to the good.

But, almost surely, nothing like adequate inroads on India's Third-Plan net-import requirements for purposes that are not project-assignable can be made within the DLF framework. Therefore, in the second place, and most important, the United States foreign aid program in India needs a major "special assistance" supplement that is non-project-oriented. By making a substantial volume of such supplementary assistance available for quick *ad hoc* allocation at the initiative of its country mission in New Delhi, the United States government can responsibly take an ambivalent position in its Indian aid negotiations. At the same time that it undertakes to meet part of India's need for flexible, non-project commodity assistance, it can insist that the rest of its aid to India be more strictly project-oriented, or at least, be funnelled into fewer, more meaningful combined commodity and technical assistance projects than in the past. And the United States can appropriately use its own provision of supplementary balance-of-payments support during the critical sixties as a basis for urging other aiding parties to follow suit.

In the third place, for the Indian and American governments to arrive at this sort of workable accommodation of the earmarking issue, it is clear that they must evolve an easier, fuller, more mutually reassuring set of procedures for joint consultation and review with respect not only to discrete projects but to the over-all design and performance of the development effort. I shall return to this subject at the end of the chapter.

Country-of-Origin Tying?

At first glance it seems eminently reasonable to require that United States dollar aid to a country like India be used for purchases from American suppliers, as the Export-Import Bank has always done and as DLF started doing in late 1959. Moreover, this is one restrictive practice that does not appear to have been American-pioneered. On the contrary, when it tied DLF loans to country-of-origin purchases, the United States finally fell in line with what every other national government assisting India had been doing as a matter of course from the beginning of its Indian aid program.

In India itself the provocation to the United States to retreat from DLF's previous "buy-it-anywhere" policy had been strong and persistent. In calendar years 1957, 1958, and 1959, for example, West Germany's annual exports to India averaged Rs. 112 crores and her imports from India, only Rs. 17 crores—figures that in themselves, an Indian aid negotiator told one of his German counterparts, accounted in large part for the American decision to convert DLF to a buy-American operation. For far more of the difference had been financed by American than by German credits.

In the anxiety over American balance-of-payments difficulties that has welled up in the United States since 1958 the desirability of requiring American assistance dollars to be spent in the United States has come to be regarded as almost axiomatic, not only by habitual critics of the foreign aid program but by many of its supporters. The latter have embraced country-of-origin tying as a comparatively harmless defensive tactic for deflecting attacks aimed at the program as a whole. They do so in good conscience, since the United States' recent balance-of-payments deficit—at least the so-called "basic" portion of it, net of short-term capital movements—is a legitimate object for concern. It is true that the balance-of-payments improvement that can be accomplished by tying American aid to dollar purchases is comparatively slight, since, even without country-of-origin tying, a substantial portion of American loans would be spent in the United States anyway, and since, even in a world generally no longer short of dollars, some of the loans spent elsewhere would indirectly facilitate additional dollar exports. Yet, feeling that even that slight improvement will help, most American policymakers presently are convinced that the tying of American aid to American exports is an eminently sensible procedure.

Leading Indian officials and businessmen were well aware of these considerations at the time DLF adopted country-of-origin tying in late 1959. One might have expected, therefore, that the move would have been accepted without any reaction. Instead, the buy-American requirement raised a furor in India, and this in a period of generally good and warming feeling toward the United States. On a trip in Mysore State, less than a month after the announcement of the DLF switch and a long distance from India's primary financial and administrative centers, I was amazed to find industrialists, even in a comparatively isolated small commercial city like Mangalore on the west coast, greatly agitated over the change. In a round of interviews in New Delhi concerning the Indo-American aid relationship six months later, when the first wave of excitement over DLF country-of-origin tying was past, I asked individually a half-dozen senior Indian aid-negotiating and planning officials which American practice, project-tying or country-of-origin tying, they would rather get rid of if they could choose. Not one of them hesitated before saying the latter.[2]

Here, surely, is a reaction that requires explanation. Is it simply a case of condemning the United States for not holding to higher standards of international conduct than everyone else? Or is there more here than is at first apparent?

The first answer that one always gets when he puts this question to an Indian is "prices"—American prices are high. While this seemingly simple assertion provides the clue necessary for unravelling the issue, it disguises more than it discloses. The high-price charge obscures some quite disparate experiences that Indian buyers have had with American suppliers. It wounds American pride and thereby triggers some fairly pointless international debating. And, except by indirection or ellipsis, it misses the crux of the problem that the DLF-AID buy-American policy has raised in India. The situation briefly seems to me to be the following:

Indians and Americans have very different groups of commodities in mind when they generalize about "American prices." Most Americans refer, at least vaguely, to the whole gamut of the domestic United States price structure. Thus gauged, United States pricing in recent years has done better on the anti-inflationary front than most of the world's other domestic price systems. But the great bulk of American prices

---

[2] This response should not, by any means, be interpreted as indicating a lack of concern over project-tying. It did, on average, reflect high hopes that DLF's project commitment would be partially relaxed through administrative interpretation. Even so, in view of the size of the Third Plan's non-project-assignable net-import gap, I personally disagree with the Indians' ranking of the two difficulties—unless, their position implicitly assumed, as suggested in the text earlier, that United States project-tied aid should be supplemented by a new program of non-project commodity assistance. Of great interest, however, is the alarm with which responsible Indians viewed DLF country-of-origin tying.

do not concern the government and private-industry buyers
in a developing economy like India's. They are interested primarily, not even in all of American export prices, but in the
prices of American machinery and industrial equipment. And,
unhappily for the image of American efficiency and competitiveness presented to the developing economies, for fifteen
years these have been the most consistently inflationary elements in the total United States price structure. During most
of the fifties they rose much more rapidly than comparable
prices in most of the other leading industrial exporting countries.[3] Thus it is that the American price structure appears
in a very unfavorable light[4] to Indian business buyers, who,
like all businessmen, are looking for bargains, and to govern-

[3] The following index numbers (in all cases 1947-49 = 100)
show the comparative annual readings for the total and selected
components of the U.S. Bureau of Labor Statistics' Wholesale
Price Index for 1953 and 1960.

	1953	1960
All commodities	110.1	119.6
All commodities other than farm products	114.0	128.3
Metals and metal products	126.9	153.8
Machinery and motive products	123.0	153.3
(Classified by stage of processing):		
Crude materials other than food and fuel	106.2	107.5
Materials for durable manufacturing	130.1	158.1
Consumer finished goods	107.1	113.6
Producer finished goods	123.1	153.7

For a comparison of price changes in the United States and
other industrial countries from 1953 to 1959 see Hal B. Lary,
"Disturbances and Adjustments in Recent United States Balance
of Payments Experience," American Economic Review (May
1961), Table 4. Among the comparisons made are these:

	U.S.	U.K.	W. Germany	Italy	Japan
GNP deflator	14	21	15	10	8*
Producers' durable equipment	22	19	5	1	n.a.
Consumer price index	9	20	12	13	10
Machinery wholesale price index	27	n.a.	12	-2	9
Index of steel prices	37	-11	10	n.a.	-13

* Change from 1953 to 1958.
n.a. Not available.

[4] While emphatic in asserting the high average cost of American equipment, the Indians also cite exceptions, American earth-
moving equipment almost always being the first mentioned.

ment of India officials, who are under heavy compulsion to economize foreign exchange.

But this is not the whole story. American officials in India, embarrassed by the high-price charge, counter with the claim that most American industrial equipment is qualitatively superior to its competitors. This appears to be so in many lines; at least some of the more experienced Indian buyers of heavy equipment think it is. But then the obvious retort is: if American equipment's net cost per unit of service compares favorably with the offerings of other suppliers, why has this fact not been more widely recognized in the Indian market? In part, the answer is that in many instances the quality differentials between American and competitive equipment have been judged smaller than the price differentials separating them. (As a top Indian negotiator said to a senior United States official, "We're willing to pay a 20-percent premium for American generators but not 100 percent"!) In addition, American officials in India are widely of the opinion that, at least until recently, few American equipment manufacturers did a good job of selling in India. They spent little time or energy promoting potential contracts; seldom presented as elaborately prepared and informative bids as their competitors did; and took few pains to demonstrate the desirable features of their equipment and to challenge traditional Indian allegiances to European, especially British, suppliers.

This comparative indifference to the Indian market was reflected above all in a lack of aggressive pricing. Thus we now return to the subject of price, but in a more meaningful way. For pricing, in merchandise as specialized and custom-tailored as exported heavy industrial equipment, is a matter of bidding. It too is custom-tailored, tactical, highly discretionary. And the range through which a machinery exporter can tailor down his bids for the sake of penetrating a new market, and still cover all of his incremental costs comfortably, is typically wide.[5] In India most American equipment

[5] For many American machinery fabricators the "rock bottom" below this cushion may still be higher than that facing some of their competitors (for example, the West Germans). If so, this point, when it is reached, poses a more stubborn problem that

manufacturers simply did not choose to play the market-winning game with much earnestness. In presenting bids to the government of India and to the few private Indian firms with whom they got in touch, they undertook to pass along at least all of the cost-plus emoluments that had become habitual in their home market. The Indians for the most part were not amenable to this, and for a time in the late fifties the United States industrial equipment business with India reached a virtual impasse.

This, I think, is a reasonably fair, although dangerously sweeping, statement of the situation as of early 1959. In the spring of that year a senior executive of one of the largest American exporters of industrial equipment remarked to a United States government official who was urging that his firm try a little harder in the Indian market, "We're getting along very nicely without India." Within six months the same company had dramatically slashed a previously "firm" bid in order to secure a major government of India contract (which it did), and this action had come to symbolize the apparent initiation of a new trend in the attitude of American equipment exporters toward the Indian market. A number of them were said to be ready to do some promotional pricing. It was at this point, in November 1959, that the buy-American move was made, guaranteeing United States exporters the custom of all future DLF loan proceeds, except for a few instances in which exemptions might be granted if borrowers could show clearly that they could not obtain needed items from American suppliers or could do so only under severe financial or other hardship.

From this point on, there was a significant disparity in the experiences of private buyers of American equipment and

---

can yield only to the sort of longer-run adjustments (a combination of accelerated productivity gains in laggard sectors of American manufacturing and increases in foreign wages relative to American wages) that probably must provide part of the solution to the general United States balance-of-payments problem. But the fact is that in the period under discussion most American equipment pricing in India had not plumbed any such depth and before it reached "bottom" in many cases, quality advantages promised to make American merchandise strongly competitive.

government buyers. A number of private Indian users of DLF dollars appear to be content with contracts they have negotiated with American suppliers since the adoption of the buy-American rule. It is significant that these DLF funds usually have not been granted on a strictly project-oriented basis, where the loan agreement itself specifies a particular set of facilities to be installed by a particular enterprise on a particular site. Instead the dollars are provided through an intermediary, a government ministry or a financial institution, for specified types of users, not for particular individual users. When a firm asks for foreign exchange, the intermediary says, "We can help you if you can work out an American deal." This gives United States suppliers a competitive advantage certainly, but no absolute security that their potential Indian customer is not going to lose patience, persuade the Ministry to find him a German, Japanese, or Swiss credit, and take his business elsewhere. Moreover, many of the private orders have been small enough and/or for sufficiently routine items so that there have been a sizable number of suppliers available in the United States alone.

In this environment American equipment exporters have seemed to continue experimenting with more strenuous competition, and my impression was that in the private sector by the late spring of 1960 complaints about American prices were considerably less prevalent than they were a half year earlier. By convincing a number of American firms for the first time that they had a chance in the private Indian industrial-equipment market, DLF country-of-origin tying may actually have strengthened competition on the supply side of that market.

But the experience of government of India buyers of American equipment has been notably different. If, in the late spring of 1960, an American asked these officials whether the dramatic price-slashing in late 1959 by a United States supplier noted above had not inaugurated a trend of more realistic American pricing, he received a vehement denial. That possibility, they insisted, had been eliminated by DLF's adoption of its buy-American rule. The trouble, they explained, was not so much with country-of-origin tying itself. Indeed that "dramatic," hopeful, and—as it turned out—rather isolated instance of price slashing by an American bidder for a major government of India contract in late 1959 had in fact involved a country-of-origin-tied dollar loan—from the Export-Import Bank. But it was not also a project-tied loan; it could have been used for a wide range of other purchases. Thus the American bidder on the particular project in question had no confidence that the government of India would not put the Ex-Im credit back on the shelf, use a different credit, and buy from another country. The American firm really had to compete. As long as the Indians had a number of such credits available from a variety of countries, they could ask for global tenders on the requirements for particular projects and have a reasonable chance of being able to accept the most desirable bid—just as they also could, of course, with project-tied DLF loans as long as the latter could be spent anywhere.

The *double tying* of loans, however—the insertion of a buy-American requirement into loans that, like most DLF loans to the government of India, also are unmistakably reserved for large individually designated projects—demolishes supplier competition. For such loans deny the buyer freedom to maneuver in either direction. He has no discretion as to what he buys, and his choice of where to buy is limited in many cases quite literally to the two or three United States firms that are prepared to fill a large Indian order for highly specialized equipment within a stated period. Such double tying creates a high degree of monopoly power for a few American machinery and equipment manufacturers. Thus it is that the DLF buy-American move was not after all, "just what everyone else has been doing all along." The problem that this poses for Americans is less its effect on India or on the United States' national image abroad than its importance for the United States' own longer-run national economic health. It seems clear that if the United States "basic" balance-of-payments deficit is going to be permanently narrowed, many American industrial exporters will have to resharpen their competitive talents. I am sure that it was not the intention of the DLF in instituting country-of-origin tying to buy a few protected markets in India and elsewhere for a few favored American manufacturers. But this, nevertheless, has been the effect, and it was a poor way to condition American exporters for the long pull.

In view of the current American balance-of-payments problem, it would be politically unrealistic—and perhaps irresponsible—to recommend complete abandonment of country-of-origin tying. But this much seems to me indisputable: *Double tying* should be strictly avoided. Comparatively little harm need be done in India by Ex-Im Bank dollar-purchase-tying as long as it is not project-tied. And the suggested new Special Assistance could carry a buy-American clause, except for commodities where American procurement is clearly infeasible. But all double tying definitely should be abandoned—either by providing, within the framework of a nominal buy-American policy that all loans for uniquely specified projects be automatically exempted from that policy, or by reversing the policy but attaching special dollar-purchase strings to those loans that do not specify individual projects. If this change is made, a further, coordinated relaxation of country-of-origin tying could then be bargained out with other aiding governments.

The Timing of Assistance and Its Continuity

To do its intended job, foreign aid obviously must be timed to fit the requirements of the recipient's development program. As the Indo-American aid program approached the start of the Third Five Year Plan, several facts were apparent: (1) Total aid requirements were due to rise radically from Plan to Plan. (2) The dearth of new project starts in the last years of the Second Plan indicated the need for a particularly heavy bunching of new starts in the first years of the Third Plan. (3) The American political and the Indian planning calendars were badly out of phase; instead of making its major move toward stepped-up support for the Third Plan in the United States fiscal year that mostly preceded India's fiscal year 1961-62, the United States, because of its presidential election, would have to delay its move at least to the United States fiscal year that began after the start of the Third Plan's inaugural year.

It was evident, therefore, even if one assumed the greatest official American enthusiasm for Indian development objectives, that the timetable of Indian needs during the early sixties was going to set a very difficult set of targets for the United States processes for budgeting, appropriating, allocating, obligating, and spending public funds. And this was apparent simply with respect to the provision of currently available aid on a year-to-year basis. But still more difficult was the matter of aid continuity, as was emphasized by many officials on both the Indian and the American sides of the relationship. It was not enough, they said, to provide adequate volumes of year-to-year aid funds through the process of annual United States Congressional appropriations. Instead, in order to inject proper continuity into its aid program, the United States government would have to find the means for providing much or most of its assistance on a long-term, multi-year basis. For long-term foreign aid commitments, such officials commonly argued, were a necessary concomitant of the kind of long-range development planning that India was attempting to implement.

Within the past few years belief in the need for long-term aid has become unchallenged dogma among many academic proponents of expanded foreign aid operations. The same principle has been strongly advanced by the Kennedy Administration, which gave it top priority in its initial foreign aid presentation to the Congress in the spring of 1961 and continues to envisage major long-term commitments as a principal characteristic of the new aid programs being formulated for Africa and Latin America.

When I looked into the question with some care in 1960, this conventional emphasis of foreign aid partisans upon the importance of long-term commitments seemed to me misguided, at least when viewed from the special perspective of the Indian aid effort. It appeared that the costs of satisfying the demand for aid continuity with multi-year dollar commitments were high and insufficiently appreciated; that the attempt to inject such continuity into the Indo-American aid program without paying the extra costs could sap, and, indeed (in the case of DLF multi-year project commitments) already was sapping, the total program's effectiveness; and that the desire for multi-year money commitments, rather than being a necessary concomitant of sensible long-range planning, was, in fact, largely a reflection of insufficiently detailed and careful planning on both the Indian and the American sides.

In the case of India, this whole issue now seems less urgent than it did in the early months of 1961. I feared then that the Administration was prepared, if necessary, to exchange an adequate expansion in the Indian program's current-year financing for expanded authority to enter into firm long-term dollar commitments. But there has been no such indication; on the contrary, the Kennedy Administration, beginning with its leadership of "Aid-to-India Club" negotiations in May 1961, has demonstrated a lively concern for near-term Indian needs. Meanwhile, moreover, it has fought—and largely lost —its first major battle in behalf of greatly expanded multi-year funds. Presumably it has been learning to live with the result. Nevertheless, the cause of long-term commitments is by no means dead. Most foreign aid partisans still assume that more multi-year obligating authority is inherently desirable and to be sought whenever the United States Congress appears receptive. A truncated summary of my somewhat iconoclastic findings concerning aid continuity in the Indian program, therefore, may still have pertinence.

In the first place, it is well to recognize that there is no sweeping necessity for linking multi-year financing with multi-year programs. In personal and business affairs many of those who venture to begin protracted undertakings do not have all of the required funds in hand before starting their projects, and there are also plenty of examples of such risk-taking in government practice. Indeed, such is the standard experience of the government of India in its domestic operations, for, like the government of the United Kingdom, the Indian government is wholly dependent for general-revenue financing of all its activities upon annual Money Bills of the Parliament, none of which has any carry-forward or non-expiring features.

There are, of course, obvious reasons why the government of India is less content to base a multi-year development program on the expectation of annual, annually expiring, appropriations by the United States Congress than on the expectation of similar appropriations by the Indian Parliament. One is the degree of uncertainty inherent in the relations between any two sovereign governments. At times when American interest in, and good will toward, India are particularly high, the Indians would prefer to see the United States convert its long-term aid intentions into multi-year grants or loans, or at least into multi-year commitments. In addition, the Indians share with all close observers of American politics uncertainty over the continuing harmony of executive and legislative views within the United States government.

United States authorities are well aware of these uncertainties, and it is because of them that, as a matter of fact, considerable multi-year financial continuity already has been injected into the Indo-American program. The device of making multi-year or non-expiring appropriations—invented as a means by which the Congress could protect certain long-lead domestic programs from intragovernmental financial uncertainty—has been extensively used in most American foreign aid programs. Likewise, the institution of the Development Loan Fund in 1957 was a move designed, for one thing, to minimize the injection of United States intragovernmental uncertainty into the provision of American capital assistance to developing economies. The idea was that the Loan Fund, having been once endowed with a substantial draft of dollar capital, could run an orderly lending program in a way that would substantially insulate the accruals of United States capital assistance to a country like India from the year-to-year vagaries of Congressional appropriations. Furthermore, where they have had multi-year appropriations or a fund of non-expiring capital to work with, the United States aid agencies have been strongly disposed to reduce the intergovernmental uncertainty in the Indo-American aid relationship by obligating their funds to uses that extend well into the future. This inclination, suiting both the Indian preference for long-term commitments and the reluctance of American officials to be subject to the charge of starting things they could not finish, has been greatest in the strongly project-oriented DLF.

The result is that many of the individual project components of the Indo-American program already have been endowed with a good deal of financial continuity. But this has been at best a mixed blessing for these reasons: First, any effort to improve an aid program's continuity by enabling it to enter into firm multi-year dollar commitments necessarily raises its cash balances of obligated but unexpended funds. Second, while those cash balances are being built up, the Congressional provision of funds must exceed the coming year's expenditure requirement if the balances are to be accumulated without encroaching upon the volume of currently effective assistance. And third, the United States Congress has in fact proved reluctant—in the cases both of DLF and of the present Administration's 1961 appeal for expanded multi-year authority—to make this kind of working-capital investment in a financial pipeline of longer than one year.

This basic point is no different whether multi-year money is supplied to the foreign aid agency by means of conventional Congressional appropriations or by authorizations to borrow from the United States Treasury (and thereby engage in the kind of "back-door financing" that presently is permissible for the Export-Import Bank). To foreign aid administrators the borrowing procedure is attractive chiefly as a means of by-passing Congressional appropriations committees. However, while an extension of the "back-door" possibility might slightly widen the total volume of aid funding the Congress would tolerate in any one year, authorizations to borrow do not in fact seem to be widely separated from appropriations in general Congressional thinking.

The reluctance of the Congress to provide the Development Loan Fund or its successor, AID's capital lending programs, with the kind of multi-billion-dollar capital endowment that would have reduced their year-to-year dependence on new appropriations has left the Indian and other country programs fully exposed to the vagaries of annual Congressional review. Moreover, by tying up in start-to-finish commitments for multi-year projects large parts of the annual appropriations they *have* received, DLF and AID have greatly narrowed the number of new project *starts* they can support in India's expanding development effort.[6]

The conventional solution that development-assistance enthusiasts offer for these difficulties is improved "continuity." That is to say, the Congress should provide the aid agency with enough extra funds to accomplish two results: First, the agency should be given enough capital to cover start-to-finish commitments on all of the annual project starts for which the Third Plan requires United States dollar financing. In addition, the aid agency must be supplied with enough extra capital to set up a "kitty" for insulating in the future its Indian (and other country) programs from a sensitive dependence upon annual appropriations.

The arithmetic implicit in this "solution" is enough to give one pause. Suppose that half of the American aid to India were to take the form of start-to-finish project loans for projects whose total foreign-exchange costs averaged three times their first-year requirements. Suppose, further, that the aid agency also were to be endowed with a liberating stock of capital equal to a quarter or a third of an average year's aid deliveries. In such a case, the increase in appropriations or authorizations that would be needed to generate a given increase in current aid deliveries would be two or three times the latter. For currently effective assistance to India to rise $400 million from one year to the next, for example, the Congress would have to effect something like a billion-dollar

---

[6] This point easily can be overstated. If the problem were to maintain a steady level of currently available aid funds, there would be no disadvantage, once the flow had started, in tying up current obligations in multi-year projects since each year the carry-in of unspent funds previously obligated would match the obligated but unspent funds carried forward to the next period. However, under circumstances like those of India's early Third-Plan years, where the requirement for aid-financed project imports jumps radically in a short period and where most of the accruing foreign-exchange costs of projects now under way already has been provided for, it greatly reduces the number of new projects the aid program can support if the bulk of a limited volume of aid is channeled into whole-cost commitments to multi-year projects.

increase in its provision of new monies. An economist might well argue that these two ways of supplying India's coming-year aid needs—one without, one with elaborate continuity protections—would have virtually the same real impact on the domestic United States economy; but it would be fanciful, nevertheless, to imagine that politically the two approaches were equally feasible.

Happily there is, it seems to me, no real need for such a short-run skyrocketing of United States appropriations and/or authorizations. For the plea for greater continuity in the Indo-American aid effort, as well as the length of the obligations that have been incurred on individual multi-year projects, is in large measure the result of weak program phasing and inadequate intergovernment communications. Assistance is solicited and received for many uses long before it is needed (and then stays earmarked and idle) while other unanticipated near-term foreign-exchange needs keep turning up, creating minor crises, and generating new demands for more "continuity" (that is, more idle balances). A more thorough and reliable year-by-year phasing of both project and non-project foreign-exchange requirements, extending at least three years into the future, would allow the United States aid-rendering agencies to ration their currently available funds to uses with the highest time priorities and, at the same time, to ready their Congressional requests for wherewithal to handle the next wave of requirements.

Project-tying makes a time-ordered rationing of aid money especially imperative where one is trying to accomplish as much as possible within a limited budget. For the more completely that excessively early allocations of aid money are earmarked as to use, the more completely they are idled. Careful and detailed project phasing needs to be coupled with an expeditious, informed, and reliable set of intergovernmental project-negotiating procedures; some of the Indians' current preference for start-to-finish commitments clearly reflects the unpredictability, as they see it, of the amount of time needed for the American processing of their loan applications. But, given improvements in this regard, there should be no insurmountable obstacle in either Indian or American eyes to financing most projects on a phase-by-phase basis. To be sure, this would inject an additional measure of uncertainty, and possibly occasional delay and waste, into the progress of some individual projects (although not a great deal, since any project in which resources have been tied up exerts a persuasive claim to be finished and rendered productive). But this cost would be small compared with the whole development effort's gain of momentum in a particularly critical period.

The real costs of the kind of hand-to-mouth financing that, it seems to me, the Indo-American program must choose as the lesser of evils for the early sixties are in hard, nerve-racking official work. When I suggested to one of the most senior and intelligent—and personally diligent—officials in the government of India that a much more meticulous kind of project phasing would permit a far more efficient fitting of annually appropriated United States funds to the time-pattern of India's needs, he heartily agreed—but then added resignedly, "But you just can't get the people responsible for particular programs to do that kind of planning until they can be assured that the foreign exchange for their projects will be forthcoming." This is shocking if true, and its source, whose statement was corroborated by others, makes me think it is. Indian development at this juncture has no time for getting caught up in such egg-and-chicken enigmas. "That kind of planning" *must* be done, and done quickly, to serve as a basis for determining the most effective uses for foreign assistance, and the initiative and the bulk of the work must come from the Indian side. But, as emphasized earlier, there is also room for a fuller official American involvement in the total Indian planning problem, and certainly there is room for American administrative efforts to get maximum benefit from given quantities of aid appropriations.

India in the past has acted too much like a man who tells his banker "I'm going to need some loans for such and such purposes one of these days—I'm not sure when, but to be on the safe side I'd be glad to have them now." The United States, on its part, has acted too much like the banker who consents —who finds it least disconcerting to meet the full requirements, near-term and far-term, of the first few respectable clients who approach him and thereby gets loaned up in a hurry, without worrying too much about whether his portfolio is as productive as it might be. At least for the time being, both Indian and American aid authorities must work hard and work together to run an effective program with relatively smaller cash balances than either, ideally, would choose.

The Design and Packaging of Technical Assistance

Technical assistance readily can become too specialized a subject to be treated competently in the present space. Fortunately, moreover, it is one on which the United States aid mission in New Delhi and its supporting personnel in Washington seem already to be doing well. Accordingly, there are just a few points—some of them reiterations—that I want to make under this heading.

It has been noted, in the first place, that the United States government's technical assistance effort in India has been extraordinarily diffuse. There are historical reasons for this, and the diffusion may have had the merit of multiplying the numbers of Indian organizations, places, and people who have had direct contact with official Americans working in behalf of Indian economic and social betterment. But the thinness of the spread of United States technical assistance activities has made it more difficult to maintain adequate cohesiveness and accountability in the program; it has limited the chance for really decisive, trail-breaking impact on those few strategically placed industries, activities, and/or areas that are exceptionally ripe for outside technical assistance; and it has invited the proliferation of poorly designed and executed minuscule ventures that neither do India much good nor add to the Indian image of American competence and effectiveness. All things considered, therefore, it is fortunate that the American aid authorities in New Delhi have decided in future to concentrate their technical assistance, in both the agricultural and the industrial spheres, on fewer, more strategic and meaningful projects, and that Washington approves.

Second, it has been noted, that the provision of capital aid to specific development projects probably has not been sufficiently exploited as a vehicle also for rendering timely technical assistance; there has not been enough packaging of the latter with the former. In part, the loss of such opportunities has been the result of poor organization on the American side of the effort, both among the several United States agencies operating in India and between Washington and New Delhi.

In the third place, however, another impeding factor has been mentioned: the Indians' tendency to underestimate their needs for outside technical assistance. With their strong appetite for independence and distaste for managerial and technical domination by Westerners, the Indians are proud of their considerable resources of trained and competent indigenous personnel; they are anxious to find jobs for the educated unemployed; and they witness the evident successes of many complex industrial undertakings that now have been wholly "Indianized." But their inclination to go it alone in technical matters can easily be overdone. Failure to make maximum use—in effective advisory, not directive, capacities—of the advanced economies' much larger numbers of specialists experienced in advanced industrial and related processes amounts to doing things the hard way. It slows the feasible pace of expansion, raises the early production costs of enterprises unnecessarily, stretches the resources of India's top technical talent too thin, and dilutes the quality of the on-the-job training available to the country's sizable and promising cadres of inexperienced younger professionals.

What of the ability of the United States, however, to deliver a greater volume of high-quality technical aid through official channels, particularly in the industrial field? On the face of it, it would appear that no nation is better equipped for this role. Moreover, as far as the United States government is concerned, there is plenty of motivation for doing a big technical-assistance job in India properly, both because of its integral importance to the general Indian development effort and because of the enduring linkages between two economies that can be generated by the sharing of industrial techniques, processes, instrumentation, technical nomenclatures, and systems of management and training. But against these a priori points must be put the fact that, from the beginning the American Technical Assistance Mission in India has been operating with substantially less, sometimes with a quarter less, than the full complement of technicians for whom jobs and salaries already have been authorized—for no other reason than the inability of the United States government to recruit enough qualified American specialists willing to accept assignments in India at the inducements provided.

In part the remedy for this shortage of specialist personnel lies in the direction of improved recruitment of individual technicians by United States government agencies. The efforts now being made by some of our graduate schools and foundations to broaden the numbers of professional Americans willing to prepare for and seek substantial tours of overseas service; adoption of less cumbersome recruitment procedures by AID; and the attainment of a sufficient sense of public responsibility by major American industrial corporations to encourage some of their gifted technicians and administrators to accept temporary technical assistance assignments with the government, not only upon retirement, but during their most productive years—all of these can facilitate United States technical assistance staffing.

However, the nub of this problem is the fact that industrial know-how mainly is the possession of private enterprises in the United States and normally does not stand at the beck and call of government. Industrial technology can be most effectively transmitted only by those organizational entities that have developed and practice it. This means that for the delivery of industrial technical assistance in India the United States government probably will need increasingly to rely on the contract device, already widely used for the collective involvement of university groups in the aid effort. As was mentioned in Chapter 8, there will be a substantial number of key industrial undertakings, especially in the public sector, where the only external participation that India needs or wants will be that of a terminating technical assistance contractor.

The United States government's ability to meet such technical assistance requirements is, for better or worse, competitively arrayed against that of governments that can, as a matter of course, exact swift and massive command performances from their nationalized industries. If American industrial firms do not want the national economic system of which they are such partisans hopelessly to disadvantage their government in this confrontation, they must be prepared to participate with alacrity, and frequently to join forces, in exercises whose only overt lures are routine technical assistance fees.

The United States aid authorities need the help of private industry in developing a broader roster of firms—operating firms as well as design and engineering specialists—that stand ready for such assignments. The United States government, however, must worry about more than the mere recruitment of businesses that are receptive to the general idea of a technical assistance arrangement. Some very careful thinking and planning is needed about the *kinds* of contractual relationships that will best serve the swift, efficient expansion, not only of physical productive facilities in India, but of indigenous organization and skills for operating the facilities.

There must be adequate coordination among all participants on the American side of each commodities-plus-technical assistance project, whether such coordination is effected through the device of a single private United States prime contractor, by a consortium of the private American participants, or by the intervention of a United States government agency as the prime contractor who assumes the responsibility for coordinating the United States participants. A proper balance must be struck between, on the one hand, empowering foreign technical participants to make good their scheduled commitments and, on the other hand, retaining sufficient responsibility for Indian personnel to make execution of the project in itself a major development experience for Indian management and technology.

The best object lesson I know of on this can be drawn from the comparative experiences of the three Second-Plan public-sector steel mills, one built under West German contracts at Rourkela in Orissa State, a second under a Soviet contract at Bhilai in Madya Pradesh, and the third by a consortium of British firms at Durgapur in the Damodar Valley region of West Bengal. These all are large steel-making units with initial designed capacities of about a million tons of ingot a year. Although they will produce different product lines by significantly different processes (particularly in the case of Rourkela's heavy reliance on the so-called "L-D Process"), they are all designed to turn out satisfactory grades of steel with modern equipment and methods. And, while each fell behind its original schedule (Bhilai, the least, Rourkela the most) and each encountered some unexpected technical difficulties (most serious in the case of Rourkela), one gathers that all sooner or later will work.

Yet these three steel projects have received radically different ratings as to their success from most Indian and foreign observers. The Russians, it is widely held, have done much the best job; the Germans, the worst. Opinion about the British performance at Durgapur is less pronounced in either direction. Hasty visits to the three projects in the spring of 1960 did not qualify me to form an independent judgment of their comparative technical merits, but they did strongly confirm in my mind the performance ranking indicated above. I discovered, however, that the differences are not due to any inherent differences among the German, British, and Russian nationalities, or between Soviet and Western economic systems. They were largely the predictable result of the widely differing contractual arrangements into which the government of India had entered in the three cases.

At Rourkela, the first of the three projects to be undertaken, separate government-of-India contracts were signed with as many as thirty-five individual German firms, and the entire burden of coordinating the project fell on the Indian management. The German contractors, apparently actuated only by the most orthodox of profit-seeking motives, were hard to bargain with, showed little concern to mesh their separate efforts most economically, adamantly resisted Indian efforts to exert some direction over their personnel, and collectively gave an uneven kind of technical training to the

Indian operating personnel who are to man the plant. According to Indian testimony, none of the individual contractors at Rourkela felt much responsibility for the "German image" to which it and its employees were contributing. Symbolically, the most luxurious looking public building in the spring of 1960 in Rourkela was a German Club, to which the project's most senior Indians had no routine right of admittance. (The British club at Durgapur was less ostentatious and, thanks to the more enclavish character of the whole British operation, less nettlesome to the Indians. At Bhilai an exclusively Russian club, it was said, would have been quite unthinkable.) The end result of the Rourkela project will be a substantial success. But the distressingly awkward manner in which the work was organized probably can be blamed for some of the technical fumbles and certainly is responsible for unnecessary delays, unexpectedly high costs, and a certain amount of bad feeling.

At Durgapur, the last of the three projects to be started, contractual arrangements were carried to an opposite extreme: the government of India entered into a single contract with an *ad hoc* consortium of a dozen British firms (which in turn did considerable subcontracting) for a finished, operable steel plant. Durgapur, in other words, was a turnkey job; full responsibility for coordinating all aspects of the construction lay with the consortium. The latter, evidently thoroughly mindful of the need for a unitary operation, was carrying forward its work efficiently. Costs compared favorably with Rourkela's, and if one can believe some of India's private steel managers, Durgapur may turn out to be the best of the three new plants technically. But the Indians on the scene, compared with their colleagues at the other two sites, scarcely felt like participants. Lacking responsible involvement in the construction as such, they found that the latter gave them little preparation for the problems of operation.

What struck me most forcefully at Bhilai, having come directly from the other mills, was not the massive and orderly plant and "township" layout (to this layman, at least, Bhilai is least impressive of the three on these counts), nor the closer approach to completion, nor the better-than-rated performances achieved by some units of the plant in their first months of operation, nor the canniness the Russians had shown in their technical design.[7] What was arresting, rather, was the extraordinarily high morale of the Indian participants in the project. They were not only enormously proud of the relatively good record that the work at Bhilai had made; they were completely convinced that this was substantially *their* accomplishment. Sharing fully, as they saw it, in each step of the work, they had gained so much in-service training and experience during the project's planning and construction phases that they were thoroughly confident of their ability to move to an entirely Indian operation of the plant in very short order.

This state of mind plainly was not the result of brain-washing; any suggestion of the latter would have been indignantly resisted by most of the senior Indians, many of whom came from stalwart private-enterprise backgrounds. Nor, I suspect, was the strict personal discipline and rigorous indoctrination in overseasmanship to which Russian personnel had been subjected decisive. The Indians found the Soviet technicians as a group almost impeccably "correct" in their behavior but, by the same token, not particularly good at fraternizing. Rather, the procedural success of Bhilai was essentially the result of faithful execution of an astutely drawn contract—a single contract in which the Soviet government undertook to provide all required imports and foreign personnel in timely fashion, to provide training for Indian operators, and to supply all of the technical guidance necessary for building a plant of the specified capabilities. But, at the same time, the contract stipulated that all line decision making, as to design and construction as well as to subsequent operations, was to be the exclusive prerogative of Indian project personnel. This prerogative, the Indians maintain, was meticulously respected; they made all of the final decisions about what was to be done, and when; they even (they insisted) had the traditional right of a boss to

[7] I was told by qualified American observers that the Soviet engineers, while installing a relatively advanced steel-making system have, unlike their German counterparts at Rourkela, opted for equipment and processes that had been thoroughly tried and tested at home. Yet they also are credited with making some fairly shrewd adaptations in their technology to suit the more labor-intensive Indian needs.

fire individual Russian technicians and occasionally exercised it.

Superficially this was a curious contract in that each party obligated itself unilaterally to responsibilities that it could not in fact perform without the cooperation of the other. But precisely this, of course, was its particular strength: the contract *forced* detailed partnership, explicit binational cooperation and agreement at every stage of the project. It was this characteristic of the arrangement that, as widely reported, was mirrored at all levels of the project organization by the dual posting of Russian and Indian counterparts to most supervisory and technical positions. Each pair was required to work as partners, formally always with the Russian in the advisory, the Indian in the decision-making, capacity, actually with the Indian assuming more and more of the joint initiative as the work proceeded.

The Bhilai model is not the only desirable means for rendering technical assistance in conjunction with project-tied capital aid. But it is a good one. It has projected the Bhilai plant into its period of initial operations with an optimistic, self-confident organizational personality instead of Rourkela's negative one or Durgapur's lack of one. Moreover, it would be absurd—it would concede far too much—for Americans to write off the Bhilai method as a peculiarly "Communist" procedure, or one that is uniquely suited to the delivery of aid by a nationalized industry. There is nothing about the essentials of the approach that should be either conceptually repugnant or administratively infeasible for any American prime contractor, private or public, who takes pains to insist that there be adequate provision for coordination on the American side of his technical assistance arrangement, and who wants the constructiveness of his procedures to measure at least up to the mark that the Russians have set in this instance.

The Personal Element in the Aid Relationship

In this era of literary fascination with "ugly" and "quiet" Americans, an explanation may be due as to why the present appraisal does not dwell more on the personal, human dimension of the Indo-American aid program. Surely the individual fiber of the Americans who man the program, as well as of the Indians with whom they deal, is vitally important. Why not then more emphasis on these matters?

Well, first, because I am afraid of them. Any detailed evaluation that I might attempt of the relationship's purely personal qualities would be excessively subjective and fallible.

Second, I am writing about India and concentrating on problems. And my general subjective impression is that the strictly personal aspects of the Indo-American relationship are fairly healthy. In one of my first conversations with a group of Indian officials, one of them cut short some circumlocutory questions with the flat statement, "We don't have any Ugly-American problem in India." This, of course, like all generalizations, was not completely correct, but a year later it still had a ring of authenticity. As I have said already, United States government operations in India probably consistently have attracted a better-than-average selection of the Americans available for under-developed-economy assignment. Most of them, I should say, show competence and earnestness in their work, are actuated by a lively concern for the particular Indian problems they face, and, with their families, develop a fairly good rapport with the culture around them. As for the human material on the Indian side of the aid relationship, I have revealed my feeling that, foibles and all, it is of very high average quality. Moreover, the Americans and Indians who are thrown together in aid operations commonly take to each other warmly (even if those Americans who have not worked overseas before suffer the familiar shock of discovering that the American *stereotype* is not universally beloved).

To be sure, the relative opulence of nearly all Americans in India is a problem. It does not endear them to their Indian counterparts, and it can be unsettling to the Americans themselves. But there really is comparatively little that can be done about this; it is an inevitable consequence of injecting upper middle-income people from the world's richest economy into one of its poorest. It would be patently foolish to try to remove this source of friction by reducing the emoluments of the

American personnel, which already scarcely offer a sufficient premium over alternatives available at home to uproot, and overcome the lingering insularity of, enough qualified American professionals. About all that can be done is to counsel self-restraint on the part of Americans and to hope for understanding on the part of the Indians. Actually there already is a pretty good measure of each. Neither the relative income gap between Indians and Americans of similar stations nor other irritants are sufficient to upset a predominantly favorable verdict on the personal aspects of the aid program.

There is a third reason, however, why I have not dwelt on these personal dimensions of the relationship: I am convinced that their relative importance is overrated. It is an old habit of American thought to linger over the personalized, individuated aspects of social problems and shy away from the formal, structural, impersonal aspects—to be interested in people more than ideas, choose the candidate rather than his party or platform, hire a man rather than fill a job. And so too, in the matter of foreign aid, one encounters time and again the injunction to get the right people and the rest will take care of itself. A central thesis of these chapters is that in a foreign aid program good people are not enough—not even good people with lots of money. There must also be sensible procedures, and it cannot be assumed that these automatically will be generated by the "right people." In the real world bad procedures can break good people, or, at any rate, frustrate, neutralize, then sour them, and in India—where we already have many of the right people—bad procedures have tended to do just this. Therefore, of the two—people and procedures—it is the procedures that require emphasis.

Summary and Conclusion: Indo-American Planning, Coordination, and Accountability

This chapter has (1) pointed to the needs for American aid-rendering machinery to consolidate the Washington administration of aid programs, adopt a country-focussed scheme of aid-agency organization, and devolve extensive negotiating and decision-making authority on the United States country mission in India; (2) argued the need for a substantial, supplementary, non-project-tied type of United States assistance to fill in the gaps and offset the rigidities with which a strictly project-oriented kind of assistance (though attractice on several counts) otherwise will encumber India's Third-Plan effort; (3) urged the case against "double tying" United States assistance both to individual projects *and* to country-of-origin purchases in the interests of maintaining competition; (4) noted that in order to protect the pace and volume of assistance against the fetish of "continuity" during the early sixties the Indo-American program probably will have to rely mainly upon more refined, reliable, and timely phasing and better intergovernmental coordination rather than upon multi-year financing; (5) examined some of the possibilities for increasing the volume and the effectiveness of the official American technical assistance flowing to India, especially in the industrial field; and (6) emphasized the need for competent personnel.

There would be little point in urging better intergovernmental planning, coordination, and accountability in the Indo-American program without first assembling such a roster of the rather more specific procedural reforms of which the program stands in need. Conversely, however, the enumeration of such steps does not quite exhaust the subject of coordination. Before concluding, I want to make three points under this heading that seem to me to deserve special emphasis.

First, the mounting of a fuller, franker, and continuing exchange concerning Indian development design is something from which both the Indian and the American governments can gain, but for which each must make adjustments in its administrative posture. The gain to the government of India need not be limited to the greater flexibility (and possibly even the greater volume) of American assistance that might follow from the reassurance that more comprehensive intergovernment planning would provide to United States policymakers. A continuing joint exercise that, subject to administrative and legislative review on both sides, would regularly program, review, and update the Indo-American aid effort could have a salutary effect on the quality of Indian planning itself. The suggestions made by the American participants in such an exercise, and even a systematic tapping of their technical programming skills, could be helpful, for example, in improving development phasing and in coordinating state and regional plans with the national development scheme. But, to reap these benefits, India may need to overcome a residual nervousness about exposing the general objectives and policies as well as the specifics of its development design to free, protracted discussion with the official representatives of a foreign government. Many senior Indian officials are confident that a broadening of the consultative role played by an aiding government need in no way threaten the autonomy of Indian planning. That will remain inviolate so long as the power of decision over indigenous Indian affairs remains unilaterally Indian. But some officials and politicians may yet need to convince themselves on this point.

On the American side, there is a legacy of diffident avoidance of such "intervention" to be overcome. Some United States officials should stop looking on Indian planning as a *fait accompli* that is both so jealously reserved a province of Indian autonomy and so technically competent in its practice that it can be neither gracefully nor usefully cross-examined. To implement a more effective intergovernment planning effort the United States needs greatly to reinforce its programming staff in New Delhi and to concentrate program design responsibilities in the latter's hands. In the United States case too, however, the rewards that such administrative reforms can yield should be sufficiently tempting. In addition to the side advantages of facilitating the preparation of annual program presentations to the Congress and reducing the aid authorities' vulnerability to their professional critics, stronger coordinated planning procedures would serve their manifest purposes. They should increase the impact of the aid dollar and give officials throughout the United States program a firmer grasp of the relation of their particular sub-programs to the over-all Indian development design.

Second, a word is needed on the impediment to easy intergovernment interchange that is posed by United States government security practices. My guess is that, even if every other condition advocated for facilitating more effective Indo-American aid planning were met, such activity would be badly hampered by a perpetuation of ICA's (now AID's) habits regarding the classification of documents, information, and ideas. As an outsider in New Delhi, I got the impression that the agency almost automatically gave every interesting piece of paper that came to hand (from outside as well as inside the agency) a security classification that shrouded it from all outside eyes, including those of Indian officials. Unless I am quite naive, the extent of this behavior could not possibly be explained on grounds of military or even broadly "strategic" security needs. Nor was it attributable to any deviousness of design in the United States program or basic distrust of the host government. My own interpretation was simply that it was a relic of the United States government's era of security hysteria in the early fifties.

Finally, as to the relationship of intergovernment (before-the-fact) planning and intergovernment (after-the-fact) accounting procedures: To the extent that the former can be strengthened, the latter can be safely and appropriately streamlined. In an administrative context like the Indian, fuller representation in the planning process is much the most effective means available to American authorities for assuring that United States monies are used responsibly. This is not to say that Indian administration is so reliable that it can be safely assumed that imports always will be put to the intended uses on the intended schedule. There is a need certainly for spot-checking and otherwise observing what physical disposition is made of aid goods. Indeed, in the case of most project assistance, such physical "end-use accounting" would be an inescapable feature of an adequate packaging of American technical assistance with American commodity assistance. But it can be asserted that the Indian government's own procedures for guarding against bulk dishonesty in the disposition of aid goods are trustworthy, and that Indian financial accounting is sufficiently elaborate and meticulous to offer a ready substitute for a mass of routine and duplicative United States government accounting.

12 FOREIGN AID'S FINANCIAL VEHICLES

In the days when individual receipt of *ad hoc* external assistance was a commonplace on the American frontier, whenever a farmer's neighbors helped him build a barn by providing aid in the form of labor, materials, and/or funds, the immediately operative characteristics of the assistance, so far as the purpose of barn-building was concerned, were given by the answers to such questions as these: How well were the kinds and quantities of in-kind services and material suited to the barn-builder's requirements? How much money did the neighbors offer? Was it offered with or without strings as to use or as to the suppliers to be patronized? Did the builder have a sensible construction schedule? Did his neighbors take the trouble to learn it and fit themselves to it—or persuade him to work out a mutually agreeable accommodation? Could their help be counted on to turn up at the appointed times? And were they willing to let the builder boss his own job, drawing, to be sure, on whatever advice they could offer and he wanted to accept?

Aside from these immediately pertinent matters—which are the ones, in the case of the Indo-American aid program, that we have just been discussing—there was also this to be asked: What future financial obligations, if any, did the barn builder incur by accepting the assistance?[1] Was the latter an outright gift, a simple loan, or something in between? If a loan, what were its terms?

In the foreign aid field, somewhat curiously, these latter

---

[1] The aided farmer might have obligated himself to make a future in-kind rather than monetary payment. In fact, if the repayment took the form of spare-time labor, of which he had an abundance but for which he had no alternative market, the situation would parallel the barter assistance rendered to India by some of the Soviet-bloc countries. But for present purposes, it makes the analogy less cumbersome to assume only that acceptance of the assistance might generate future "financial" obligations.

questions are commonly said to constitute the problem of "aid financing." This is even superficially descriptive only from the viewpoint of the aided party, who, lacking sufficient foreign exchange of his own, must try to get enough grants, loans, or their substitutes to "finance" the imports he needs. Even from this recipient's perspective, the real issue in financing net imports is more to get the assistance itself than to worry about its grant or loan format. From the viewpoint of an aiding government, the problem of financing foreign aid is the same as that of financing any other public outlay; it requires collection of taxes and/or creation of credit within the aiding government's own economy—issues that it is futile to discuss in the context of one comparatively small government expenditure program.

Our present very different subject is the one that would logically remain if the United States already had decided to render a stated volume of assistance to India on a stated timetable and had determined all aspects of its intrinsic form. In this event the issue of how the aid should be distributed among grants, ordinary loans, and alternatives in between, and of what the "terms" of the non-grants should be, would be a matter simply of deciding what financial forms or vehicles should be employed for conveying the assistance.[2]

Although the importance of the matters we are about to discuss commonly is exaggerated, this does not justify any slighting of them here. For one thing, my claim of primacy for the procedural problems involved in rendering and receiving assistance is premised on a tacit assumption that the choice as to forms of conveyance at least falls within certain limits. For example, there would be no point in worrying about any of the other characteristics of aid to India that could be conveyed only in the form of non-renewable one-year hard loans; assistance of such brevity would be tantamount to no assistance at all.

[2] For a more detailed analysis with respect to world-wide American foreign aid programs of many of the issues that this chapter raises with respect to the aid-to-India program, see Robert E. Asher, *Grants, Loans, and Local Currencies: Their Role in Foreign Aid* (The Brookings Institution, 1961).

Moreover, the point just implied—namely, that the conveyance form actually is an integral part of the total aid package —has a great deal of practical relevance for American policy-making. The United States Congress actually seldom, if ever, determines the other basic aspects of a country aid program and then, finally, turns to the choice of financial vehicles. It may, in fact, do the very opposite—set up a "development loan fund" with carefully drawn conveyance characteristics and leave most of the other procedural characteristics subordinate to, or to evolve from, this determination of vehicle.

Further, so far as the significance of the financial-forms question in the Indian case is concerned, excessive use of hard loans could readily pose a most tangible obstacle to orderly development by generating more future obligations than India will have the dollar capacity to meet. Finally, the vehicular choices are important because some of those that have been made in the past are leading to unwieldy accumulations of blocked United States rupee holdings that could lure future policymakers into serious errors.

The Traditional Choice: Grants or Ordinary Loans?

The basic choice as to vehicle that an aiding government has is between an outright gift and a loan in the usual sense— that is, one that provides that the borrower shall subsequently repay the lender in the latter's currency within a given period and with interest payments analogous to those required by private lenders. The outright grant is the simpler vehicle, and it shares the uncomplicated logic of the ordinary domestic government outlay—namely, that it is worth it to the American people to spend, say $400 million on economic development in India in fiscal 1963, just as it may be worth it to contribute $100 million to highway development in Indiana.

But the grant, since it is not to be repaid, is also in a significant sense the more expensive way of rendering a given amount of current foreign assistance. Most parliaments, if told that it is a matter of indifference whether they give India $400 million or just provide her with the use of $400 million for a limited period (charging interest for that service), will choose to part with their liquidity rather than their assets, and the United States Congress is no exception. Selection of the loan rather than the grant vehicle has no immediate advantage for American taxpayers, but eventually the flow of repayments and interest, by facilitating increased American imports (it being assumed that United States commercial policy remains neutral), should permit taxes to be set at somewhat lower levels than they otherwise responsibly could be.[3]

The impulse to economize is the predominant reason that aiding governments, including the United States, prefer to make loans and be repaid wherever they can. But there also are other reasons. There are the special considerations that obtain where an appropriating authority wants to institute a revolving fund for the long-run benefit of foreign development activity. Here the originating legislature does not "want its money back." But if one thinks of the fund it appropriates as a non-expiring asset, it does determine that the asset shall be dedicated in perpetuity to aiding a series of developing economies through their periods of greatest need.

[3] If one assumes certain domestic political rigidities, he can arrive at the opposite conclusion. For example, if United States tariffs were increased or other commercial-policy action taken to prevent the influx of loan-repayment-financed imports, then the opportunity for taxpayers responsibly to reap the future advantage that a present choice of loans instead of grants holds out to them would evaporate. Or again, as a result of similar commercial policy difficulties, it is possible that an added inflow of Indian debt repayments ten to thirty years hence would be counted, not a boon to the United States balance-of-payments problems of that era (as it would be counted right now), but the kind of aggravation that it would have been considered in the early fifties. Or further, since India's repayment obligations will encroach on her own growing but limited ability to finance imports, it can be argued that, if the United States continues to find it advisable to support a given pace of Indian economic development, choosing hard loans as a vehicle for current assistance will only raise the size of the future bills that American taxpayers are asked to foot—not for *net* assistance but for *fresh* assistance to India; and in terms of American politics it is the fresh-assistance requirement that is the painful one. Nonetheless, there is a residual plausibility in the idea that in the long run a hard loan would leave the lending government better off than would an equivalent grant.

These revolving-fund institutions may have a second characteristic, as in the case of the World Bank: They may be empowered to augment their funds of recirculating government capital by going for subscriptions into the private capital market. By this device the choice of loans as the vehicle for transferring public capital becomes a catalyst augmenting the export of private capital. Moreover with the passage of time, both the revolving-fund feature and the independent borrowing power of such institutions assure them a measure of independence from the annual moods of the national legislatures that set them up. This achieves what probably can be regarded as the ultimate purpose of these institutions—namely that they should serve as government-contrived substitutes for the withered portions of the highly developed private international banking system that served many of the foreign-credit needs of the world's then-developing economies in the era prior to 1914. This last point emphasizes what admirably useful institutions such agencies as the World Bank and the United States Export-Import Bank are. But also like their names it emphasizes their specialized character; they are designed to serve only the "bankable" portion of a developing economy's foreign-exchange requirements.[4]

Some of the reasons that Americans advance for preferring loans to grants as aid vehicles are less logical. In particular there is the reiterated claim that "loans are more businesslike." If this phrase refers to the motivations of the aiding government, it is plainly irrelevant. For it is not the business of government to be "businesslike" in its motives. The United States government does not provide assistance to India in order to earn interest. If this were its purpose, it would do better to lend the funds at home or better yet reduce taxes and let the taxpayers do their own lending or spending. It is true that government loans have more of the superficial stigmata of private loans than do government grants—but this is equally irrelevant.

[4] "Bankable" is an ambiguous adjective, however, that should not go undefined. We shall return to it in a moment, when I shall argue that whether a loan to a particular project is bankable really cannot, in a context like the Indian, be separated from the issue of the economy's total capacity to repay hard loans.

Even the most nearly defensible reading of the "more-business-like" phrase—the contention that being forced to repay with interest will stimulate the recipient to use the assistance more efficiently and productively—is unpersuasive in a case like the Indian. If the immediacy and urgency of the domestic needs for increased production and for narrowing the economy's future dependence upon assistance are not enough to promote efficiency in development, it may be doubted that much marginal stimulus will be afforded by deferred repayment obligations that are spread over extended periods. In any case, if the aiding government wants to promote development efficiency, it can do far more by engaging in effective intergovernment planning and by attaching the right conditions to the acceptance and use of the assistance itself.

Nevertheless, whatever the reasons, the fact remains that the majority preference in the United States is for using conventional loans as the mode for conveying foreign assistance wherever feasible. Moreover, at times in the past, nationalistic pride has caused the government of India to abet rather than resist this American inclination. Thus in the Indo-American program the choice between grants and loans reduces, in practice, to the question of how far the pro-loans bias can safely be indulged in the light of the Indian economy's probable future capacity to service ordinary international loans.

The relevant consideration for deciding this question frequently is misconstrued. The "bankability" of the foreign-exchange requirements of different specific development projects sometimes appears to be graded on the basis of their prospective domestic profitability, or of the net increases in output and real income that they are expected directly to yield. Such appraisals of the repayment prospects on foreign loans made to a central government miss the point on two counts.[5]

[5] It should be emphasized that, in taking this position, I do not mean to deny that authorities that make hard loans, like the World Bank, by following careful consultation and review procedures with respect to specific projects, especially of types with which they have accumulated extensive engineering and other experience, can give the recipient some valuable technical assistance. Indeed I already have singled out this opportunity for packaging technical

In the first place, so far as domestic productiveness is concerned, their criterion is too narrow. If allowed to mature during the life of a longer-term loan, an investment in education, let alone in road transport or additional contour bunding, may contribute at least as much to the total national output as would an equivalent investment in the most productive fertilizer factory or steel plant. Admittedly, whether the national government can in fact recapture enough such indirect gains in domestic real income to honor its debt obligations depends upon the degree of fiscal discipline it is able to impose on the economy. But so does its ability to capture enough of the real gains from the most directly productive project; even those of a wholly-owned public enterprise may be allowed, by irresponsible cost-price policies, to slip through the government's fingers. The fact is that, if domestic productiveness were the appropriate criterion, it could be argued that the government of India's total net-import requirement for the Third- and Fourth-Plan periods, is "credit-worthy" in the ordinary international banking sense.[6]

But, in the second place, domestic productiveness is *not* the appropriate criterion for judging loan-repaying capacity. The real question is the Indian economy's prospective foreign-exchange position, and as will be recalled from earlier chapters (see particularly Chapter 4, Tables 3 and 4), India's best hopes in this regard are far leaner than is its outlook for domestic output and income. Under the existing program net foreign-exchange requirements are projected as rising to peak levels of some Rs. 500-600 crores annually by the end of the Third Plan and as not diminishing substantially during the Fourth Plan. Moreover, as was emphasized in Chapter 9, these projections already assume the most vigorous expansion in exports that it is possibly realistic to anticipate. Thus it is abundantly clear that during the sixties India will have no

---

together with capital assistance as the greatest advantage of project aid. My present point, however, is entirely separate: It is that the probable domestic productiveness of a particular project (which can be improved by good project design) is not the relevant criterion for judging a country's ability to repay the foreign loans it receives for financing the project.

[6] Provided that some of the credit were of quite long term.

apacity for meeting more conventional-loan repayment and ervicing obligations than the amount its plans presently budget or that purpose—unless additional obligations are directly off-et by extra foreign assistance.

The Third Five Year Plan budgets Rs. 550 crores for for-ign debt repayment, and the great bulk of this will be claimed y obligations that already had been incurred by the start of he Plan period; there is very little provision for repayment of ew conventional-loan indebtedness incurred during the Third 'lan itself—unless the initial installments are postponed until fter 1965-66. As a matter of fact, the Plan makes compara-ively little provision for fresh conventional borrowing even of his latter sort. For under existing obligations, since virtually o old loans will be fully retired during the first half of the ixties, annual repayments already are bound to rise through-ut the Third-Plan years and to remain at high levels through-ut the Fourth Plan—when, as we have just noted, the na-ion's foreign-exchange position will continue to be under eavy pressure.

Two assumptions are necessary before the finding that India as scant capacity for paying additional foreign-exchange debt harges during the sixties can be translated into the conclu-ion that the country has scant capacity for accepting fresh onventional (or "hard") loan assistance. First, it must be ssumed that such loans cannot be refunded *ad infinitum*. fter a fashion, of course, the aiding countries could make he hard-loan vehicle convey all of the assistance India needs f they would keep on issuing enough new loans to cover, be-ides net assistance, most of the charges falling due on old oans. But this, from the Indian viewpoint, would be a most npalatable procedure. It would push the achievement of self-upport farther and farther into the future, and it would, to say he least, add a disquieting element of financial insecurity to evelopment planning. Nor does the making of loans that will ave to be paid off by fresh borrowing make any real sense rom the viewpoint of the United States. It leaves the assistance b unnecessarily undone; it creates the problem for a sub-equent Administration and Congress of deciding whether an dditional aid appropriation should be made if the original aid intent is to be made good; and in the end it may even be hard to tell whether the aiding government is not having to make fresh loans to finance the payment of the interest it is owed.

A second assumption is necessary before one concludes that an inability to make extensive additional repayments means an inability to do much additional conventional borrowing. It concerns loan terms. One can conceive of interest rates so low and amortization periods so long that loans of any required magnitude could be squeezed within limits set by maximum supportable annual debt charges. As we shall be noting shortly the United States presently is seizing upon just such an escape from India's repayment-capacity dilemma. But for the moment let us continue to suppose that we are talking about conventionally "hard" dollar loans of the sort that India thus far has been given by the World Bank and the United States Export Import Bank. During the fifties credits to India from these two sources had an average duration of 13.1 years, an average interest rate of 5.1 percent (weighted in both cases by loan sizes). These average terms combine to produce an annual debt charge that is just about 10 percent of the principal. At these terms, India's debt repayment budget for the Third and Fourth Plans might support something on the order of $1½ billion of additional borrowing. This is a crude estimate, but it needs no more refining to make its significance abundantly clear—if one remembers that India's non-P.L. 480 net-import requirements for the sixties are on the order of $10 billion.

In United States policy circles in recent years it has become increasingly fashionable to couple enlightened appraisals of aid needs with a preference for loans instead of grants. For India, at least in the sixties, such a policy line makes no sense if one means conventional loans at conventional terms. Such loans cannot begin to do the needed job.

And yet grants are felt to be political anathema in Washington. Such is the dilemma that has been heavily responsible for stimulating American foreign policymakers to invent three disguises for needed but politically unseemly overseas grants: (1) the so-called "sale" of aid commodities in exchange for overseas blocked deposits of local currencies, (2) so-called "soft" dollar loans repayable in similarly blocked local cur rencies, and (3) conventional loans (that is, dollars repayable in dollars), whose terms have been so extraordinarily liberalized as to make them adequately "soft."

The Camouflaging Devices

The last of the devices just listed, an invention of the Kennedy Administration, was the last to be used. It is a comparatively harmless device. As a practical matter, it appears to me that 2 percent, forty- and fifty-year loans are scarcely distinguishable from grants. Certainly they are virtually shorn of the conventional loan's repayment and revolving-fund advantages. But such "loans" have few serious unwanted side effects, and if a way is needed to sugar-coat grants, this new way rather plainly is the best. It has been devised as a substitute for the other kind of soft loan by those who have realized the latter's shortcomings. Moreover, the criticism of arrangements that cause the United States to accumulate the balances of blocked local currencies that is implicit in the new-style "soft loan" (dollars repayable in dollars, but over a greatly extended period) applies as much to blocked-currency "sales" of United States surplus farm commodities as it does to the old-style soft loan. Thus I may appear to be flogging a dead horse to carry on, as I do in the balance of this chapter, about the two older blocked-currency varieties of grant disguises. However, the facts are that the present Administration has shown no actual disposition to desist from using the blocked-currency sale as its principal device for distributing United States food surpluses overseas; that, even if both old-style soft loans and P.L. 480 blocked-rupee sales of American food should be abandoned forthwith as aid vehicles, their past uses already have created mounting United States rupee balances that pose serious problems; and that the pitfalls besetting the blocked-currency vehicles are not yet widely enough recognized, either in India or in the United States, to assure the avoidance of these dangers. Thus the following critique, I suspect, is still worth spelling out.

First, to make clear the theory behind the blocked-currency

vehicles: Suppose one of our frontier ancestors, Jones, undertaking to build a barn, had refused an ordinary loan from his neighbor, Smith, because of inability to repay. Smith, for his part, stubbornly refused to make Jones a gift of what he needed. But he did agree to supply it to him under either of two arrangements. Under the first arrangement Smith would sell Jones supplies in exchange for vouchers that entitled the bearer to a stated number of hours of Jones' labor—vouchers, however, that could be used only for work done on Jones' premises and on projects and at times to which Jones agreed. Or, second, Smith would make Jones a money loan that was repayable, as to both principal and interest, in the same kind of vouchers. Contemporaries of the two would have called Smith's position pretty childish, or something stronger to the same effect, unless you explained that Smith had a wife who had put her foot down against all further give-aways; yet she was sufficiently concerned with keeping up appearances to find his subterfuges relatively acceptable, even when she saw through them.

The foregoing, to the best of my understanding, is analogous, point-for-point, to the manner in which the United States government has been conveying the majority of its economic assistance to India during the past half-dozen years. Perhaps the analogy should be amended to indicate that the blocked-currency camouflages have had almost as much semantic appeal for Jones (the government of India) as they have had for the aiding party. But the American purpose in adopting the disguises—to appear less free-handed overseas and more businesslike at home—is the same as Smith's. And Jones' labor vouchers exactly fit the case of the rupee deposits that accrue to United States government account in exchange for the surplus foods and other agricultural commodities supplied to the government of India, or as payment of interest and principal on old-style soft Development Loan Fund (DLF) loans. These rupees, by agreement, are inconvertible; they cannot be used for buying Indian exports; they cannot (with a minor exception, noted below) be used in India except for purposes and projects to which the Indian government agrees; and their contribution to such purposes obviously represents no fresh or additional commitment of American resources to Indian development, over and above the original assistance that gave rise to the rupee funds.

Moreover, there is no need, in the Indo-American case, to extend the analogy to cover the possibility that the prospering condition of the aided economy some day will allow the United States' blocked rupee holdings to be made convertible, thereby "hardening" the soft loans after all. As far into the future as anyone can dimly make out the Indian export-import outlook, the only sensible assumption for current United States policymakers is that India's trade position never will become buoyant enough to allow us to bring home the blocked rupee holdings—as dollars or commodities—that meanwhile we shall have been accumulating.

One might spin out various complaints about the intangible effects of the blocked-currency vehicles. I suspect, for example, that by perpetuating the fire-sale image of surplus-foods disposal, sale of such food for blocked rupees has been distracting American policymakers from some rather basic rethinking about the role of American agriculture in the world economy during the remainder of this century. Likewise, I would argue that the soft-loan disguise caused DLF to adopt a banker's attitude and act like an agency dispensing slightly modified hard loans instead of adopting the very different attitude that suited its actual function—that of the United States government's principal instrument for dispensing slightly modified development grants. But these are elusive matters that others may find much less discernible or serious than I do. The one concrete, unmistakable set of difficulties that the blocked-currency aid vehicles have produced in the Indo-American aid program is that surrounding the administration of the United States rupee funds to which they have given rise.

The Phenomenon of Blocked Rupee Funds

The rupee payments that the United States receives from the sale of P.L. 480 commodities to the government of India give rise to essentially the same kind of funds as do the rupee proceeds from DLF's (old-style) soft loans. However, DLF loan repayments have not yet attained nearly as formidable proportions as have P.L. 480 rupee proceeds. And the latter, unlike the former, have an evident kinship to the "counterpart funds" that have become such a familiar feature of American foreign aid programs throughout the post-World-War-II period.

The standard counterpart fund, often associated with an aid grants program providing consumer goods or raw materials imports, serves as a depository for the proceeds from the local sales of aid goods. It has been generally accepted that the title to such funds lies with the aided government. However, in negotiating its provision of aid goods, the United States retains partial rights of decision over the disposition of the local-currency funds which their sale produces. Typically, an agreed small portion of the funds is allocated for meeting the local-currency expenses, especially the local labor expenses, that the United States government incurs in administering the aid program.[7] The remainder of the funds, reserved for indigenous development purposes, can be spent only for purposes to which the United States and the aided governments jointly agree.

There is one narrow but deep difference between the local-currency receipts that accrue under the P.L. 480 and the DLF programs, on the one hand, and, on the other, the ordinary counterpart fund: The former are exclusively the property of the United States government. In a sense, this is only a technicality. And yet, as will be emphasized at the end of the section, it is this fact of technical ownership that, by inviting the United States to ascribe an illusory power and substance to its rupee holdings in India, prompts the worst anxieties about their long-run mismanagement.

---

[7] To this minor extent the arrangement becomes neither a grant nor a loan but the kind of barter transaction (common in Indian-Soviet bloc relations) in which the aiding government provides needed commodities in exchange for available local services and commodities for which the aided government could not otherwise find an export market.

Otherwise, the formalities of the disposition of P.L. 480 sales proceeds are substantially the same as those of a standard counterpart fund. The rupee proceeds from the P.L. 480 imports are immediately deposited to a United States Treasury account in India.[8] Each of the individual sales agreements between the two governments has stipulated that a stated fraction of the proceeds (the figure has varied but has averaged about 15 percent) shall be available for the United States government's unilateral use in meeting its rupee expenses in India. Another minority fraction—in earlier agreements, as much as 11 percent; in later and larger agreements, as little as 5 percent—is reserved for jointly agreed uses of the kind specified by the Act's "Cooley Amendment"—namely, loans (1) to United States business firms or local affiliates of such firms for business expansion in India and (2) to any firms establishing operations or facilities that, it is deemed, will promote the marketing of United States farm products in India. The majority balance of the rupee proceeds (in earlier agreements, some 72 percent; in recent agreements, 80 percent of the total) is to be loaned or granted by the American government to the Indian government for jointly agreed development uses. In the early agreements only about one-fifth of this majority fraction of the rupee proceeds was earmarked for grants, the remainder being destined eventually to be repaid into the United States Treasury's rupee account, presumably for repetitive lending. More recent agreements specify a 50-50 split between grants and loans for these United States rupee transfers to the government of India.

The mechanics for disposing of the rupee proceeds that DLF receives from its dollar loans to India are simpler but

---

[8] As a matter of fact, the proceeds are deposited *before* the aid goods are sold internally. The government of India pays for the commodities upon arrival at Indian ports, usually obtaining short-term credits from the Reserve Bank for this purpose. Then it uses the internal sales proceeds to retire these short-term obligations.

Until mid-1960 the United States Treasury rupee deposits were in commercial banks, almost exclusively in the nationalized State Bank of India. Thereafter it was agreed to transfer them to the Reserve Bank of India (the central bank). They draw interest in the latter, as they did in the former.

also, compared with the P.L. 480 arrangement, less clearly specified by the enabling legislation or in the Loan Fund's individual dollar-loan agreements. In this case there appears to be no question of earmarking fractional portions of the proceeds for local United States government expenses or for special loans to United States affiliated firms. It is clear that the rupee proceeds shall all go to uses that, in due course, shall be jointly agreed upon by the two governments. Presumably the uses all will be internal ones of a development character; and presumably the vehicle for disbursing these rupee funds is to be, unexceptionally, the interest-bearing loan. However, both of these last points (the second of which, like the loan portions of rupee disbursements under P.L. 480, suggests the prospect of endlessly mounting United States rupee holdings) remain uncertain, as does the question of who the recipients of DLF's rupee loans will be—only the central Indian government, or also specific enterprises, financial institutions, and lesser governmental bodies?

There is one obvious difference between the rupee-repayment aspects of soft loans, on the one hand, and, on the other, either the P.L. 480 arrangement or a conventional grant-counterpart fund: In the soft-loan case more time elapses between the original import of aid goods and the deposit and subsequent disbursement of the rupee payments to which the aid goods (or dollar loan) give rise. Actually, there are some time lags in all these cases. But in the counterpart and P.L. 480 operations they are, or in principle can be, short enough so that it often seems plausible to discuss the functions and proprieties of local-currency fund management as though the lags between the receipt of the aid goods and the disbursement of their rupee proceeds did not exist.[9]

On the surface there appears to be nothing seriously improper about these arrangements. What, then, is wrong with them? In the most immediate sense, the trouble is that they produce friction between the two governments and, in the case of the Indian government, anxieties that threaten seriously to

[9] As a result, as we shall be noting in a moment, there is much less confusion about the economic effects of soft-loan repayment than of the other two arrangements.

impede the smoothness of the aid relationship. If one insists on a more analytical answer than this, he is apt to discover, I think, a kind of layering of issues running from ones that are loudly debated but superficial, at the top, to ones that are little articulated but fundamental, at the bottom. I shall mention five of these, ranked in descending order of prominence but ascending order of importance: (1) the allegedly inflationary effects of expenditures of blocked rupees, (2) the extent to which the operation of the rupee funds delegates to a foreign government control over indigenous development activities, (3) the sheer administrative nuisance of the arrangements, (4) the progressive accumulation of United States rupee holdings that present procedures seem to assure, and (5) the mounting dangers of proprietary delusion as this accumulation proceeds.

1. From time to time there have been vociferous complaints from some Indian government officials that the expenditure of United States P.L. 480 rupee holdings is dangerously inflationary. (This complaint has not to my knowledge been extended yet, with equal force, to the prospective disbursement of DLF's rupee receipts.) It is argued that expenditure of the P.L. 480 rupees, at the time it occurs, is unmatched by any fresh injection of real resources into the economy. Some United States officials have vehemently denied the charge, often reasoning from the assumption, mentioned a couple of paragraphs back, of simultaneity between the arrival of aid goods and the expenditure of the rupee funds to which they give rise.

Actually there need be no mystery about the economic effect involved here. The importation of surplus American foodgrains into India and their sale have a dual anti-inflationary effect that is both powerful and immediate. First, there is a supply effect; by adding to local supplies, the aid goods lower the food prices that given volumes of food demand will call forth. Second, there is a demand effect; as the government accepts payment for the sale of the foodgrains, it withdraws private purchasing power from the circular flow of income just as surely as it would do if it were collecting additional taxes.[10] Thus foreign provision of food or of other scarce consumables creates an opportunity for noninflationary internal development outlays that otherwise would not exist. It is also true, however, that this opportunity must be seized at the time it arises or it will be lost. It cannot be stored up. All of the anti-inflationary offset that receipt and sale of a particular consignment of P.L. 480 imports provides is, perforce, set against the expansionist effect of the internal spending (including that for development programs) being done at the time the imports are sold. If there is more offset than is needed to neutralize any tendencies that such current spending may have to raise consumer prices, the result may be some current price declines; but there cannot be any transference of "unused" anti-inflationary potential to the future.

Thus, when United States officials try to justify the noninflationary character of P.L. 480 rupee outlays on the ground that the funds originated three (or six, or eighteen) months earlier from inflation-resisting imports, and Indian officials reply that all of this is past history and has no bearing on the present inflation issue, the Indians, strictly speaking, are quite right. And, of course, they are also right when they note that the contribution of United States rupee holdings to the Indian government (which originally issued the currency) does not in itself constitute any real contribution to Indian economic development; exactly the same result could be accomplished by additional Indian deficit spending.

But none of this supports the impression that those who object to the "inflationary" effects of United States blocked-rupee spending seek to create. In the first place, current rupee outlays, if one wants to keep his books that way, *can* be legitimately set off against, and can be rendered "noninflationary" by, *current* sales of P.L. 480 imports—not those in the past that

---

[10] It will be noted that P.L. 480 imports that are used for adding to the government's food stocks have only the supply effect, unless the need to make rupee payments to the United States for these increments in its food inventories causes the government of India to collect more taxes than it otherwise would. This is most unlikely. However, by providing better cushions against domestic shortages due to bad crops, the supply effect of such additions to stocks may be overwhelmingly important.

generated the funds now being spent, but those being made at the present time.

Second—a more general and conclusive point—a developing economy, especially one like India's that also is experiencing a fairly rapid monetization of transactions previously conducted, and of savings previously held, in nonmonetary forms, requires a rapidly growing money supply. In India this means that in any case the growth process itself requires the government to make sizable continuing expenditures of newly created funds. Up to a limit that well exceeds the rate of United States rupee outlays *thus far,* the growing productive capacity of the economy can readily absorb this new-money spending without general inflationary consequences. Under these circumstances, there is no good reason on inflationary grounds why the government of India should not use United States rupee holdings in their present amounts when it has undertaken in good faith to do so. It is simply a matter of arranging its budget to use these funds instead of borrowing so much from the banks.

2. When I reached India in mid-1959, I was convinced that all of the arguments about the inflationary effects of P.L. 480 rupees were a cover for a less articulate but deeper Indian antipathy to the degree of joint control with India over some wholly indigenous development projects that the scheme seems to give the United States aid authorities. Some United States officials at that time were complaining that the Indian authorities seemed systematically to have been withholding their approval from P.L. 480 rupee projects, thereby forcing the P.L. 480 funds to pile up in the State Bank, where they were deposited. At the same time, the government was borrowing from the same bank approximately equivalent amounts and going ahead with the same kinds of projects to which the P.L. 480 funds might have been allocated. This seemed like the tactic of an astute government that simply wanted to do its own "inflationary" spending without having the United States exercising any control over project choice and design.

Moreover, the tendency to consider the P.L. 480 operation as a sort of "counterpart-fund" arrangement invited the assumption that the American authorities really sought some measure of control over indigenous development activity. For unquestionably the achievement of such partial control—albeit presumably for wholly benign, unselfish reasons—has been the major purpose of the United States government in establishing grant-counterpart arrangements in connection with foreign aid programs in other countries. The United States has wanted to make sure that its consumable aid goods are sensibly "priced into" the aided economy and, this having been done, that the opportunity thereby created for noninflationary internal development outlays is not frittered away. Or in more sophisticated situations, where this last is not a serious risk, the United States has wanted to influence the mixture of internal development activities in what it has regarded as desirable directions.

Thus it appeared in mid-1959 that the Indian and American governments, while arguing over the inflationary effects of P.L. 480 rupee outlays, were silently grappling over the issue of United States control. But I am now convinced that this interpretation was mostly mistaken. In the first place, some of the appearance of "silent grappling" was inadvertent. The Indian government's "unilateral borrowing" from the State Bank of amounts equivalent to the United States deposits being immobilized therein was not necessarily a shrewdly calculated tactic. The actuating impulse may have been simply the routine desire of the State Bank managers to show a good profit and loss statement by using idle, interest-bearing deposits to buy interest-yielding government securities. And the government's use of these funds for what could have been P.L. 480 projects may have been due simply to a desire to get on with some scheduled work without the administrative delays incident to P.L. 480 financing. On the United States side, moreover, the responsible TCM officials seemed little concerned to use the P.L. 480 operation as a device for partially controlling some indigenous development activity. The funds, they felt, were essentially a by-product of an American policy choice made for domestic political purposes, and their concern was chiefly just to dispose of the rupees in a responsible, legally correct manner.

In the second place, in any event, the control issue has been downgraded by the fact that the Indians recently have re-discovered a way to play strictly according to the P.L. 480 rules and yet virtually to by-pass any effective United States direction of indigenous development activity. And the Americans have been acquiescing readily. Since mid-1959 the appropriation of P.L. 480 funds to jointly agreed uses has considerably accelerated. The procedure basically has been for the Indian government to present to the United States authorities a long list, drawn from the next phases of its development plan, of projects requiring local financing and to say, in effect, "These things are going to be done anyway. Which ones would you like to finance?" American officials have selected certain projects, and agreements have been made. To be sure, the United States has sometimes secured modifications in selected projects and occasionally has persuaded India to accept alternatives to those on the list, but it has not exercised any major initiative as to project choice.

In the third place, the lack of overt Indian misgivings about the control implications of prospective disbursement of DLF rupees suggests that the encroachment on their development autonomy is not, after all, what really worries the Indians with regard to United States rupee holdings. For if one accepts the thesis that it is unlikely that DLF rupees will ever become convertible, the United States' purpose in requiring rupee repayment in this case is peculiarly susceptible to being interpreted as control-motivated. And yet there do not seem to be serious Indian complaints on this score. I suspect that in this case, as also now in the P.L. 480 case, sophisticated Indian officials have come to the view that very little in principle is lost by letting the United States get the credit for some earthen dams, godowns, and other rupee-expense projects that are going to be built anyway.

Where the P.L. 480 arrangements come closer to raising a really substantive control issue is in the preferment (required under the Cooley Amendment) of American and American-affiliated private firms doing business in India and of firms facilitating the local marketing of American farm products. For this undoubtedly skews whatever provision of finance to private business the government would otherwise choose to make, and it may even deny India a certain amount of foreign exchange by preventing particular American firms from using dollars to buy the rupees required for local investment outlays when they are beginning operations in India. However, the Indian government now recognizes and, on balance, approves the trend toward joint foreign-Indian business ventures; and it realizes that most incoming American private capital will be recruiting its "counterpart" rupee capital through an Indian partner anyway. Cooley-Amendment loans may help a little to stimulate the inflow of externally-financed equipment and technical assistance that foreign private investment can bring, and, at any rate, their percentage claim on P.L. 480 funds has been very small, especially in more recent agreements. The increase in jointly approved assignments to particular users since mid-1959 suggests that the Indian government is not greatly exercised about them.[11]

3. In the eyes of Indian officials, American procedures for disposing of blocked rupee funds have been more of an impediment to the expeditious administration of locally financed development projects than a threat to the autonomy of the indigenous Indian effort. In the past the rigid application of formal United States government accounting practices to rupee outlays has caused a cumbersome, duplicative mass of paperwork. One can only hope that these procedures now have been adequately simplified. Plainly if any part of the Indo-American program's financing needs to be thoroughly streamlined, it is this one.

[11] One reader of an earlier draft of the present paper has offered an important amendment to its discussion of the "control issue" in P.L. 480 rupee financing:
There is a real possibility of . . . frictions developing as a result of efforts by the states to work directly on the U.S. mission to get P.L. 480 money for pet projects. The U.S. mission has already been placed in the middle of a squabble between West Bengal and the Center over P.L. 480 funds for urban development in Calcutta and refugee resettlement. States are likely to try this more often. Not only American Congressmen but also Indian politicians begin to believe that it is real money after a while.

4. One begins, finally, to strike toward the root of Indian anxieties about United States blocked-rupee funds when he asks about the future of the funds. How long will they remain in United States hands, and how long will they continue to grow?

In India, as we have seen, a majority fraction of the earlier P.L. 480 proceeds, nearly half of the proceeds arising under more recent P.L. 480 agreements, and presumably all of the DLF rupee proceeds have been reserved for revolving fund use, compounding with the passage of time. All of the United States government's rupee receipts earn bank interest from the time of their receipt to their initial disbursement; and those disbursed as loans thereupon start earning loan interest in perpetuity, except for intermittent periods when, having been repaid and not yet reloaned, they earn bank interest again. Moreover (again, presumably), all of the interest earned by the United States rupee loan funds accrues to the loan funds themselves and cannot be appropriated to other purposes. An extrapolation of present practices would suggest, not only that the United States rupee holdings in India will grow enormously over the next two or three decades, as a result of assistance already committed to India or likely to be rendered during the next five years, but that they are slated to remain permanent United States government assets and to accumulate indefinitely.

There is a quip current in New Delhi that, thanks to the workings of its rupee funds, the United States soon "will own a majority of the Indian money supply." The prospect is not as bad as that, mainly because we are talking (we hope) about an economy that also will be growing at a compound rate of increase. But the outlook is, nevertheless, thoroughly bizarre. By the end of the Third Five Year Plan, as a result of the loan-fund allocations from the United States surplus food sales that already have been made to India or that are now committed to the end of the Third Plan, plus the early payments of principal and interest on the soft ("Development Assistance" and DLF) dollar loans made up to and during the Third Plan, plus the interest that already will have accrued on United States rupee funds and loans by 1965-66, United

States rupee holdings are likely to have an aggregate value of Rs. 800 crores or 900 crores. If India can avoid substantial inflation between now and then, this might be equivalent to, say, one-fifth of the total Indian money supply (demand deposits and circulating currency) at that time. If all existing legal arrangements surrounding the funds held firm, it would not be surprising if this fraction rose to one-third during the succeeding quarter-century, as a result of the fresh injections of rupee capital being made by the continuing payments of principal and interest on outstanding DLF loans and of the compounding of these increments once they accrue.

Additional P.L. 480 rupee sales or old-style soft loans during the Fourth-Plan period and after would tend to push this fraction higher. On the other hand, it would be lower to the extent that there is significant price inflation.

5. We may be fairly sure that the United States government is not really going to own a third of the Indian money supply, or any amount near that, in 1990. The important question is whether such an outcome will be forestalled in a painless, civilized manner or only after some crises that seriously strain the relations of the Indian and the American governments and impede the progress of Indian economic development.

The latter is the basic concern that sophisticated Indian officials feel about the rupee-fund arrangements. They reason that if the funds continue to mount as rapidly as predicted, it may, indeed, become fiscally embarrassing to the Indian government to find employment for all of them. For example, in order to make noninflationary use of all of the new United States rupee loans that would be coming to hand in some years, it might be necessary, not just to forego some conventional deficit spending, but to run a substantial surplus in the rest of the Indian budget. And this would be at least as difficult politically in India as it would be here. Accordingly, as the accumulation proceeded, the Indians would be inclined to quarantine more and more of the United States rupee holdings—to force them to pile up idly by refusing to consent to uses requiring joint agreement. It is such a situation that Indian officials fear might become explosive before it is finally resolved by measures that would put the funds, once and for all, out of existence.

The responsible United States authorities in New Delhi tend to be impatient with such Indian anxieties. These are American officials who by now have become thoroughly erudite in the topsy-turvy economics of United States rupee funds. They are quick to say that "of course" United States rupees add no real resources to the Indian economy, that accumulations allowed to reach the proportions I have suggested would be plainly "monstrous," and that "obviously" the funds, sooner or later "simply will have to be extinguished." Such officers take the Indians' fears as almost a personal affront to their own good sense and integrity. They say, in so many words, "They (the Indians) should know we'd never use the funds for purposes they don't approve. Why, we even lean over backwards to clear all of our unilateral United States uses of the funds with them in cases where we are under no obligation to do so. Moreover, if they have any remaining doubts, it is time for them to consider the control issue the other way around. All they have to do to prevent uses they don't like (other than the limited category requiring only American approval) is to with- hold agreement."

In a legalistic sense, this last point is decisive. The govern- ment of India's veto power over the uses proposed for Ameri- can blocked rupee balances is legally a complete defense against excesses. The Indian government can allow the United States rupees to pile up in quarantine and print rupees to pay the interest on them indefinitely without the slightest disloca- tion of the economy. The Indian officials admit this and also admit to no doubts of the reasonableness of their immediate American counterparts. But they push the argument to the level of practical politics.

The Indians point out that not all members of the United States Congress, any more than all members of the Indian Parliament, are as sophisticated about the peculiarities and limitations of the United States government's rupee holdings as are the American officials directly concerned with the prob- lem. The critical fact, they feel, is that of United States pro- prietorship. To many American Congressmen rupee notes that belong to their government may seem just as real a claim to resources as do dollars. How can they be sure, the Indians ask, that at some future time, when enormous numbers of rupees pile up in United States coffers, well-intentioned American politicians will not insist on giving India, say, a "wholly United States-financed" doubling of her university system, or insist on using United States rupees to finance heavy Indian exports to Africa? And how can they be sure, the Indians persist, that when such a time comes their own politicians will not acquiesce to some extent—for the sake of general good relations with the United States, or to strengthen their plea for more real United States assistance, or in response to domestic political pressures? The result, they conclude, could be grossly to overburden indigenous real resources and/or to force an economy with a chronic foreign-exchange problem into making unrequited exports that it could not afford.

As corroborating evidence, the Indian officials point to the ideas for third-country uses of local-currency receipts which the United States Congress has included in both its surplus-food and its soft-loan legislation, and especially to the expansive notions along these lines that characterized much of the original Congressional thinking about the International Development Association: "If we can't bring our rupees home, at least maybe we can give them as aid to Indonesia."

I must say that I find these Indian anxieties disturbingly persuasive. Endlessly mounting United States government rupee holdings are, at the very least, an invitation to folly. It is like keeping a Christmas tree lighted with old-fashioned candles around the house. Nothing may happen, and it may for a time be ceremonially necessary. But a circumspect householder would do well to get rid of it as quickly as possible.

Conclusion

I end this chapter with the uneasy sense that I may have spoken too bluntly about the elaborate financial pretenses in which supporters of United States development assistance have encased their programs for domestic political reasons. Perhaps this is a case where a friend of foreign aid, and, more specifically of aid to India, should avoid calling a spade a spade. However, I cannot quite believe that is so. At any rate, it seems to me that the circumstances of the Indian case make it so essential to urge a change in the attitude in the United States toward grants that, in order to make this point, it is worth even running the risk of arousing fresh opposition to the substance of development assistance.

No instant abandonment of the camouflaging devices, of course, is possible. However, the shift of project aid from old-style soft loans to conventional loans with greatly stretched-out terms represents, as we have seen, a major step in the right direction. In addition, the following seem to me steps that would improve the vehicular aspects of the Indo-American program.

1. If, as suggested in the preceeding chapter, a substantial portion of non-project-tied "special assistance" is among the American contributions to India's Third Five Year Plan, clearly this should be conveyed as grants.

2. Authority should be sought and the decision made to supply at least a sizable fraction of India's receipts of non-relief surplus foods on a grant rather than a rupee-sales basis, and the possibility should be explored of renegotiating part of the Third-Five-Year-Plan Indo-American foodgrains agreement accordingly.

3. AID should be empowered, if it chooses, to disburse some of its original rupee receipts of DLF loan repayments as grants to the government of India instead of as rupee loans —and it should so choose.

4. In subsequent P.L. 480 sales agreements, more of the proceeds should be assigned to grants-to-government, and less to loans-to-government, uses.

5. Legislative authorization (where necessary) should be sought and administrative decisions taken to check the cumulative growth of the United States rupee loan funds (a) by

allowing rupee loan repayments to be redisbursed as grants and (b) by providing that all interest earned by rupee loans shall accrue to general United States rupee holdings (from which they can be granted) rather than as additional loan fund capital.

6. American aid authorities should be empowered generally to rely upon the Indian government's accounting of its uses of United States rupees, and every effort should be made to simplify rupee disbursement procedures.

It is perhaps appropriate at the end of a study like this one to point up the major conclusions that have been reached and at the same time to emphasize some of its limitations.

Omissions and Qualifications

I would warn first about the topics that have been slighted. While the concern of the book has been with the whole phenomenon of Indian development and with the relationship of the United States thereto, its focus has been confined to a few critical issues that by no means exhaust the terrain. Many of the slighted subjects—the irrigation program, for instance, the nation's energy requirements, the whole matter of public enterprise management, and many other subjects—clearly lie within the study's analytical framework. Their neglect has been due only to limitations of space.

However, subjects have been omitted also that fall largely or entirely outside the present framework and yet have major significance for Indian development. For example, there is the matter of Indo-Pakistani relations. Not long before I went out to India in 1959 a senior United Nations official assured me that it would be nearly fruitless to expend analytical energies on India's development prospects until there had been some accommodation of the disputes between India and Pakistan, especially over the Kashmir and over the management of the Indus River. This view, once I was on the scene in India, seemed to me grossly exaggerated, and in any event, there seemed to be a conspicuous improvement in Indo-Pakistani relations in 1959-60. Latterly, however, evidence of renewed friction between the two countries added plausibility to my UN informant's contention. At any rate, it is well to note that here is a dimension of the Indian development problem that the present discussion has entirely omitted.

Also slighted are the massive subjects of literacy and, more broadly, of India's educational strategy and programs. Clearly these are issues of the very greatest moment for any truly comprehensive appraisal of Indian development needs. This is so even if one were disposed, as I am, to emphasize the costs as well as the benefits of education and the need, accordingly, to fit educational programs within a realistic total-resources budget and to enforce a tough-minded, production-oriented set of priorities upon the composition of such programs.

I have given little attention to the training of skilled manpower—a matter that, while it can be logically subsumed under the heading of education, has such immediate operational bearing upon economic development that it usually receives separate emphasis. The rapid multiplication of technical and organizational skills is a vital concern of industrializing economies the world over. As indicated, India's supplies of skilled manpower and its present capacities for training probably are somewhat larger, not only in absolute numbers but relative to its requirements, than those of most other poor countries. Accordingly, I have tended to dwell on other more pressing problems and scarcities—or rather (more accurately) not to dwell on the training aspect that runs through most of the problems I have emphasized. It would be a gross error to conclude from this, however, that further development of skilled manpower is unimportant in the Indian case or that those engaged in training can afford to slacken their efforts even slightly. It remains true for India, as for any emerging economy, that economic development, most simply construed, consists in increasing the productive capacities of the population, and that these capacities depend even more upon the skills of the work force than upon the stock of tools with which it has to work.

The most glaring omission in this discussion has to do with the population problem. In examining the Indian planning aggregates, of course, I have taken account of the unexpected acceleration of population growth during the fifties and of the projections for the sixties. But very little space has been given to the longer-run prospects for India's population, to the manner in which the growth rate will be retarded (as plainly, sooner or later, it must be), or to the part that the government of India (or other agencies) will manage to play in this process through the propagation of birth control.

This is an omission for which I would enter a positive defense. For in this case thoughtful Americans stand in some danger of letting what obviously is a problem of tremendous importance—perhaps overriding importance in the sweep of history—distort near-term policy. In India there is little that the United States government, quite aside from its own political inhibitions with respect to birth control, could conceivably contribute to an attack on the birth rate. The Indian government, as we have seen, has strong purposes in this regard; it is little restrained by formal religious or ideological inhibitions; virtually no technical assistance will be required in this area; and the direct resource requirements for a vigorous population control effort are inconsequential. What is needed, however, is a change in mores of a most sensitive and delicate kind, and this is going to take time. In the long run the government's efforts will be assisted by a natural "standard-of-living effect" as, with rising incomes, people begin to realize the material advantages of smaller families. But meanwhile it is unthinkable that either the government of India or such suppliers of assistance as the government of the United States would, for demographic reasons, slow up their attack on the Indian death rate via public health programs.

Therefore, while accelerated population growth persists in India, this would be the very worst time for Americans to fall into the delusion of thinking that it would be useless to try to promote an expansion of production in India until the "population explosion" has been brought under control. This notunfamiliar thesis gets the priorities exactly backwards. Until an effective population policy can begin, slowly and hesitantly, to take hold, the need for a production expansion in India—which the United States can materially assist—is doubly urgent.

The warnings addressed to the reader in these final pages must extend to what the book does say as well as to what it does not. Some of the present discussion, based as it is on firsthand impressions now two years old, may be dated, and some of the commentary on government operations may reflect the limitations of the outside observer who, no matter how close his associations, never completely can share the vantage point of those bearing responsibilities within a government.

More generally, it is only fair to admit that an essay of the proportions of this one must base its arguments at many points upon mere glimpses of reality. Repeatedly in surveying as broad a subject as that of Indian economic development, a seeker after insights may think he has found some. But he can never be sure immediately. In a few cases, by accumulating data or additional direct observations, he may be able to submit his hypothesis to a quasi-scientific test. But the usual procedure is to assemble tentative, mostly untested hypotheses, together with some findings and speculations of others, into some kind of pattern that the investigator then proceeds to "try out" on other students of, and participants in, the field. This trying-out process is never quite done. It entails the successive submission, revision, and resubmission of a diagnosis to the criticism of others and to the challenge of new observations and events. The purpose is to bring the hypothesis into progressively closer accord with reality, always on the hopeful premise that reality itself has an internally consistent pattern that only requires discerning.

The argument of the present volume has, through discussion and through the circulation of papers and drafts, already been subjected to considerable winnowing and revision. However, for many of its aspects the trying-out process has only fairly begun.

Conclusions

Practical-minded readers, especially those with decision-making responsibilities, however, are apt to lose patience with such an attitude. For men of affairs seldom are willing to settle for forecasts or promises of further study of a problem; they demand one's best judgments now. And in this, of course, they are usually quite right, since their decisions so often have to be made before all of the data are in and all of the underlying hypotheses safely established. Certainly this is the case with Indian economic development in the sixties, concerning which, as we have seen, a new time for decision is plainly at hand, in both New Delhi and Washington. Nor are most of the larger issues to be decided so delicately balanced that any great amount of courage is needed for the academic researcher to voice practical judgments about them.

The following, accordingly, are the principal conclusions —briefly summarized—at which I have thus far arrived about the Indian development process. All but the last are discussed in the preceding chapters.

1. The unique dignity of the Indian development experiment and the unique importance of its success to the United States stem from India's faithful adherence thus far to a constitutional mode of development. That she will continue to follow such a course, however, is far from certain; her fidelity to constitutional methods is due for a most strenuous testing before this decade is over. The political outcome is apt to depend markedly on the near-term progress of the present regime's economic development scheme, which calls for particularly heavy inputs during the current decade.

2. As a piece of macroeconomic calculus, the principal strategy that is incorporated in the Second and Third Five Year Plans (and presumably will be also in their successors) is basically sound and fairly well spelled out in its details. It would be self-defeating for American policy to resist an "excessive" emphasis on heavy industry in India. The scheme's subsidiary strategy—to mobilize redundant rural manpower—has to date been far less satisfactory; success in this area will require the encouragement of India's friends and, in particular, more imaginative uses of American surplus foods. But, in general, the design of the development effort eminently warrants American support. It requires extensive dollar assistance in the sixties, probably somewhat more than is officially admitted.

3. The detailed procedures for rendering United States government assistance, and for determining the forms of its financial conveyance, need careful study and revision. Particularly at this time, it is important that concern over its own balance of payments not cause the United States to make hastily-conceived adjustments in procedure that gain very little for its own balance of payments at the price of greatly constricting the effectiveness of its foreign assistance.

4. The most difficult of the essential policy adjustments that must be made by the United States and other Western powers, if they are to assist India's effort to attain a sustaining domestic economic expansion under conditions of self-support in the international market, are in the realm of commercial policy. Western parliaments are apt to find it extremely distasteful to facilitate the access of nontraditional manufactured exports from India, and from other similarly situated countries, not only to third markets but to their own (Western) markets. But if the objectives of the Indian and other development efforts are to be realized, such access is essential, and the United States and Western European countries would do well to start trying to obtain the necessary domestic political consent.

5. The most difficult of the policy adjustments facing Indian authorities are the exceptionally complex but urgent reforms that appear to be indicated in the field of rural development. At present the greatest danger of a general breakdown in the development effort probably lies in this quarter. A reasonably definable series of policy changes is evidently needed and is being undertaken to some extent in agriculture. But it is very doubtful that these can be successfully pursued except as part of an integrated restructuring of the whole rural scene that tries determinedly, and with administrative innovations, to strengthen the agro-industrial, administrative nuclei of local economic regions and to experiment aggressively with a policy of town-centered industrial location. (I regard this last as the most tentative but also probably the most important of the book's major hypotheses. Happily it is one that invites experimental implementation.)

6. Indian planning has stopped short thus far of achieving an adequately articulated nexus with plan administration, and Indian public administration has yet to become fully activist and development-oriented as required by the nation's economic objectives. While many influential Indians are far from impervious to these problems, the concerted attention of the nation's top political leadership—as well as the sympathetic understanding and, where appropriate, the intelligent assistance of such aiding parties as the United States—are needed.

7. American private enterprises can be by far the most effective vehicles for carrying American industrial knowhow and managerial techniques into the Indian economy. Their potential in this regard will be realized if the Indian government will maintain and further implement its recognition of their worth for these purposes; if the United States government can act to increase the involvement of American firms in technical assistance contracts as well as in equity ventures; and if American firms themselves continue (as many have been doing) to discern their opportunities both for rewards and for service in India, instead of bogging down in ideological irrelevancies.

8. Finally, to end on a pious note: Indians and Americans particularly need to curb their prejudices against each other. It happens, for a variety of reasons that I shall not attempt to examine, that the two nations, each looking through its own parochial lenses, see images of each other that often are mutually irritating. The result is a certain latent waspishness—a comparative incapacity for tolerance—in the relations between the two countries that injects unnecessary friction into their joint efforts. And yet these images—the unexamined, often subconscious premise of many Indians, for instance, that Americans in the abstract are affluent, materialistic, belligerent, and insensitive, and the assumption of many Americans that all Indians tend to be mystical, pacifist, sanctimonious, and wily— are at most the crudest caricatures of a few of the "average" qualities of two extremely diverse peoples. The images are not only inaccurate but woefully incomplete. They entirely ignore the enormously important values the two nations share, and they ignore the exceptional compatibility that Indians and

Americans so commonly demonstrate when thrown together as individuals. It is my own impression, indeed, that few friendships, given the opportunity, grow so easily and spontaneously as do those between individual Indians and Americans.

Henceforth, therefore, it will be well for the cause of orderly economic development in India, and for the United States' heavy stake in that cause, if Indians and Americans see more of each other as they really are and less of each other's stereotypes. The cause is a noble one, and with intensive, imaginative effort—and a little good fortune—it can succeed. But its success will depend, among many other things, on a high quality of Indo-American collaboration that can scarcely be sustained in an atmosphere of aimless ill humor.

ANCHOR BOOKS

GOVERNMENT AND POLITICAL SCIENCE

ARON, RAYMOND On War, A171

BARKER, ALAN The Civil War in America, A274

BELL, DANIEL The Radical Right, A376

BROGAN, D. W. Politics in America, A198

BURKE, EDMUND Edmund Burke: Selected Writings and Speeches, ed. Stanlis, A334

CHEVALIER, MICHAEL Society, Manners and Politics in the United States, A259

FRANK, JEROME Law and the Modern Mind, A350

FROMM, ERICH May Man Prevail?, A275

HAHN, WALTER F., & NEFF, JOHN C. American Strategy for the Nuclear Age, A224

HANDLIN, OSCAR Race and Nationality in American Life, A110

HEARD, ALEXANDER The Costs of Democracy, A288

HOOVER, CALVIN B. The Economy, Liberty and the State, A241

HUNTER, FLOYD Community Power Structure, A379

KIMBLE, GEORGE H. T. Tropical Africa: Land and Livelihood, Vol. I, A303a

——— Tropical Africa: Society and Polity, Vol. II, A303b

KISSINGER, HENRY A. Necessity for Choice, A282

——— Nuclear Weapons and Foreign Policy, A152

LENSKI, GERHARD The Religious Factor, A337

LETWIN, WILLIAM, ed. A Documentary History of American Economic Policy Since 1789, A280

LIPSET, SEYMOUR MARTIN Political Man: The Social Bases of Politics, A330

———, TROW, M. A., & COLEMAN, J. S. Union Democracy, A296

LUBELL, SAMUEL The Future of American Politics, A71

MARX, KARL, & ENGELS, FRIEDRICH Basic Writings on Politics and Philosophy, A185

MILL, JOHN STUART John Stuart Mill: Essays on Politics and Culture, ed. Himmelfarb, A373

MILLER, PERRY, ed. The Legal Mind in America, A313

NEGLEY, GLENN, & PATRICK, J. MAX, eds. The Quest for Utopia, A326

NEHRU, JAWAHARLAL The Discovery of India, A200

PIERSON, GEORGE W. Tocqueville in America (Abridged), A189

ROOSEVELT, JAMES, ed. The Liberal Papers, A290

SERGE, VICTOR The Case of Comrade Tulayev, A349

SIBLEY, MULFORD Q., ed. The Quiet Battle: Writings on the Theory and Practice of Non-Violent Resistance, A317

SOMERVILLE, JOHN, & SANTONI, RONALD, eds. Social and Political Philosophy: Readings from Plato to Gandhi, A370

TOCQUEVILLE, ALEXIS DE The Old Regime and the French Revolution, A60

VERNON, RAYMOND Metropolis 1985, A341

WASKOW, ARTHUR The Worried Man's Guide to World Peace, A377

WILSON, EDMUND To the Finland Station, A6

ANCHOR BOOKS

EUROPEAN HISTORY

ANCHOR BOOKS

9